MW01615041

An Educator's Guide to Assessing Threats in Student Writing

Based on research from the threat-assessment community, this important resource addresses the challenge of assessing concerning online communication, written narratives and artistic works at schools, colleges and universities. Drawing from the collective fields of law enforcement, law and psychology, the authors expand on evidence-based practices to help student-affairs staff and K-12 educators best assess the validity of these communications and develop intervention and management plans. Concepts are supported through numerous examples of social media posts, written fiction work, emails and examples from past attacks, as well as averted plans. Appropriate for the classroom, Behavioral Intervention Teams, frontline teaching staff and administrators, this new resource will ensure an evidence-based approach to early assessment and intervention.

Brian Van Brunt is a partner in The NCHERM Group and president of the National Behavioral Intervention Team Association (NaBITA).

W. Scott Lewis is a partner with The NCHERM Group and the cofounder and advisory-board member of ATIXA (the Association for Title IX Administrators) and NaBITA (the National Behavioral Intervention Team Association).

Jeffrey H. Solomon is vice president of K-12 and Safety Initiatives at The NCHERM Group and also serves on the advisory board of the National Behavioral Intervention Team Association (NABITA).

An Educator's Guide to Assessing Threats in Student Writing

Social Media, Email and other Narrative

Brian Van Brunt, W. Scott Lewis and Jeffrey H. Solomon

Routledge
Taylor & Francis Group

NEW YORK AND LONDON

First published 2021
by Routledge
52 Vanderbilt Avenue, New York, NY 10017

and by Routledge
2 Park Square, Milton Park, Abingdon, Oxon, OX14 4RN

Routledge is an imprint of the Taylor & Francis Group, an informa business

Library of Congress Cataloging-in-Publication Data
Names: Van Brunt, Brian, author. | Lewis, W. Scott, author. | Solomon, Jeffrey H., author.
Title: An educator's guide to assessing threats in student writing : social media, email, and other narrative / Brian Van Brunt, W. Scott Lewis, Jeffrey H. Solomon.
Identifiers: LCCN 2020019613 (print) | LCCN 2020019614 (ebook) | ISBN 9780367428594 (hardback) | ISBN 9780367430665 (paperback) | ISBN 9781003001096 (ebook)
Subjects: LCSH: School violence--Prevention. | Threats of violence--Evaluation. | School prose.
Classification: LCC LB3013.3 .V36 2021 (print) | LCC LB3013.3 (ebook) | DDC 371.7/82--dc23
LC record available at https://lccn.loc.gov/2020019613
LC ebook record available at https://lccn.loc.gov/2020019614

ISBN: 978-0-367-42859-4 (hbk)
ISBN: 978-0-367-43066-5 (pbk)
ISBN: 978-1-003-00109-6 (ebk)

Typeset in Perpetua
by SPi Global, India

Visit the eResources: www.routledge.com/9780367430665

To Jerry and Diane Van Brunt,
    The swift and hurried, bushy-tailed, chestnut brown fox
    Bounds above, in lingering hurdle, over
    the tremendously lethargic and somnolent dog.

    Thanks for your support over the years!

                                                                    BVB

To Dad (Pops),
    Who taught me "the measure of a man."

                                                                    JHS

To my partner, Kim:
You will never know how much your support means; I will always keep trying to show you, though.

To my kids, Jordan & Justice,
May you grow up in a safe world; and, as you do already, work to make it safer, more loving and more inclusive.

I love you all.

Contents

Preface

This book addresses the challenge of assessing concerning online communication, written narratives and artistic works at K-12 schools, colleges and universities. The early identification of risk factors has been well-established in the literature to prevent mass shootings and targeted violence. We expand on evidence-based practices aiding student-affairs staff and K-12 educators to better analyze the risk of a violent attack when a student communicates violent ideations through email, written narrative and social media. Having a research-based process is essential given the challenge of sorting the risk of violence from artistic expression, frustration or developmentally young behavior unrelated to an attack plan.

Given the challenging nature of this topic, we adopted a case-example approach to teaching. Concepts are supported through numerous examples of social media posts, written fiction work, emails and examples from past attacks, as well as averted plans. Appendix B contains a list of the cases that are included in this study. The authors hope this material will prove useful in learning the assessment concepts as well as for future researchers looking to build upon this work.

The book is divided into three sections: (1) **Foundational Concepts**, a discussion of the growing use of social media and a review of foundational elements of violence-risk and threat assessment, (2) **Assessment and Intervention**, a review of the assessment and intervention processes when a concern is identified from a K-12 school or college/university and (3) **Adopting a Continuous Management Approach**, a discussion of contagion effect, post-intervention running a press conference. Several case examples will be used to help identify and practice these assessment and intervention skills.

Appendix A includes a set of tabletop learning exercises for elementary school, middle school, high school, community college and four-year college settings. Each example will include a one-page narrative, questions for group discussion and *Advice from the Experts* section, including insights from law enforcement, student conduct/discipline, legal and psychological perspectives. These are designed to increase the fidelity of the reading and training to ensure practical application of the materials in everyday life.

It is the authors' hope that this book assists those in education, behavioral intervention, threat-assessment and CARE team roles have better access to the research related to the assessment of written content. As the use of social media increases and mass shootings continue, having well-informed faculty and staff trained in the current best practices of violence-risk and threat assessment is a wise choice for educators and those tasked with violence prevention to invest their time in to ensure an evidence-based approach to early assessment and intervention.

E-Resources

Supplementary resources can be downloaded, printed, copied and/or manipulated to suit your individualized use. You can access these downloads by visiting the book product page on our website at www.routledge.com/products/9780367430665:

- Appendix A: Tabletop Exercises
- Appendix H: Preparing for the Interview: What To Do Before, During and After the Interview
- NaBITA Risk Rubric

Contributors

Makenzie Schiemann is the vice president of the National Behavioral Intervention Team Association and a senior associate consultant with The NCHERM Group (TNG). She earned her B.S. in Education from Ashland University, her M.S. in Educational Psychology, Community Counseling from Southern Illinois University, and is currently a doctoral candidate in the University of South Florida Ph.D. program for Higher-Education Administration. Makenzie has chaired a behavioral-intervention team and delivered non-clinical case management at both a small private and large public university. In these roles, Makenzie worked directly with students who presented a risk or threat to the campus community to reduce the risk and ensure students received quality support to enhance their overall personal and academic success. Makenzie has previously served on the leadership team for the Higher-Education Case-Manager's Association and is currently an editor for the Journal of Campus Behavioral Intervention.

Amy Murphy, Ph.D., is an assistant professor at Angelo State University and program coordinator for the M.Ed. in Student Development and Leadership in Higher Education. She was formerly the dean of students at Texas Tech University and has more than 20 years of student-affairs administrative experiences. Dr. Murphy coauthored *A Staff Guide to Addressing Disruptive and Dangerous Behavior on Campus* and *Uprooting Sexual Violence in Higher Education: A Guide for Practitioners and Faculty.* She is the 2019 president of the National Behavioral Intervention Team Association (NaBITA) and writes and presents regularly on current issues in education related to safety and wellness.

Dr. Lisa Pescara-Kovach is an associate professor of educational psychology at The University of Toledo where she also serves as the director of the Center for Education in Mass Violence and Suicide and chair of the Mass Violence Collaborative. Lisa has a B.A. in Psychology, M.A. in Experimental Psychology and Ph.D. in Experimental Psychology with a minor in Child Clinical Psychology. In addition to her work at the university, she is an advisory-board member for the

National Behavioral Intervention Team Association (NaBITA), a web-content creator for the ALICE Training Institute and the regional Crisis Intervention Team (CIT) "Fundamentals of Mental Health" trainer. Within her local community, she is the cofounder and lead member of the Northwestern Ohio Critical Incident Stress Management (CISM) team and serves on the advisory board of the Lucas County Suicide Prevention Coalition. Her work on media contagion, female shooters, threat assessment and post-mass shooting context cues has been featured in *Salon*, *The Hill*, *The Californian*, *Diverse Issues in Higher Education*, and the *Colorado Sun*, as well as peer-reviewed journals.

Nicole Morgan is a Licensed Professional Counselor (LPC), holding active counseling licenses in Oregon and Florida, and has worked in a variety of settings including higher education and community mental health organizations completing risk assessments and crisis intervention. She coordinates NaBITA's Special Research Team (SRT) and was instrumental in collecting and analyzing the over 200 case examples in this volume.

Darryl Armstrong, Ph.D., is the president and senior facilitator with L. Darryl ARMSTRONG and Associates Behavioral Public Relations LLC. He is a former corporate and government executive who has managed crisis and issues management throughout his 45-year career. He and his wife have operated ARMSTRONG and Associates for the past 25 years. Dr. Armstrong developed and champions the use of the Collaborative Informed Consent model of communications and public engagement. He holds degrees in behavioral psychology, neurolinguistics and communications/journalism. Dr. Armstrong is available for consulting and speaking engagements on a limited basis. He is currently developing an online webinar series for distance learning. www.ldarrylarmstrong.com

B. Kay Miller-Eaton Armstrong is the senior consultant with ARMSTRONG and Associates with more than 25 years of experience. She is a former teacher and corporate manager in public engagement and community relations. She holds degrees in teaching and German linguistics. Ms. Armstrong works with communities across the United States using the Collaborative Informed Consent model to ensure dialogue between clients and stakeholders. Ms. Eaton-Armstrong is available for workshops, consulting and speaking engagements on a limited basis. www.ldarrylarmstrong.com

Dr. Jim Kerley is a retired university president. He served 25 years in presidencies in Kentucky and Florida. Dr. Kerley is the author of *Leadership Lifeline*. Dr. Kerley is available for limited speaking engagements.

Leslie Lillard is a senior associate at Nusura, an emergency and crisis-management technology firm in Denver, Colorado. Ms. Lillard has two decades of professional experience in emergency management and risk and crisis communications, with specialized expertise in disaster response and recovery leadership, as well as congressional and intergovernmental relations. www.nusura.com

Jacques S. Whitfield, J.D., is a seasoned human resources executive with over 19 years of experience in human resources management. Whitfield recently completed a six-year tenure as the chief human resources officer for the Yuba Community College District. Whitfield was responsible for the management and oversight of the human resources operations for the district and is credited with revitalizing and streamlining the human resource operations for the Yuba Community College District. Whitfield is a subject-matter expert in performance management, employee engagement and state and federal EEO compliance matters. He is highly accomplished in successfully working with others to develop professional skills and improve employee effectiveness through training and development. Whitfield is a frequent speaker, trainer and presenter.

Jim McCamy has 25 years of experience in emergency management at the local, state and federal levels. He has served as a manager in the public and private sectors in planning, directing and evaluating emergency operations and crisis plans.

PART I

FOUNDATIONAL CONCEPTS

Chapter 1

The Challenge that Faces Us

Let's begin with a story. The following was turned in to a high school English class for a creative writing assignment. As you read it, consider what your reaction would be as a member of a school's behavioral intervention team (BIT), threat assessment team or campus assessment response evaluation (CARE) team.

As I walked through the broken door entrance to the final military installation, I realized that this hellish experience was almost over. The invasion was stopped, all of the aliens were dead, and whatever wasn't dead was waiting for me ahead. While I was leaning against a granite wall in a large calmly lit room, I scanned over the dozens of marine bodies that scattered the floor in front of me. A last, futile, stand that wasn't enough to ward off the alien attacks. Bullet shells sprinkled the floor, on top of the carpet of blood. I must go on, to fight whatever waited ahead, I am the only one left on humanities side of the battle. The bright room ahead suggested that I wouldn't have anywhere to hide once I showed myself. I almost laid down beside my fallen comrades and just went to sleep, as some of them appeared to be. But that would mean that they bad guys would win, and I just could not allow that to happen. So I gathered up all the bullets and superior firepower I could scavenge off the dead soldiers, or what was left of them, and prepared myself for the last battle.

As I entered the last military base on the moon, I came upon a hellish sight. Bodies of my former marine buddies were scattered across the stone floor. The deathly dark glow of light from above was barely enough to notice the blood and flesh splattered on the large slabs of granite that passed for walls. The platoon had tried to barricade themselves in, but with the alien fire coming through two gigantic windows and with a blitzkrieg of monsters in the small doorway between the windows, the marines couldn't hold them. Arms, legs, and heads were tossed about as if a small child turned on a blender with no lid in the middle or the room. Some were burnt off, some torn, some eaten. Even though the mass of alien bodies outside the room was at least 10 times the marines', they still fell. I must be crazy to fight this was; I must be out of my battered mind. How could one soldier stop all of these monsters? There must be some way out of here that doesn't involve firepower. It is just too much, all the death and destruction. It's pointless, there's no way, no way at all. I can't fight anymore, let them take Earth, I'll stay here on my little moon, along with my squad of dead soldiers.

The words we write shed light on the thoughts and passions within our minds. We write, create and share ideas to allow others the opportunity to gain insight into our emotions, desires and future dreams. There is no more human quality than sharing our ideas and feelings with others. There has never been a time in the world's history where the sharing of ideas through writing, narrative, email and social media has occurred at such a rapid pace and at such an unprecedented volume. This new generation of students has been given a megaphone of creative self-expression through the internet, smart phones and video capabilities.

Communication is no longer limited by distance, but rather occurs in a manner that previous generations would attribute to magic. Through this new avenue of expression, students share optimistic and joyful sentiments and a hope for attention and shared connection. While there are certainly positive advances in this new way of communicating, there are also significant challenges. Debates have become more harmful and objectified, radical ideas challenge the status quo more quickly, extremist viewpoints that encourage violence or segregation are on the rise and "fake news" and misinformation have driven the need for validating content.

Against this backdrop, students in K-12 and college/university settings are increasingly using social media, written narratives, emails and the creation of graphics and video content to communicate a dissatisfaction with their lives. This dissatisfaction may contain threats of violence, incitements to gather others to revolt or targeting of individuals or institutions for radical overthrow, change or destruction. These may be direct threats, veiled accusations, conditional ultimatums or rage-filled rants or commentaries. Layer on to that the ease with which all of this can be done anonymously, and educators are left with a challenge of sorting out if the communications are truly related to potential violence or rather an artifact of the student's development age, lack of awareness of consequences, an attempt to gain attention, or to troll/intimate others.

This book will provide educators and behavioral intervention, threat and CARE team members a clearly defined process to assess, rate and intervene on concerning communications shared on social media, in email, videos, creative writing assignments and other written narratives. We will review these concepts from the three major fields working to assess threats and better prevent violence: law enforcement, psychology and student conduct/discipline. A core element in the process of violence risk and threat assessment is gathering information and analyzing the potential threat from a multidisciplinary perspective. Simply stated, we do this work better when we look at the issue from a wider, more diverse set of experiences, rather than limiting this to a single point of view (Federal Commission on School Safety, 2018; National Threat Assessment Center [NTAC], 2018; Van Brunt, 2012, 2015a).

A central challenge is separating a true threat, what we call "leakage," that provides school officials a clue to stopping an attack prior to its implementation from other content that may be disturbing, threatening or hurtful, but lacks any actual intent or lethality of an attack occurring. The added challenge for schools, colleges and universities is the need to be correct in their assessment 100% of the time. A failure to assess the social media content accurately and corresponding lack of appropriate intervention in the Stoneman Douglas High School shooting on February 14, 2018 (Appendix B: 114) created a missed opportunity to avert violence. An overreaction to a student's threats occurred when Justin Carter (Appendix B: 78) made a threat to a fellow gamer on his Facebook page on February 13, 2013, and resulted in several months of jail time and five years of house arrest prior to a reduction of his charge to a misdemeanor in 2018 (Pinsof, 2013; Sanders, 2018).

A successful violence risk or threat assessment neither underestimates nor overestimates the risk or threat. It is not concerned with predicting future violence through probability statistics, but rather assessing a threat and/or concerning content with an awareness of research, an understanding of transient versus substantive threats and an analysis that mitigates explicit and implicit bias and balances the interplay between evidenced-based risk and protective factors (Calhoun & Weston, 2009; Deisinger et al., 2008; Meloy et al., 2011; Turner & Gelles, 2003; Van Brunt, 2015a, 2016). These assessments work best when they are used as a part of a multidisciplinary team with an emphasis on evidenced best practices. Team members should be knowledgeable about their population, the BIT/CARE model, concepts related to threat and violence risk assessment, bias awareness and mitigation, and engage in ongoing training (Van Brunt et al., 2018).

The story shared at the start of the chapter was written by Eric Harris, prior to his attack at Columbine (Appendix B: 20). The question that plagues educators or those involved in violence risk assessment is could this story have provided a clue or a catalyst for further assessment of the author who ultimately killed so many at Columbine? How do we sort through writing that is a red flag or leakage prior to an attack versus writing that may be disturbing but unrelated to any type of violence? In other words, how do we separate out troubling, violent content in stories, emails and social media posts and accurately categorize a level of threat and a future course of action? Any approach must be cognizant of time and cost, be built upon a research-based model and bring together various stakeholders and departments.

The direct answer is the development of a clear and consistent process informed by research and knowledge of past attacks. This process would advertise and encourage the community to share any concerning content forward to a behavioral intervention, threat assessment or CARE team. Once the team has the information, they should apply an evidence-based rubric and analyze the material in context through a multidisciplinary team approach (Cornell, 2010; Deisinger et al., 2008; Deisinger & Scalora, 2016; Randazzo & Plummer, 2009; Sokolow et al., 2014). Once the risk level is established, the team draws from a range of interventions that involve student conduct/discipline, counseling, 504/ADA/ IEP support, involvement of law enforcement and/or an off-campus criminal process to collaboratively reduce the risk of violence (Federal Commission on School Safety, 2018; Schiemann & Molnar, 2019; Van Brunt et al., 2018).

In the following sections, we will highlight the importance of a multidisciplinary approach to threat assessment and behavioral intervention. We will discuss student conduct/discipline and legal perspectives, psychological and educational perspectives, and the law enforcement and threat assessment perspectives. This will demonstrate the importance of working together when completing these types of assessments and developing successful intervention plans.

STUDENT CONDUCT/DISCIPLINE AND LEGAL PERSPECTIVES

There are two prominent legal issues that are immediately considered when any expression, written or spoken, may result in some action that could be considered adverse to a student. They are the First Amendment's protection of freedom of speech and the Fifth and Fourteenth Amendment's due process protections (U.S. Const. Amend. I, V, IVX). All states have similar due process protections in their state laws and constitutions and, even though private schools are generally not held accountable under the First Amendment, those protections have been eroding in the courts, and California extended free speech protections to private schools as well. Many private schools also offer these same protections to students as part of their contract to them in their student handbooks or institutional policies. Differences also exist between regulations allowed in K-12 settings as opposed to higher education.

First, we have to understand that not all speech is protected; three examples of unprotected speech would be:

- Harassing speech: Speech that would rise to the level of sexual harassment,
- Dangerous or disruptive speech: Yelling "Fire!" in a crowded theater or doing a sit-in that blocks the courthouse steps, and
- True threat: Speech that meets the true threat test. The test, taken from law enforcement and court decisions, is explained more in Chapters 5 and 8

(Elonis v. U.S., 2015; Virginia v. Black, 2003). True threat is "when the speaker means to communicate a serious expression of intent to commit an act of unlawful violence to a particular individual or group of individuals." Court says, "The speaker need not actually intend to carry out the threat. Rather, a prohibition on true threats protects individuals from the fear of violence and the disruption that fear engenders, as well as from the possibility that the threatened violence will occur" (Virginia v. Black, 2003, pp. 1547–1548). This can also include intimidation.

That said, there are genuine concerns when individuals (in our cases, students, faculty and staff) are disciplined or otherwise subjected to an adverse act on the basis of speech. The Fifth and Fourteenth Amendments of the U.S. Constitution require educational entities provide due process prior to removing a person's "life, liberty, or property" (U.S. Const. Amend. V; U.S. Const. Amend. IVX). The courts have held that students have a property interest in their educational opportunities (Goss v. Lopez, 1975); thus, adverse actions by the school, such a discipline or conduct, may be depriving the student of "property." Any state action that impacts the property of an individual requires due process.

Campuses and districts will find themselves subjected to a two-part analysis any time this issue is raised. The analysis is a simple one on its face, but can quickly get more complex, as explained in later chapters. Once an action has been taken (and challenged), the analysis is as follows:

1. Was the speech protected?
2. Was the student afforded adequate due process?

While the first question seems simple, there are a number of considerations that help answer it beyond the harassing/disruptive/threatening question above. Where was the statement made or written, often referred to as Forum Analysis (Perry Education Association v. Perry Local Educators' Association, 1983)? What was the context of the speech? Who said it? Who was the comment made to or about? Was it humor or satire? Does it encourage illegal activity, such as drug use in a K-12 setting (Kaplin & Lee, 2014)? Was there behavior that occurred in addition to the speech that violates other aspects of conduct codes or law? Does it advance and show the practice of discrimination, such as a fraternity with a "No Blacks allowed" sign, and it is connected to broader, systemic issues of discrimination? In later chapters, there will be more examination of these questions in different examples.

Whether the speech was protected or not, the due process analysis applies if adverse action is being considered. In other words, the speech may not be protected (i.e., it is determined to be a true threat), but the school's action may fail to meet the standards of adequate due process (or, at a private school, a fundamentally fair process) and the school may be held liable for that action. At the basic level, due process requires notice (of an allegation) and an opportunity to be heard (Dixon v. Alabama State Board of Education, 1961; Goss v. Lopez, 1975), but anyone who works in campus discipline knows that it goes well beyond that. This has been well established by the courts interpreting the Constitution. Any interim measures, hearings, investigations, etc. will be examined, as well as all procedures and policies. The terms used most commonly in these matters are "substantive due process" and "procedural due process" (Seal v. Morgan, 2000).

This means a school needs to have and consistently follow sound policies and procedures, and they must document the actions taken and the rationale for those actions in order to show they were based on evidence and are impartial and fair. Administrators should also be mindful of bias for and against certain students and employees based on a myriad of factors, as that impacts the due process analysis as well. Imagine, a student references her desire to "accompany" a dead body to "the retort." On its face, it may seem like suicidal ideation that may require an assessment. But it has to be contextualized. Where was the speech made? What other things has she written or said? What else do we know about her? This case is explored in detail in Chapter 5.

At beginning of the chapter, a student is asked to write a creative story. He does. If the school were to read that and, solely based on the story, take some adverse action such as in-school suspension, that would likely not withstand the Free Speech analysis. There is no direct threat, it is not in and of itself disruptive and it is not harassing. Stephen King likely wrote some amazingly terrifying essays and stories but never became a school shooter. It is not difficult to imagine a teacher reading that and saying something to the effect of "I am too scared to have him in my class anymore. He is always acting creepy, and now this!" Removing him from the class on the basis of "creepy" and this essay—which is in line with the assignment—will also not likely survive the free speech analysis. And, as is often the case, when done so without an opportunity for a hearing on both the action and the speech, fails the due process analysis. Assessing the writing in more detail and having a conversation with the student about their motivation for the writing, however, is the heart of the BIT/CARE process.

Schools find themselves in the unenviable position of having to balance their actions to avoid underreaction and overreaction. The multidisciplinary team approach to this clearly offers protections, as it allows for an objective analysis of statements, writings and behaviors. Obviously, in an immediate crisis—the person is running down the hall waving a knife and threatening to stab people or actually doing so—there will not be time for a meeting to discuss free speech and due process. Law enforcement will be called, and the school will deal with the aftermath. Thankfully, schools are less likely to have to confront that scenario, but more likely to have essays, statements and social media posts to analyze and then balance actions with social constructs, norms and mental health issues, etc. These are things that multidisciplinary teams and conduct offices with sound policies, procedures and objective rubrics are designed for.

PSYCHOLOGICAL AND EDUCATIONAL PERSPECTIVES

In addition to considering conduct, student discipline and legal issues related to free speech and due process, it is essential to understand the elements related to developmental and personality considerations when assessing written content. Students with mental illness often present differently, and when an educator is attempting to sort out the difference between leakage related to an actual violence plan or a reactive, poorly considered, potentially trolling posting on social media or story written in class, establishing a baseline for mental illness, differences in language, and understanding how affective and predatory violence factor in are essential tasks.

When assessing the risk for violence in written materials, it is essential to have a multidisciplinary team that is well-versed in risk and protective factors for violence, such as those outlined in Chapters 3 and 4. While these risk factors include some mental health conditions such as depression and substance use disorder in addition to hopelessness, paranoia, delusions and suicidality, they make up a small percentage of the overall risk factors related to violence (Van Brunt & Pescara-Kovach, 2019). Despite the common misperception, there are statistically far more people with the same mental health disorders, such as depression, PTSD, or Asperger's, who never go on to commit violent acts (Choe et al., 2008; Langman, 2009, 2015). Targeted violence and mass shootings are better understood through the lens of multiple risk factors that include mental illness as one of many pieces to the puzzle (Langman, 2017).

Those assessing risk content based on writing and social media posts should have an understanding of the two different kinds of violence. *Predatory violence* (also known as targeted, instrumental, mission-oriented, tactical and strategic violence) describes those who do not act based on the immediacy of their emotions, but rather plan over weeks, months and years, acquiring the data needed to carry out their assault (Meloy, 2000, 2006). They create drawings of the target, obtain detailed blueprints, conduct photo surveillance and post social media content and/or a written manifesto. Their writings, emails, stories or social media content may indicate an obsession with a particular target who is considered to be responsible for their ill fortune. Unlike affective violence, predatory violence is driven by targeted, thoughtful planning, often based in the harboring of past wrongs, and the development of a plan of attack (Meloy, 2000; O'Toole, 2002; Van Brunt, 2012, 2015a).

Affective violence is different. Affective violence is an adrenaline-driven process that occurs as part of a biological reaction to stressors leading to the production of adrenaline, an increase in the heart rate, rising body language and behavior and communication indicators that we can identify and measure (Hart, 1995; Grossman & Siddle, 2000). Behaviors occur in the immediacy of a stressor and are often poorly considered and rash. When analyzing social media posts or impulsive writings, we must understand the difference between those created out of fear, rage or an immediate flush of emotion and those written with a calm, prearranged single-mindedness to punish, right a wrong or make a larger, societal statement. A common problem when schools assess a social media threat is the failure to take into account whether this was a poor decision to post something in a moment of rage, or instead, a thoughtful expression of a hardened point of view.

Another common misstep K-12 schools and colleges/universities make is to assume that a mental health assessment will be sufficient in most cases and will address the risk of potential violence following a written threat or concerning content shared online or in class. Mental health assessments are primarily focused on diagnosis, development of a treatment plan, assessment for medication refer- rals and an assessment to determine whether or not the student meets the criteria for an inpatient psychiatric admission. When the school relies exclusively on this type of assessment and does not pursue a violence risk or threat assessment, there is a danger of cross-communication. The school assumes the risk has been assessed when that was not actually the type of assessment provided. An example of this miscommunication occurred prior to September 13, 2017, when a 15-year-old was suspended for writing notes, sharing threats and concerning social media posts (Appendix B: 108). He was required to complete a counseling assessment and was allowed to return prior to the completion of the assessment. Upon his return, he shot three students, killing one and is currently on trial (Clouse, 2017). The presence of a behavioral intervention team and conducting a violence risk assessment rather than a referral for a counseling assessment would likely have created a different outcome.

As we will explore in Chapter 3, there are numerous risk factors that relate to targeted violence. Very few of these involve mental illness-related concerns. Beyond suicidality, hopelessness, desperation, substance abuse, social isolation and explosive reactions, the more relevant risk factors look at fixation and focus, action and time imperative, injustice collecting, catalyst events, violent fantasies, lack of remorse, glorification of violence and objectification of others (Van Brunt, 2012, 2015a). While having an understanding of psychological motivations and mental illness can be useful in supporting the threat assessment process, it should not replace this process.

From a psychological perspective, it would be helpful to explore the story at the start of the chapter through the lens of a fantasy rehearsal. Was this written with a relishing of being the space marine or carrying out a similar attack? Was it related to the topic assigned? Was there an intention or reaction desired when read by the teachers or class? Is this writing the tip of the iceberg when it comes to the student's fascination with war, aliens and graphic violence? Was this inspired by the playing of the first-person video game *Doom*™? Are the violent themes related to a mental illness such as Asperger's or autism spectrum disorder (ASD), obsessive compulsive disorder (OCD), schizophrenia or bipolar mania? From an educational perspective, did the student have a history of this behavior? Is there an existing individualized educational plan (IEP)? While both psychological and educational perspectives provide some potential insight, neither tell the whole story. Once the information is shared with the team, multiple perspectives and areas of expertise should be applied to establish the level of risk and develop a plan of intervention.

LAW ENFORCEMENT AND THREAT ASSESSMENT PERSPECTIVES

When assessing written threats, it's easy to keep reports siloed with campus police, public safety or off-campus law enforcement. The challenge is making sure that all threats are viewed appropriately in our communities with all the stakeholders who may share a piece of the puzzle. This means that all threats are referred to the BIT, thus allowing us to "gather data" on the potential risk.

Working together is essential as law enforcement agencies, and certainly campus-based agencies, may be limited in their knowledge of dealing with threats and specifically with written threats. This is usually a specialty assignment tasked with a detective within the agency. Law enforcement should not be the sole evaluator of a written threat. There are several reasons for this. Most campus-based police/campus safety departments have limited staffing and even fewer detectives. If there is not a moderate or high-level treat, there may be a time delay in response. It is also limiting to view the threat from that single perspective rather than through a multidisciplinary team (Federal Commission on School Safety, 2018; NTAC, 2018; Sokolow et al., 2014; Van Brunt, 2012) The ideal approach is to lean into these teams as a consultant body to improve data gathering, assessment of risk and development of intervention plans. Through this approach, there remains the autonomy of the law enforcement criminal process and communication with additional security and intelligence organizations.

Understanding the nature of transient and substantive threats is useful, as schools receive varied levels of written threats, from writings on bathroom stalls, social media posts, student journals and writings made in public spaces such as residence halls. Dewy Cornell (2010) describes these as **transient and substantive threats**. *Transient threats* do not express lasting intent to harm someone. They wear off in a short period of time; further explanation makes it apparent that the true threat of violence is over or never existed. In contrast, *substantive threats* are defined as a continuing intent to harm someone. The risk of violence extends beyond the immediate threats or writings. The risk continues to be heightened after the incident or confrontation. If there is any doubt to whether a threat is transient or substantive, caution would dictate treating the threat initially as substantive.

The team should not only be concerned about the presence of a threat, but also should be evaluating the context and meaning. Knowing the difference between transient and substantive threats, applying a risk rubric to every case and consistently providing a structured professional judgment approach to assessment (Hart & Logan, 2011; Smith, 2007; Van Brunt, 2015b, 2016) can save time and resources while separating transient threats from the more concerning substantive threats that should be prioritized.

When determining if a threat is transient or substantive threats, **the context of the threat must be considered**. Imagine a soccer game. As the teams line up on the prior to the start of the game, a forward from the home team yells "we are going to kill you guys today!" The context of this threat is in relation to a sporting event, and it is unlikely there is a real intent to harm anyone. This is a transient threat. While it may be an inappropriate comment given the current climate, it is not a conduct violation in most cases and certainty not a criminal offense. Context is important.

What if, during the same game, the same forward on the home team makes the same threat—however, there are additional behaviors of concern. Perhaps the forward receives several intentional fouls during the game, or he follows the opposing team into the locker room during halftime, taunting players and trying to get a reaction. We may see behaviors after losing the game, such as following the opposing team's bus and taunting them or throwing a water bottle at the bus while yelling derogatory comments. This same student then makes an offhand comment to a teammate such as, "I am going to get even with those elite assholes." This behavior would be more concerning and understanding the context would help the team see this as more substantive in nature.

Law enforcement has a unique focus on their work and **threats should be seen from a multidisciplinary team approach**. If law enforcement is the only campus entity investigating a written threat, they will be limited in their range of responses. Most law enforcement agencies, whether they are campus-based or outside, will take the perspective of determining the presence of a crime. If the threat does not reach the level of a criminal threat, a limited incident report will be generated and filed in the department with no follow-up or opportunities for interventions.

Leading law enforcement organizations stress the importance of maintaining a low threshold for reporting concerning behaviors (NTAC, 2018). It's better to receive information earlier at a lower risk level than to receive it later at a higher one. BIT and CARE teams who do not have a law enforcement officer are at a disadvantage and may miss an opportunity to share information and/or intervene at this level.

The most effective model to assess and manage threats is one that is focused on prevention; preferably one that incorporates a threat assessment capability within the team. A BIT should encourage reporting of low levels of concerning behavior with the goal of developing an intervention plan as soon as possible (Sokolow et al. 2014; Van Brunt, 2012). This allows us to prevent small problems from becoming large ones, especially if they are left unattended or only attended to when they reach the "threat" level. The same can be said for your team receiving information on concerning behavior from your community. Focusing on prevention encourages your community to report behaviors that a traditional "threat" based team would not get, thus enhancing your capabilities for early intervention.

CONCLUSION

As we bring this chapter to an end, there are two central thoughts that are important to understand when assessing concerning content. First, all community members, teachers and faculty must be trained to share information forward with the behavioral intervention, threat assessment or CARE team. It would be a critical error for the reader to finish this text and use their newly found knowledge in a vacuum. **Information about a potential threat or troubling content found online or in a class writing assignment MUST be shared forward with the team for assessment and intervention.** These teams are discussed in detail in Chapter 7, but as an overview, they consist of five to ten faculty and staff who meet weekly or twice a month to review concerns shared with the team by the larger community of faculty, staff and students. These teams follow a three-phase process of (1) gathering information, (2) applying an evidence-based risk rubric and (3) developing and deploying intervention strategies. Unlike other teams in K-12 or college/university communities, these meet regularly to review cases and are separate from student discipline, individualized educational plan (IEP) meetings, critical incident stress management (CIMS) or mental health teams. They act as air-traffic control for various departments around campus to reduce siloed information and better assess and manage threats through a collaborative process.

Second, **any violence risk or threat assessment process must understand the context of the threat**. It is critical to develop an awareness of unconscious, implicit bias as well as explicit bias when determining if a threat is transient or substantive, "hunting" or "howling." Written content, videos and art projects are clues to further assess leakage and the potential of putting a threat into action. Assessing the context and the validity/truthfulness of the concerning content is essential. Any writing can be taken at face-value, and assumptions and judgments may lead to incorrect and indefensible conclusions. We must be cautious, however, to understand any data in a violence risk or threat assessment within the context of the case. As philosopher Alfred Korzybski wrote, "The map is not the territory" (Kendig, 1990, p. 299). This means taking into account age, developmental stages, generational diversity, political affiliation, family and upbringing, religious attitudes, language ability, surrounding geography, closed community attitudes and racial and/or socioeconomic factors. It is essential to apply the Goldilocks principle; that is, responding in a manner that is neither too hot nor too cold.

To further drive this point home, read the following from a student who was asked to write what they learned following court-ordered anger management. This is a common approach to a developmental conduct/discipline process. He writes the following:

> The anger management class I took was helpful in many ways. I feel the instructors were well qualified for this class and the class size was not too big. I learned several things about how drugs and alcohol contribute to violence, and how to avoid using drugs and alcohol. I felt like the class was focused more on people who had committed violent crimes and people who use drugs and alcohol, rather than being more broad. Nevertheless I still learned what anger is, how to recognize it, and how to deal with it. Violence is expensive, along with anger. Committing violent crimes brings forth fees, bills, and punishment that have very deep affects on that person, not to mention the emotional turmoil it causes. I learned to four stages of anger; tension building, verbal escalation, physical escalation, and opportunity for change. I believe the most valuable part of this class was thinking up ways to control anger and for ways to release stress in a non-violent manner. Things such as writing, taking a walk, talking, lifting weights, listening to different music, and exercising are all good ways to vent anger. We also discussed the positive and negative results of anger and violence. Another thing we discussed was "triggers." Triggers are defined as warnings or symptoms that one experiences when getting angry. Things like quick breathing, tunnel vision, muscles tighten, and teeth clench. I feel that all of the suggestions can all be helpful, but the main part of anger management comes from the individual. If the person does not want to control his/her anger, then it can be a problem. The person must want to control his/her anger and actually want to not be violent or angry. It all starts in the person's mind. I have learned that thousands of suggestions are worthless if you still believe in violence. I am happy to say that with the help in this class, and several other diversion-related experiences, I do want to try to control my anger.

Many will see this writing as positive and demonstrates that the author had learned some lessons in their anger management class. It may surprise you to learn this was also written by Eric Harris, one of the attackers at Columbine and the same author from the creative fiction story that started this chapter. While he says all of the correct things in this writing, he is clearly writing this to complete a court diversion program rather than as a heartfelt epiphany. Conducting a more complete violence risk assessment would have been a more valid way to assess his risk for future violence.

As we move forward, we will discuss the growing use of social media by the current generation and how better understanding these contextual issues will assist those being tasked to complete violence risk and threat assessments as part of their work.

GLOSSARY OF TERMS

As educators become more versed in the behavioral intervention, threat assessment and CARE team process to better assess the risk and determine the intervention in a particular case, having an awareness of key terms will prove helpful.

Leakage is the communication to a third party of intent to do harm (Meloy & O'Toole, 2011). In violence risk assessments, there are often opportunities to detect leakage during the initial interview. Targeted violence is rarely spontaneous, and this offers an opportunity for others to overhear or observe potential leakage that could then be used to prevent an attack. The presence of this kind of leakage prior to an attack gives evidence to support the idea that those who plan this kind of mass-casualty violence often plan, fantasize and talk about the event prior to an attack. Attending to leakage offers an opportunity to thwart a potential assault.

Silo(ing) occurs when departments or individuals hold on to information in isolation without working collaboratively. These isolated communications occur when each department focuses on their own individual mission, policy and rules without seeing themselves as part of a larger, more complex system. Communications that focus primarily on a single department to the detriment of seeing threat assessment and behavioral intervention as larger, community-based approach are said to be operating in a "silo." Much like the tall grain silos that are spotted throughout the Midwest, they are single structures serving their function, separated from the larger overall system (Meloy et al., 2011).

Catalyst Events are recent occurrences in the subject's life that involve a sense of stark change. Some examples would include the death of a parent, the loss of a job, losing a position in an academic program, not making the cut for a sports team, suspension or expulsion from school, failing a pledge to a fraternity or sorority, police charges or loss of an intimate relationship. The danger here is that the catalyst event can become the match to a pool of gasoline, accelerating the movement towards violence (Van Brunt et al., 2017).

Legacy Tokens are writings or media content prepared by a perpetrator prior to an attack that are typically designed to be found following the attack as a way to share a message. The legacy token is a manifesto, written text, online blog, video project, piece of art, diary or journal created prior to an attack and left for someone to find after the attack. It clarifies the motives of the attacker or better defines the attacker's message of infamy. A legacy token merits study by those involved in violence prevention because it can help them be better prepared to engage with others who intend to harm (Smith, 2007; Van Brunt, 2015b, 2016).

Costuming is the process of creating a persona or mask that defines or hides the true identity of those planning violence. There are two explanations for the type of clothing and accessories mass shooters choose. First, this is an individual who is dressing tactically to complete a mission. Few retailers that sell tactical vests, knee pads, thigh rigs, and harnesses offer colors in red, pink or yellow. Choices are more typically black, olive drab and camouflage. Colors and styles are designed to allow wearers to have easy access to their weapons as well as to blend into surroundings. Shooters choose these items for similar reasons. The second reason shooters outfit themselves in this style of tactical gear is more psychological in nature. Meloy refers to this as *identification warning behavior* (Meloy et al., 2011).

Zero-Tolerance Policies refer to a straightforward separation based on a single incident of weapons possession or violent threat/rhetoric. Simply separating a subject from school or work under the authority of a zero-tolerance policy creates the potential to take an upset, frustrated individual and escalate them into a rage-filled and potentially vengeful attacker. Careful assessment, intervention and monitoring are the tools that are most effective in mitigating threats of violence in the community. While separating a subject from campus or work may give an illusion of safety, there are numerous examples where angry, disgruntled and disempowered individuals came back to campus or the workplace to seek their revenge (O'Toole, 2000; Scalora et al., 2010).

Hardening the Target is the process of making a target more difficult to attack. This occurs when buildings create a single point of entrance, use closed-circuit television cameras (CCTV), build reinforced doors, install automatic locks, create sign in/sign out policies or have armed school resources officers (SROs). Many attackers have shown in their journals that they specifically consider these factors when carrying out an attack.

Objectification and Depersonalization are ways of distancing oneself from a target and are common techniques used to avoid any lasting emotional connection that might distract from completing the mission at hand. Objectification and depersonalization are risk factors, as they allow the aggressor to dehumanize the intended victims. The seeing of another as separate from oneself is one of the building blocks necessary prior to carrying out a rampage shooting or another extreme, violent event (Van Brunt, 2012, 2015a).

Trolling is the term for posting or writing concerning content in order to get a reaction from others. Trolling, when it has a threat quality, is predominantly a transient or "howling" type of threat, with little evidence of an intent to complete the action. An example of trolling is the message below, written on a Resident Advisor's white board at a college (Figure 1.1). This was reported to the BIT/CARE team and

FIGURE 1.1

the school attempted to locate the individual to no avail. They offered a program on suicide prevention for the hall and discussed with students the importance of attending to suicide risk, even if it was meant as a poorly crafted joke (Van Brunt & Solomon, 2019).

Affective Violence is the result of a progressive, biologically driven path towards physical violence. It is poorly planned and a reaction to environmental stressors. Affective violence is based upon the primal instinct of fight or flight, fueled by adrenaline and characterized by someone losing control and ultimately attacking a victim (Grossman & Siddle, 2000; Hart, 1995; Howard, 1999)

Predatory (Instrumental, Targeted, Mission-Oriented) Violence, in its extreme form, is described as an intent-driven, planned attack. This aggression occurs when a subject becomes isolated, disconnected, lacks trust and feels threatened and frustrated by a perceived attack. They plot and plan their revenge and execute their plans with a militaristic, tactical precision (Van Brunt, 2012). This violence is a result of a planned, intent-driven action that is more commonly exhibited by a subject engaging in mission-oriented, instrumental violence such as a mass shooting (NTAC, 2018). Predatory violence involves a more strategic, focused attack and a desire to complete a mission.

MOVING FORWARD

In the next chapter, we will explore the growth of technology and social media as it relates to threat assessment work. This communication style has become much more common, from texting to TIkTok, and practitioners need to have an understanding of how this contextually shifts the work we do related to determining the lethality of communication.

ADDENDUM

The following citations are included here to allow the reader the opportunity to engage in the author's exercise prior to knowing who wrote the stories. These are both included in the reference section as well as in Appendix B: 20.

Citations for the space marine story at the start of the chapter: Short Story about a Massacre, Eric Harris January 17, 1999. Gyldendal Uddannelse (2006). Columbine and Beyond. Page 43-44.

Citation for the anger management paper written at the end of the chapter: Langman, P. (2019). Diversion Records of Eric Harris. Retrieved on November 28, 2019 from https://schoolshooters.info/sites/default/files/eric-harris-diversion.pdf

REFERENCES

Calhoun, F., & Weston, S. (2009). *Threat assessment and management strategies: Identifying the Howlers and Hunters.* Boca Raton, FL: CRC Press.

Choe, J., Teplin, L., & Abram, K. (2008). Perpetration of violence, violent victimization, and severe mental illness: Balancing public health concerns. *Psychiatric Services, 59,* 153–164.

Clouse, T. (2017). Accused Freeman school shooter told detectives that everything went "exactly as intended". Retrieved on November 30, 2019 from www.spokesman.com/stories/2017/sep/27/prosecutors-add-more-than-50-new-assault-charges-a/

Cornell, D. (2010, January/February). Threat assessment in the college setting. *Change Magazine,* pp. 9–15. Retrieved from www.changemag.org.

Deisinger, E., & Scalora, M. (2016). Threat assessment and management in higher education in the United States: A review of the 10 years since the mass casualty incident at Virginia Tech. *Journal of Threat Assessment and Management, 3*(3–4), 186–199.

Deisinger, G., Randazzo, M., O'Neill, D., & Savage, J. (2008). *The handbook for campus threat assessment and management teams.* New York: Applied Risk Management, LLC.

Federal Commission on School Safety. (2018). *Final report on the Federal Commission on School Safety.* Retrieved on February 24, 2020 from https://www2.ed.gov/documents/school-safety/school-safety-report.pdf

Grossman, D., & Siddle, B. (2000). Psychological effects of combat. In L. Kurtz (Ed.), *Encyclopedia of violence, peace and conflict.* New York: Academic Press.

Harris, E. (1999, January 17). *Short story about a massacre*; Stilling, L. and Tang, L. (2006). *Columbine and beyond* (pp. 43–44). Gyldendal Uddannelse.

Hart, A. (1995). *Adrenaline and stress, the exciting new breakthrough that helps you overcome stress damage.* Nashville, TN: Nelson Press.

Hart, S., & Logan, C. (2011). Formulation of violence risk using evidence-based assessment: The structured professional judgment approach. In P. Sturmey & M. McMurran (Eds.), *Forensic case formulation* (pp. 83–106). Chichester, England: Wiley-Blackwell.

Howard, P. (1999). *The owner's manual for the brain: Everyday applications from mind-brain research* (2nd ed.). Austin, TX: Bard Press.

Kaplin, W. A., & Lee, B. A. (2014). *The law of higher education* (5th ed.). San Francisco, CA: Jossey-Bass.

Kendig, M. (1990). *Alfred Korzybski: Collected writings, 1920–1950.* Englewood, NJ: Institute of General Semantics.

Langman, P. (2009). Rampage school shooters: A typology. *Aggression and Violent Behavior*, 14, 79–86.

Langman, P. (2015). *School shooters: Understanding high school, college, and adult perpetrators.* New York: Rowman & Littlefield.

Langman, P. (2017). A bio-psycho-social model of school shooters. *Journal of Campus Behavioral Intervention*, 5, 27–34.

Langman, P. (2019). Diversion records of Eric Harris. Retrieved on November 28, 2019 from https://schoolshooters.info/sites/default/files/eric-harris-diversion.pdf

Meloy, J. (2000). *Violence risk and threat assessment: A practical guide for mental health and criminal justice professionals.* San Diego, CA: Specialized Training Services.

Meloy, J. (2006). The empirical basis and forensic application of affective and predatory violence. *Australian and New Zealand Journal of Psychiatry*, 40, 539–547.

Meloy, J., Hoffmann, J., Guldimann, A., & James, D. (2011). The role of warning behaviors in threat assessment: An exploration and suggested typology. *Behavioural Sciences & the Law*, 30, 256–279.

Meloy, J., & O'Toole, M. (2011). The concept of leakage in threat assessment. *Behavioral Sciences and the Law*, 29(4), 513–527.

National Threat Assessment Center (NTAC). (2018). *Enhancing school safety using a threat assessment model: An operational guide for preventing targeted school violence.* Washington, DC: U.S. Secret Service, Department of Homeland Security.

O'Toole, M. E. (2000). *The school shooter: A threat assessment perspective.* Quantico, VA: National Center for the Analysis of Violent Crime, Federal Bureau of Investigation.

O'Toole, M. E. (2002). *The school shooter: A threat assessment perspective.* Quantico, VA: FBI.

Pinsof, A. (2013). Teen terrorist or Facebook prankster? Online gamer in jail on charge of posting a "terroristic threat" on Facebook. Retrieved on November 28, 2019 from https://www.austinchronicle.com/news/2013-07-12/teen-terrorist-or-facebook-prankster/

Randazzo, M., & Plummer, E. (2009). *Implementing behavioral threat assessment on campus: A Virginia Tech demonstration project.* Blacksburg, VA: Printed by Virginia Polytechnic Institute and State University.

Sanders, A. (2018). Felony charges dropped in "Facebook threat" case Justin Carter pleas out to class A misdemeanor. Retrieved on November 28, 2019 from https://www.austinchronicle.com/daily/news/2018-04-06/felony-charges-dropped-in-facebook-threat-case/

Scalora, M., Simons, A., & Vansly, S. (2010, February). Campus safety: Assessing and managing threats. *FBI Law Enforcement Bulletin*, 79(2). (Federal Bureau of Investigation, Washington, DC, pp. 1-10.)

Schiemann, M., & Molnar, J. (2019). *A practical guide to case management in higher education.* King of Prussia, PA: The National Behavioral Intervention Team Association.

Smith, S. (2007). *From violent words to violent deeds? Assessing risk from threatening communications.* Diss Abst Int. 68, 1945B.

Sokolow, B. A., Lewis, W. S., Van Brunt, B., Schuster, S., & Swinton, D. (2014). *The book on BIT* (2nd ed.). Berwyn, PA: The National Behavioral Intervention Team Association.

Turner, J., & Gelles, M. (2003). *Threat assessment: A risk management approach.* New York: Routledge.

Van Brunt, B. (2012). *Ending campus violence: New approaches to prevention.* New York: Routledge.

Van Brunt, B. (2015a). *Harm to others: The assessment and treatment of dangerousness.* Alexander, VA: American Counseling Association.

Van Brunt, B. (2015b). Violence risk assessment of the written word (VRAW²). *Journal of Behavioral Intervention Teams (JBIT)*, 3, 12–25.

Van Brunt, B. (2016). Assessing threat in written communications, social media, and creative writing. *The Journal of Violence and Gender*, 3(2), 78–88.

Van Brunt, B., Murphy, A., & Zedginidze, A. (2017). An exploration of the risk, protective, and mobilization factors related to violent extremism in college populations. *Violence and Gender*, 4(3), 81–101.

Van Brunt, B., & Pescara-Kovach, P. (2019). Debunking the myths: Mental illness and mass shootings. *Journal of Violence and Gender*, 6(1), 53–63.

Van Brunt, B., Schiemann, M., Pescara-Kovach, L., Murphy, A., & Halligan-Avery, E. (2018). Standards for behavioral intervention teams. *Journal of Behavioral Intervention Teams (JBIT)*, 6, 29–41.

Van Brunt, B., & Solomon, J. (2019). *Threat case studies*. King of Prussia, PA: The National Behavioral Intervention Team Association.

Chapter 2

A New Way of Talking: Social Media and the New Generation

Perhaps you have heard, or maybe even have said, the following:

- The problem with today's youth is they don't talk to each other anymore and just text! They don't know how to interact with anyone.
- The internet is the worst of who we are, just look at these Facebook posts; they are horrible. Political memes, racist posts, being exposed to white-supremist beliefs!
- Our kids have a screen attached to their face all the time. Look at TikTok, WhatsApp, Snapchat. It's all sex and foul language. These need to go!

As with many things in life, the truth lies in the middle. The internet, texting, smartphones, gaming systems, social media and applications (or apps) are all ways of spending our time by interacting and communicating with others, each of which have positive and negatives features. For every student who attacks a campus and references an online "involuntary celibate" (incel) Reddit group or white-supremist website, there are hundreds who connect with friends from afar, using social media to connect and share with others. For each student who is bullied and teased on social media, there are dozens who use this to plan social groups, support each other and increase connection. Technology continues to grow and change, creating chatbots that address suicidal thoughts and content, support groups and apps that offer access to early alert reporting, protection from sexual assault, and access to online therapy and resources for groups that have historically had problems finding reliable information on LGBT resources, varied religious thoughts and sexual education.

Social media in the hands of the younger generation is a tool, neither good nor bad. It is a method used to communicate, interact and be entertained. We will not stop the escalation of violence, bullying, intolerance and racism by having everyone unplug and talk more. Social media creates a *different* way of connecting with others,

---

Special thanks to Dr. Lisa Pescara-Kovach, Ph.D. for her contributions to this chapter.

not necessarily a negative one. For each student who is harassed, teased and bullied on social media, there are others who receive support, care and access to information and people they would have never been able to meet without these tools.

In the remainder of this chapter, we will review the types of social media that are most common and how they are used by the newer generation of students in our schools and colleges. We explore how social media has been used to spread white-supremacist ideology, hatred and efforts to radicalize some towards violence and terrorism.

TALKING ABOUT MY GENERATION: OK, BOOMER

As we dive into the world of social media and online communications, we want to review some of the traits and qualities of the younger generations as they make use of this technology. As administrators, law enforcement, teachers and counselors assess and intervene, having a better understanding of motivations and social media usage patterns improves the contextual analysis of threat.

Each year, seemingly to depress large groups of college faculty and staff, the Beloit College Mindset list is released. Well, it was, until Beloit College passed the preverbal torch to Marist college in 2019. The current list (McBride, 2020) contains examples of things the incoming college class of 2024 experienced:

- The Tech Big Four—Apple, Facebook, Amazon and Google—are to them what the Big Three automakers were to their grandparents.
- Apple iPods have always been nostalgic.
- The nation's mantra has always been: "If you see something, say something."
- Thumb, jump and USB flash drives have always pushed floppy disks further into history.
- Oklahoma City has always had a national memorial at its center (p. 1).

A generation can be defined as the aggregate of all people born over a span of roughly 20 years. Strauss and Howe's work in *The Fourth Turning* (1997) helps us move beyond this quantitative, time-based definition by understanding the commonalities of childhood and early adulthood and the historical events they experience together. Our newest additions, beyond our Mature, Boomer, Gen-X and Millennial (Generation Y or Echo Boomers) generations, are in some flux. The cluster of names for our current youth are iGen, Gen Z and Gen Alpha. As with any newer generation, there remains debate on the name. When asking a 17-year-old sitting next to me on the couch at the time of this writing, she responded with, "Alpha… bitch!" So, there may not be great assistance available from the current generation regarding their name.

For a reference point, Millennials have often been described as lazy, unmotivated and lacking initiative to complete assignments and work tasks. The argument we make here is that this perception—exemplified by the extreme, not the mean—coincides with our collective frustration around our opinions on iGen, Gen Z and Gen Alpha. When we simplify to single examples or frustrations, we become the proverbial grandparent shaking their fist: "Stop playing that rock-and-roll music so loud! Get off my porch!" And yet, there are more commonalities between the generations than differences. They communicate in a different way, in a manner that often seems odd, less-than or problematic. But as the great humanistic philosopher and psychologist Carl Rogers (1977) wrote, "The clue to understanding their behavior is that they are striving, in the only ways that they perceive as available to them, to move toward growth, toward becoming. To healthy persons, the results may seem bizarre and futile, but they are life's desperate attempt to become itself" (p. 8). This "striving to become" is what we see with each new generation: young people attempting to sort out a complex and ever-changing world. Yet, under it all, they seek what we sought: friendship, connection, fame, success, love, glory, meaning, safety, acceptance, excitement, comfort, passion, understanding and peace.

SOCIAL MEDIA APPS

Now that we have discussed generational use of social networking, we will outline some of the technology and applications available to our students. A challenge in writing on this topic is that because so much of the social media landscape shifts so frequently, some of the information in Table 2.1 will already need updating. The most dangerous qualities of social media are found in those that create anonymous content that bullies, threatens and escalates others to violent action with no ability to hold the writer accountable. While most companies work hard to cut out racist and extremist content, this often occurs after a matter of days or weeks, often leaving that content available and unchecked. A popular app that had many an administrator in primary and secondary education losing sleep at night was YikYak. We won't explain YikTak here, as it is dead and buried, and for those who were familiar, you understand the happiness of its demise. Sadly, apps like Vent, YOLO and Gab have risen to take YikYak's place.

Terminology is also important, albeit mercurial, when understanding online communication. For example, **meme** is short for mimeme, derived from the Greek mīmēma and referring to an idea, behavior or usage that is shared from person to person in a society. Alternatively, **GIF** stands for a Graphic Interchange Format and is a series of pictures combined without sound to create a small movie clip. **Emojis** are popularly understood small graphics, symbols and icons that are used in text conversations such as email, social media and text messages.

Let's look at four social networking sites to better understand how they relate to potential threat. While each have positive aspects, the following sections point out how these tools can be used to bully, share extremist thoughts and incite violence. In the **Snapchat** review, the nature of the app becomes central in understanding

TABLE 2.1 A Primer on Common Social Media Apps

Application	Description	What to Know
Facebook	A social networking site that allows users to create posts and share pictures, videos and live streams. Can be public or limited in terms of privacy.	Losing popularity with younger groups and not as common in primary education settings.
Twitter	A social messaging site where users share brief messages called "tweets" for those who follow them on Twitter. Optimizes scan-friendly approach, allowing users quick looks at topics.	Designed more as a one-way method of communicating, used in many threat cases at the moment of attack.
YouTube	The most popular site to share videos. May be used commercially, as a video podcast or channel, or may be clips from movies and television. Clips can allow for user comments or have this feature turned off to limit comments.	Several recent attacks have involved manifestos uploaded to YouTube as well as live-streaming attacks. There is also the question of exposure to extremist content.
Instagram	One of the largest social networks that allows users to share photos and videos. It allows direct messaging with friends. Allows users to like posts.	Similar to Facebook, more picture- and video-oriented in terms of posting. Numerous cases of threat.
Snapchat	Both a messenger platform and social network. Snapchat messages disappear after a few seconds. More common with younger users.	Used to communicate more securely between groups; known for its disappearing content. It can't be used on the regular web, only as a mobile app.
YOLO	This is an anonymous question-and-answer app that is used within the Snapchat platform. It allows users to make anonymous comments on user's content.	Concerns around bullying and threats have increased with the roll-out of this addition to Snapchat in 2019.
TikTok	Allows users to post 15 seconds of content or string stories together. Built around music clips, trending video challenges and pranks, creativity is pushed to the limits. There is often sexualized and vulgar content, which has caused the app to concern parents.	A growing trend that often has numerous trolling, transient posts. The app is popular with the under-24 crowd.
WhatsApp	WhatsApp is a messaging app that allows users to share text, pictures and video without cutting into cellular text or call allotments. It is popular internationally through Wi-Fi.	Used frequently outside of the United States to communicate free of charges.

continued…

TABLE 2.1 continued...

Application	Description	What to Know
Discord	Discord is an app for teens and adults primarily interested in gaming. It allows users to create groups and text, chat or share videos and pictures with each other.	A common app for gamers in high school and college. Allows users to build private, invite-only groups.
Whisper	A social networking app that assigns users random names with a gallery of fonts and photos to choose from. Users post confessions and, according to the app, have a chance to express their pent-up frustrations.	Anonymous apps lack accountability and become a challenge for law enforcement when identifying and mitigating threats.
iFunny	A collection of GIFs (short clips without sound), pictures, memes and videos. Allows users to collect content.	Concerns around bullying and racist and misogynistic content.
Reddit	A specialized discussion-board site and app that allows users to talk about various topics and share content with each other.	Some boards have questionable content related to threat, violence, bullying and racists themes. Starting place for the incel discussion boards.
Vent	An app designed to allow users to anonymously "vent" their frustrations. The company describes it as a social diary to express how you really feel. The app closely follows the YikYak and Whisper designs.	If there were an app designed to frustrate school officials and threat assessment professionals, centered on the anonymous posting of intense feelings, this would be it.
Myspace	A social networking site that predates Facebook and allows users to create a webpage to interact with others.	An older site that still remains in somewhat limited use.
4chan 8chan 8kun 8kun.top	4chan is an information-based discussion board that allows for anonymous sharing of videos, memes, text and pictures. 8chan is a more notorious version of 4chan, which recently changed its name to 8Kun and 8kun.top. Anonymous, the hacker group, started out on 4chan.	Similar concerns as other sites that allow anonymous posting. Multiple campus shooters have posted threats and extremist/racist content. The El Paso attacker (Appendix B: 143) posted his manifesto on 8chan.
Gab	A more unrestricted social network similar to Twitter that has few restrictions on what users are able to post. There is no overall moderation, but rather upvoting and downvoting by users. It is not supported directly for iPhone users, but there is a work-around through other apps.	Common with users who are concerned their right-wing, anti-Semitic content would be censored. This was used by the attacker in the Pittsburg synagogue shooting (Appendix B: 135).

the context of a recent threat analysis. **Chan sites** can provide discussion forums often utilized by white supremist, racist and alt-right users as well as potentially serving as a posting ground for attackers' manifestos prior to an attack. **Discord** can allow for communication between neo-Nazis, homophobic users and white supremacists. **TikTok**, one of the most popular social media apps, has hashtags related to #schoolshooting with over 16.8 million views as of March 2020.

SNAPCHAT

There was a recent threat case in California that centered on a student who was being teased by other students in a group. The student received a Snapchat from the group of students that had some bullying content. The student became angry, found a paper towel and Sharpie and wrote down a list of the names of those who sent the Snapchat. They can be seen in Figure 2.1. There was an exchange of words, and a BIT/CARE report was created after the student was accused of giving the bullies "death glares" in a meeting. When police discussed the case with the student during a wellness check, he admitted to having knives in his room (in response to the police's question about weapons). He said he collected them, and they can be seen in Figure 2.2. Three of the knives in question are considered felony weapons in California. These are the two butterfly knives and an automatic opener.

The case is an interesting one. Immediately, there is a tendency to hear "list" and jump to the idea of "hit list." In this incident, it was not the case. The list was made quickly, on an object near the phone where the Snapchat came in. The student grabbed the nearest paper towel and the nearest writing implement, a Sharpie on the table. He wrote down the list to hold the students accountable for

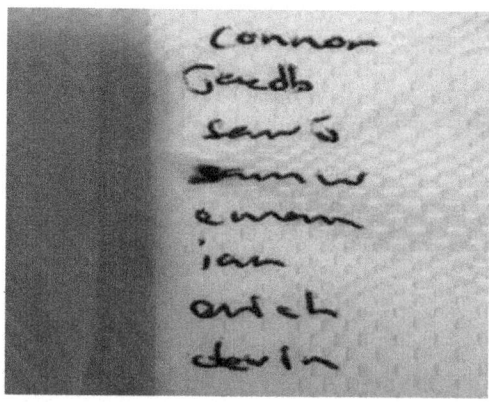

FIGURE 2.1 Snapchat case: list of names.

FIGURE 2.2 Snapchat case: confiscated weapons

their teasing in the video. Why did he need to write this down? Because he knew Snapchats disappear, and he wanted to make sure he had a list of the men involved so he could hold them accountable. There was no plan to hurt them; instead, this was a reaction to bullying and teasing that involved the making of a list of students he wanted to hold accountable.

The knives are another matter. In California, the three knives are not considered legal. Having any knife in the residence hall on campus is a violation of the student conduct code. While concerning he had these knives in his room, he said they were something he collected with a family member and that he had not said anything about hurting people with them. The illegal knives were purchased in a neighboring state, where there were legal. The student was unaware the butterfly and automatic knives were illegal in California. He was able to return the knives to his family home and did not face criminal charges for possession of them on campus.

This case highlights the importance of understanding the nature of the social media apps and communication tools. Since Snapchats disappear, he made a list. As he was interviewed by police out of an abundance of caution, he admitted to having a collection of knives in the room. There was no threat in this case, only a weapons-possession conduct code violation, which moved the student to probation and monitoring. Without an understanding of Snapchat's qualities, this case could have been a miss.

FAMILY DINNER WITH SOCIAL MEDIA

Welcome to the Social family's dinner, where Great-Grandma Myspace sits with her family, reminiscing about her youth. She shares how she used to be able to reach people around the world and even highlight her singing talents

27

with her own social-networking application. She tells the family about her specific likes, dislikes and other clues to who she is. She beams when speaking of all the friends she "talks" with when they visit her.

Great-Grandma Myspace is abruptly cut off by Grandpa Facebook, who immediately starts talking about how he spends his time with old friends who love to keep up with his family and share war stories, the best ways to change the oil in the car and travel advice. He tells Great-Grandma Myspace that it seems odd that she would open herself up to so many strangers instead of talking to a smaller group of people she chooses. She tells him that she can always chat with friends and share recipes during private conversations.

Uncle Twitter chirps up, "Move over, Boomers. I can do all of that, and I don't need to interact with people. I just tell my friends what I'm thinking or doing. Who wants to do all of what you do when I can just say what I want and be done with it?" He then goes on and on about hashtags, which just confuses Great-Grandma Myspace and Grandpa Facebook. He tells them he just hits the pound symbol and then just smaller groups hear what he has to say, like his buddies who are into #SuperBowlSunday or #fishing. Both Great-Grandma Myspace and Grandpa Facebook say that it would be too hard to keep track of all of that and want to know more about recipes and pictures of their grandchildren. Not to be outdone, Aunt Instagram begins her account of how she has the best of both worlds because she shows people pictures of food that she likes and then also includes a recipe. She tells them she doesn't have time to read long stories.

Suddenly, two unfamiliar faces appear at the door. Nobody knows who they are, but they notice their clothes are matching and they seem to be finishing each other's sentences. "Hi, can I help you?" says Grandpa Facebook. "Um, yeah, I'm Cousin Chris and this is my partner, Cam. You might not recognize us, but we feel like we know you because we've seen your social media. Would it be OK to join you for dinner?" Because she wants to let everyone taste a few of her new recipes, Great-Grandma invites them in for dinner. But things start getting odd... Being the social bird that he is, Uncle Twitter asks how they met, what their hobbies are and what they do in their spare time. They already know quite a bit about everyone else, so it is time to get to know them.

Chris starts talking first and says, "Oh, we met on 8chan, but when 8chan was taken down, we switched over to 4chan, but 8chan is now 8kun and sometimes we use 8kun.top and we're back on it." This sentence is followed by quizzical looks. Seeing this confusion, Cam starts talking about 8kun, despite Chris trying to stop the conversation for some reason. Cam explains that 8chan is essentially a place where you can control your own conversations and talk about anything you choose. No one understands anything they are saying.

From the end of the table, Brother Tik and Sister Tok laugh to themselves. Brother Tik says, rather loudly, "hit or miss?" and everyone looks over to him quizzically. Sister Tok makes this noise, "SKSKSKSKSSSKSKKS," and then says, "and I oop."

The end.

CHAN SITES

Another trend is that a large number of anonymous Chan sites have become safe zones for violent youth to post hate-filled views and launching pads for manifestos related to attacks, as with the El Paso (Appendix B: 143) and Christchurch (Appendix B: 138) attacks. Those who are running *8kun.top*, previously *8chan* and *8kun*, make it very clear that those who run the site are speaking indirectly towards those who shut them down when they were known as *8chan* and *8kun*. At the very top of the home page, it reads, "Welcome to 8kun. Speak freely – legally." Then further down the page:

> Anonymous pamphlets, leaflets, brochures and even books have played an important role in the progress of mankind. Persecuted groups and sects from time to time throughout history have been able to criticize oppressive practices and laws either anonymously or not at all
>
> (8kun.top citing Supreme Court Justice Hugo Black, *Talley v. California*, 362 U.S. 60).

Their audience and posters are often disenfranchised with the popular sites and are looking for places to discuss common interests without fear of censorship, like with the social media platform Gap. On *8kun.top*, there is even a link to an option to bypass government censorship. Users are all different, with groups divided up in communities. In terms of threat concern, there are a growing number of white supremacy groups, and those who admire them, who share their ideas on the /Pol/ group (Garsd, 2019). Garsd stated, "/Pol/ stands for politics, but this is an extreme right-wing, racist community" (2019, p. 1). Garsd continues by describing the /Pol/ community as having the goal of radicalizing users. She shared, "Community members offer tips on weapons, discussions about the best translated version of *Mein Kampf* and pictures of mass shooters portrayed as saints" (Garsd, 2019, p. 1).

DISCORD

A recent report in *ProPublica* revealed that Atomwaffen Division (AWD) uses *Discord*, which is a private, confidential, online chat service originally geared toward video gamers (Thompson et al., 2018). Atomwaffen, which some feel is a harmless white supremacy group, is actually growing in membership. Its leaders work through social media to recruit new members. In addition to Discord, Atomwaffen uses *Ironmarch.org*, on which the founder of the group, Brandon Russell, announced,

> The ATOMWAFFEN DIVISION is a group comprised of many members, and has been many years in the making, at least 3 years. Our exact numbers are not to be talked about too publicly but we are over 40 members strong. Large concentration in Florida, various smaller chapters throughout the US, such as Chicago, Texas, and New England, Boston, New York, Kentucky, Alabama, Ohio, Missouri, Oregon Virginia, and a few others.
>
> (Southern Poverty Law Center, 2018, Para. 14)

This neo-Nazi group is dangerous. It has the power to influence those at risk of becoming violent. In fact, a raid of a member's residence revealed material to make explosives in addition to makeshift detonators, electric matches and two sources of radiation. Further, Samuel Woodward, a member of Atomwaffen, is said to be responsible for the murder of Blaze Bernstein, a gay, Jewish college student. Woodward murdered Bernstein and buried the body. It seems the news was leaked to the authorities, and from here it is important to realize the type of posts being shared among neo-Nazi groups and others who are walking the pathway to violence. Subsequent to the death of Blaze Bernstein, Atomwaffen members expressed their support for the killing of a gay man and the disdain for whoever leaked the information that implicated Woodward. But the posts do not end there. ProPublica discovered 250,000 messages shared via Discord among AWD members (Thompson et al., 2018).

TIKTOK

TikTok has been described as, "The app where Gen Z vies for 15 seconds of fame." (Schwedel, 2018, p. 1). TikTok is the most widely used form of social media and, while it was created to be harmless way to share music and make videos, it has led to some controversy. Video clips on TikTok typically involve users dancing, singing, joke-telling and pranks. Yet, there is a dark side to TikTok. Anastasia Basil (2018), a writer and concerned parent, describes the day she accessed Musical.ly, which is the former name for TikTok, as follows:

> There are #killingstalking musical.lys, which are dark-themed (artistic? emo?) videos showing boys putting knives to girls' throats. There are #self-harm videos that show suicide options — bathtubs filling, images of blades, a child's voice saying she doesn't want to live any more. I saw a boy with a bleeding chest (yes, real blood). I saw a young girl whose thighs were so cut up I had to take a break from writing this article. A long break. The images

are deeply upsetting. There are #cutter and #triggerwarning and #anorexic videos. Musers with eating disorders hashtag videos using proana (code for pro anorexia.) I found over eleven thousand #selfhate videos. It goes on and on. Each hashtag is its own magical wardrobe, a portal into a world where it's always winter but never Christmas

(Basil, 2018).

In addition to what Basil describes above, there are disturbing hashtags related to school shootings. In a recent post, a student made a video with finger-gun gestures and gunshot sound effects pointing at three schools in Florida (Appendix B: 170). It's easy to find videos with the #schoolshooting hashtag. As of March 2020, the #schoolshooting hashtag reached approximately 16.7 million views on TikTok. Many of the videos are created as a way to cope with the fear that comes with being part of the school-shooting generation. Other clips depict students hiding in classrooms, standing up after a shooting has ended, and there are several in which teenagers and college-aged students use the "better outrun my gun" lyrics from the song, "Pumped Up Kicks."

Because TikTok is open for anyone and everyone, it is easy to find vulnerable, lonely youth who become dependent on TikTok, almost addicted to the content. Just a few months ago, TikTok shut down 24 accounts because they were spreading ISIS propaganda through their videos. Depicted, and accessible to all TikTok owners, were videos of dead bodies, shouts of allegiance to ISIS and other sensationalized portrayals of terrorism. The open, anonymous and quick method of creating an account and posting content creates opportunities to expose other users to violent and concerning content. While TikTok monitors its users and content, the nature of the app will always leave the company in a reactive, rather than preventative, posture. If there is a silver lining threatening texts, they do provide administrators, law enforcement, counselors and teachers an opportunity to monitor social media content to better inform a violence risk assessment. This is particularly effective when paired with educational and awareness programming for all students in order to increase the potential for someone in the community to share a concerning post.

ADVICE FOR PARENTS AND EDUCATORS ABOUT ONLINE COMMUNICATION

- Ask the child or teen what social media sites they use.
- Select options to block inappropriate content or review content prior to delivery.
- Use a strong password that includes uncommon words, upper- and lowercase letters, numbers and a symbol. Do not use the same password for multiple sites.

- When the app or website allows, set who they can receive or send messages to or friend requests from.
- Establish an age limit and check their privacy settings, ensuring their profile is set to private.
- Be careful about postings of pictures or videos that expose vulnerabilities or personal data.
- Don't accept friend requests from people you don't know.

MOVING FORWARD

Having explored the use of social media by the new generation, we are now better suited to understand the vector, or way information is shared. When the content of the text, videos, memes, GIFs and videos on social media contain threatening or concerning themes, this allows administrators, teachers, counselors and law enforcement to better analyze the nature of the concern. In the next chapter, we will review common risk factors for targeted, or mission-oriented, violence.

REFERENCES

Basil, A. (2018). Porn is not the worst thing on Musical.ly. Retrieved on March 12, 2020 https://humanparts.medium.com/porn-is-not-the-worst-thing-on-musical-ly-5df07ab842af

Garsd, J. (2019). Site's ties to shootings renew debate over internet's role in radicalizing extremists. Retrieved on March 12, 2020 from https://www.npr.org/2019/04/29/718373524/sites-ties-to-shootings-renews-debate-over-internet-s-role-in-radicalizing-extre

McBride, T. (2020). The Marist College mindset list, class of 2023. Retrieved on March 13, 2020 from https://themindsetlist.com/2020/02/the-marist-college-mindset-list-class-of-2023/

Rogers, C. (1977). Carl Rogers on personal power: Inner strength and its revolutionary impact. New York: Delacorte Press.

Schwedel, H. (2018). A guide to the app Tik Tok for anyone who isn't a teen. Retrieved on March 12, 2020 from https://slate.com/technology/2018/09/tiktok-app-musically-guide.html

Southern Poverty Law Center. (2018). Atomwaffen division. Retrieved on March 28, 2020 from https://www.splcenter.org/fighting-hate/extremist-files/group/atomwaffen-division

Strauss, W., & Howe, N. (1997). The fourth turning: An American prophesy. New York: Broadway Books.

Thompson, A.C., Winston, A., & Hanrahan, J. (2018). Inside Atomwaffen as it celebrates a member for allegedly killing a gay Jewish college student. Retrieved on March 12, 2020 from https://www.propublica.org/article/atomwaffen-division-inside-white-hate-group?utm_campaign=sprout&utm_source=youtube&utm_medium=social&utm_term=atomwaffen

Chapter 3

Risk Elements for Predatory Violence

In the simplest terms, those assessing threat or violence risk are tasked with understanding the interaction between an individual's risk and protective factors. Like a teeter-totter on a playground, risk and protective factors are generally in three states: (1) high risk/low protective, (2) low risk/high protective, or (3) risk and protective balanced. When assessing the violence risk related to social media, emails, class writings and other online content, educators must develop an understanding of risk and protective factors for predatory violence before understanding their relationship in a particular case. This chapter will review risk factors and Chapter 4 will review protective factors.

As mentioned in Chapter 1, there are two types of violence that are important to differentiate between when assessing written or social media content. This distinction is vital when evaluating the difference between an emotionally reactive writing or social media post and one that is leakage being shared prior to a targeted attack. The National Behavioral Intervention Team Association (Sokolow et al., 2019) has created a risk rubric that is useful for K-12 schools, colleges and universities to better understand the escalation spectrum of both affective and predatory violence (Appendix J). This assists behavioral intervention teams (BIT) and campus assessment response evaluation (CARE) teams (discussed in Chapter 7) to better identify and measure these observable behaviors and determine an overall level of risk from mild, moderate, elevated or critical. Interventions are then built upon the assessment of risk.

An easy place to start is understanding the much more common *affective violence*. This violence is rooted in an adrenaline-driven, biological reaction to aggression, which leads to the production of adrenaline, an increase in heart rate and the resulting body language, behavior and communication indicators (Grossman, 1996; Grossman & Siddle, 2000; Hart & Logan, 2011; Hart et al., 2011; Howard, 1999; Meloy, 2000, 2006). This progression from calm to rage-filled is described further in the National Behavioral Intervention Team Association (NaBITA) Risk Rubric (Sokolow et al., 2019; Appendix C) and more specifically on the D-Scale in Appendix J. Affective violence is reactive and impulsive, driven by perceived or actual threats and/or fear. An individual trying to manage and respond to this mixture of vulnerability and physiological responses, prompted largely by the release of adrenaline, often responds with unpredictable, spontaneous affective violence (Howard, 1999).

Predatory violence, in contrast, is the result of a planned, intent-driven action that is more commonly exhibited by terrorists and those engaging in mission-oriented, instrumental violence such as a school shooting. This violence involves a more strategic, planned attack and a desire for the individual to complete a mission (Meloy, 2000, 2006; Meloy et al., 2011, 2014; O'Toole, 2014; Van Brunt, 2015a). As educators, we should attend to those who are isolated, disconnected, lacking trust and often feel threatened or bullied. In contrast to affective violence, students on a predatory-violence pathway often plan their revenge and execute plans with militaristic, tactical precision (Meloy, 2000, 2006; Meloy et al., 2011, 2014; O'Toole, 2014).

Such violence develops over time, with those on its path often sharing or "leaking" information about their plans to others (O'Toole, 2014). This leakage often occurs in the form of writing, emails, texts and social media posts. This rarely happens all at once, but rather follows a stage-by-stage progression providing behavioral intervention and threat assessment teams the potential opportunity to prevent the harm. When violent writing or social media content is discovered or shared hinting to a potential attack, it should be explored and analyzed. This is one of the central recommendations in a 2008 report to the Massachusetts Department of Higher Education by O'Neill, Fox, Depue, and Englander: "Writings, drawings, and other forms of individual expression reflecting violent fantasy and causing a faculty member to be fearful or concerned about safety should be evaluated contextually for any potential threat" (pp. 32–33).

Targeted violence may be a bit of a misnomer in the sense that the term does not imply a specific target, but instead references threats that are predatory, premeditated, planned and methodically executed rather than those that are spontaneous and more likely to emerge without leakage and therefore without warning. O'Toole (2014) describes those intending targeted violence as individuals who are mission oriented.

> Mission-oriented shootings are hardly impulsive crimes. They are well-planned and can involve days, weeks, months, even years of making preparations and fantasizing about the crime. The planning is strategic, complex, detailed, and sufficiently secretive to minimize the risk of being detected and maximize the chances for success. The planning does not occur in a vacuum—during this phase, mission-oriented shooters make many decisions, including the types of weapons and ammunition they will use and where to obtain it, the clothes they will wear, the location of the assault, who

the victims will be, what they will do at the location, and the date and time of the shooting (p. 9).

NaBITA's risk rubric (Sokolow et al., 2019; Appendix C) addresses this process of violence by providing delineated stages to engage with the individual and gives an opportunity to move them off the pathway to violence (Calhoun & Weston, 2009; Fein et al., 1995). Each of the four levels can be observed on the E-Scale in Appendix J and allows schools, colleges and universities to develop appropriate interventions with law enforcement, campus housing, student conduct, disability services, counseling and others trained to identify and intervene.

When assessing writing or social media content, a central question must be resolved. Is this an affective, emotionally driven process or one more situated in a predatory violence process? This discussion parallels the difference between transient/substantive and hunting/howling types of threats, detailed below. Is the writing or social media post indicative of a larger attack plan, or is the impulsive, emotionally driven action intended to troll or intimidate others? To better understand these concepts of risk, let's explore some of the more common risk factors for predatory violence.

RISK FACTORS

Many researchers have discussed the various risk factors related to targeted violence. These have included the Federal Bureau of Investigations (O'Toole, 2002), the National Threat Assessment Center (NTAC) (2018), the United States Postal Service (USPS) (2007), NaBITA (Sokolow et al., 2019) and the Association of Threat Assessment Professionals (ATAP) (2006). Some of these factors are listed here in Table 3.1.

A key aspect of understanding risk factors is the importance of seeing these in combination, like puzzle pieces coming together to create a larger meaning. As with a puzzle, one piece alone is not particularly useful. It's when these pieces combine that the factors begin to be clarified and help to understand the risk. When assessing threats in writing or social media posts, there are several primary factors educators and BIT/CARE team members should be aware of to better determine the likelihood of violence.

QUALITY OF THREAT

When a threat is discovered, the educator or BIT/CARE team members need to determine if the threat is leakage or simply a poor decision by the student, perhaps related to feelings of powerlessness, a desire to intimidate or trolling of others to garner a reaction. *Leakage* is the communication to a third party of an intent to do harm to a target (Meloy & O'Toole, 2011; Van Brunt, 2016).

TABLE 3.1

Direct threat	Indirect threat	Lack of mental support	End of a relationship
Access to weapons	Lack of peer support	Explosive reactions	Inability to date
Hardened thoughts	Lack of family support	Intimidates others	Hopelessness
Social isolation	Loss of job	Lack of empathy	Last-act behavior
Victim of bullying	Decline in academics	Polarized thoughts	Legacy token
Substance abuse	Acquiring weapons	Glorified violence	Feeling persecuted
Authority conflict	Suicide attempt	Lacking remorse	Leaking attack plan
Fixation on target	Focus on target	Action plan for attack	Time frame for attack
Fantasy rehearsal	Rejection	Financial loss	Catalyst event
Feeling trapped	Poor anger outlets	Fame-seeking	Objectification

The most direct warning sign for suicide or mass murder-suicide is often the individual's leakage of intent (Meloy et al., 2014; National Institute of Mental Health, 2017; NTAC, 2018). Most attackers share statements about their intent prior to their attacks (Horgan et al., 2016; Lankford, 2013; Meloy & O'Toole, 2011; Meloy et al., 2014; Pollack et al., 2008; Van Brunt, 2012; Vossekuil et al., 2002).

While the presence of a ***direct threat*** of violence should be understood in the larger context of the writing, identifying the presence of a threat should be seen as an aggravating factor in terms of the larger violence risk assessment process. However, this should be balanced against the data. We know the majority of communicated threats do not lead to actual violence (Scalora et al., 2010; Turner & Gelles, 2003). This balance is important when assessing social media and written threats. Simply making a threat does not mean the student in question is likely to carry it out. Calhoun and Weston (2009) share this important reminder: "Writing letters is easy; shooting someone or setting him on fire presents a considerably more difficult challenge" (p. 29).

Threats can be direct, indirect, vague or as part of a conditional ultimatum. A direct threat made in the Parkland attack (Appendix B: 114) included a social media post that read, "I'm going to be a professional school shooter." Conditional ultimatums create a condition that must be met in order for the attack to take place.

An example of this would be, "If you don't give me the grade that I deserve, then I will teach the next class with my Glock 9mm." Students might make "threats" as a way of expressing anger, controlling or intimidating others, communicating frustrations or expressing hopelessness.

While the majority of directly communicated threats do not lead to violence, the contextual risk factors should be explored relating to the case at hand. Scalora et al. (2010) write: "Unlike disruptive and other forms of aggressive behavior, violent or directly communicated threat always requires immediate investigation and evaluation. While most communicated direct threats do not end in violence, this can only be determined after directly questioning and assessing the student in question" (p. 5). The only way to determine the nature of the violent speech (or text) is to conduct a threat assessment and interview the student to determine the exact nature and likelihood of the threat—again, understanding the threat in the larger context of its occurrence.

Threats are either transient or substantive. *Transient threats* are statements that do not express a lasting intent to cause harm. In contrast, a *substantive threat* is a statement that expresses a continuing intent to harm someone. Transient threats are often made rashly in the immediacy of the moment and lack intent. These threats make up approximately 70% of threats made in primary and secondary schools (Cornell, 2010). Substantive threats extend beyond the immediate incident and require more intensive attention and intervention.

These concepts are similar to Calhoun and Weston's (2009) concepts of hunting and howling. *Howlers* make threats or create concerning posts that have no likelihood of being acted upon. *Hunters* intend to use lethal violence to right some perceived injustice. These threat qualities are explained further in Chapter 5.

Another important aspect of threat is to determine the *lethality* of the threat. Lethality has two qualities: the actual danger of the threat being carried out leading to death and the access to lethal means to carry out the attack. While this may not be readily apparent in the writing sample or social media content, assessing the lethality of a threat is an essential part of a thorough violence risk assessment.

Fixation and focus can best be described as an individual identifying a specific target. This is a target in real life, who is identified in the writing sample or social media post. Turner and Gelles (2003) indicate the presence of fixation and focus in a threat increases the overall risk level.

Fixations are strongly held beliefs and obsessions about a certain group being responsible for the pain or suffering a student is feeling. *Focus* narrows the attention further, like a camera lens moving to draw an image into increasing clarity. An example of this may be fixating their anger onto teachers and then further narrowing and focusing this to their math teacher. These beliefs and obsessions relate to the idea of grievance and injustice collecting, discussed later in this chapter. Blame is cast on a group or individual in a grandiose or sweeping manner.

For example, in 2002, a Gulf War veteran (Appendix B: 24) entered his nursing college, killed his professor in her office and then went into two class-rooms, finding and executing two more professors in front of their classes as they were administering an examination (New York Times, 2002). Prior to the attack, he bragged to classmates that he received a concealed weapon permit and noted that he had failed a class in nursing and had to retake it. A year and half before the attack, he threatened to "end it all" and to "put something under the college."

Prior to the attack, he wrote a letter to the press entitled "From the Dead," explaining his motives and targets. He wrote, "I guess what it is about is that it is a reckoning. A settling of accounts. The University is filled with too many people who are filled with hubris. They feel untouchable. Students are not given respect nor regard. It is unfortunate but the only force that seems to get any attention from the University is economic force. One instructor asked why I didn't go to the health center [to get help with his depression]. I replied that it cost money and I would get kicked out of the program if I was candid" (Van Brunt 2012, p. 4). This case is one of many where we see writing that describes past injustices and justi-fies the attacker's violent actions.

Action and time imperative require the educator to identify content in the writing sample or social media post that has a tendency toward a specific time or place for the attack (Turner and Gelles, 2003). Is there is specific information mentioned that offers insight into when an attack might likely occur? This can be specific, such as "The day of reckoning will occur at 4 p.m. on Thursday," or more vague, like "I don't have much restraint left, if you keep treating me like this I am going to snap one of these days." In 2006, a student sent an instant message to a friend about his plans to carry out an attack the next day. The message said he wanted "to finally go out in a blaze of hatred and fury" (Van Brunt 2012, p. 24). The attack was averted by police and they recovered a homemade bomb and CD detailing how to make bombs from his home.

In the fall semester of 2016, an individual wrote the time, date and details of an attack on campus on the wall of a bathroom (Van Brunt & Solomon, 2019) (Figure 3.1). The case was a challenging one in that the threat was made anonymously and cameras were not present in the bathroom. While the threat was not acted upon and appears to be an example of trolling, it was taken seri-ously by law enforcement and a plan was developed to set up a camera outside of the bathroom and set up hourly checks to review the bathroom for new graffiti. This was unsuccessful, perhaps as the individual saw the increased surveillance.

Finally, the threat may take the form of a *conditional ultimatum*. This sets up an if/then scenario; "do this or else," or "if you do this, this will happen." The implication is if the target of the writing or social media post does not comply

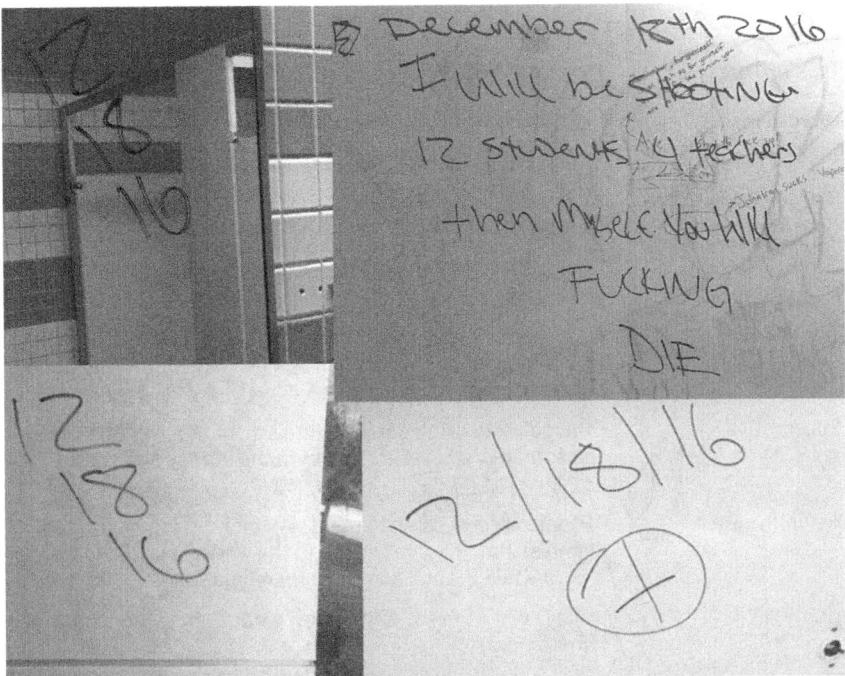

FIGURE 3.1

with the author, they will take action. In 2007, David Stebbins sent a threatening email to University of Arkansas staff members. Beyond the threatening content, this email, quoted below, offers a clear example of a conditional ultimatum. His threats caused grave concern on campus, though no attack took place (Appendix B: 48).

> So, listen up, you fucking retard, you fucking inbred, cocksucking [sic] piece of shit. I'm not asking you, and I sure as hell am not asking you kindly: You have sixteen business hours—you have until 5PM this Tuesday evening—to do the following:

1. Override the student accounts office (that is why I am talking to you, because, if anyone has the authority to do that, it's you).
2. Remove my suspension. Make it so that, officially, I was never kicked out against my will in the first place; I withdrew on my own.
3. Allow me to re-admit myself to the University of Arkansas on the spot, no applications, no fucking interviews, no jack shit.
4. Send me an email telling me that the above three have been accomplished.

TABLE 3.2

Type of Threat	Example
Direct	"I'm going to blow up the school's library."
Indirect/vague	"Something bad will happen to the library."
Direct with action/ time imperative	"I'm going to blow up the school's library at 3pm on Tuesday."
Conditional ultimatum	"If you don't give me the grade I want in class, I'm going to blow up the school's library."
Transient	A student throws books in the library when frustrated about an assignment and writes in black permanent marker on the library whiteboard, "Burn this down!"
Substantive	"I'm going to bring gasoline into school in a Nalgene bottle and spread it all over the books in the library and start a fire."
Howling	"People need to listen to me. I am not going to be treated like this! I'm going to set fire to this entire world and watch it burn while I laugh and roast marshmallows."
Hunting	"I have what I need. And I know what I am going to do. #fire #library"
Vague, but direct	"Something bad is going to happen soon in the library."
Direct, but vague	"I know how fire can spread, so maybe think about investing in some fire extinguishers."

All of them must be completed by Tuesday, June 15, 2010 at 5:00 PM CT. If they are not, I will sue you in your individual capacity and collect $50,000 in punitive damages from you. Thank you, and go to hell. Sincerely, David Stebbins Harrison.

(Pavela 2013, p. 8)

A summary table with some examples of the different kinds of threats is provided in Table 3.2 to assist the reader in better understanding the various nature of threat quality.

WEAPONS KNOWLEDGE/ACCESS

When assessing threat, another consideration is the actionability in the writing sample, email, story or social media content. *Actionability* refers to the concept of access to means and materials to make good on a particular threat. For example, a student may threaten to shoot up the college gymnasium, but the violence risk level is mitigated if they have no weapon access or knowledge and no ability to acquire a weapon. If the student had access to guns or firearm mastery (say from military or other training) or an ability to acquire a weapon from friends or work, these would be considered aggravating factors to the assessment. In a study of targeted violence from 2007 to 2017, the National Threat Assessment Center (2019) found that most of the attackers gained access to firearms in the home or from the home of a relative, both secured and unsecured. While firearms are of particular concern, a threat assessment should explore if a student has access to any weapons, not just guns.

The following case involved a college student in a math and probability class writing some concerning comments on their test (Van Brunt & Solomon, 2019). The professor shared the test with the BIT/CARE team, as the student referenced several details about a weapon in response to a question. This can be seen in Figure 3.2. The writing was discussed with the student. According to the student, when the math dividing 623/2500 led to .249, it triggered the student's memory and he wrote the statistics down from the *Call of Duty* video game on the exam. He denied having any weapons and acknowledged it was a bad decision to write that on the exam. Recalling this data from memory indicates the student played a good amount of the game, but this was with friends and did not seem to be an issue of fantasy rehearsal for violence.

The following is a short list of weapons commonly used in attacks or referred to in written content and on social media. This is not a definitive list, but rather a starting place for those without firearms experience.

- **Long Gun**. This is a military or law enforcement reference to a rifle or shotgun.
- **Magazine**. Commonly and wrongly referred to as a "clip," this is usually a plastic or metal tube that contains bullets that feed into the weapon.
- **Semiautomatic**. This is either a handgun or rifle that has a magazine that feeds ammunition into the weapon every time you pull the trigger.

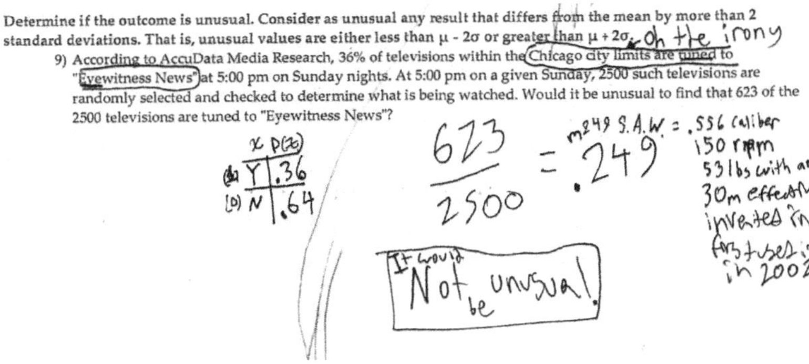
Determine if the outcome is unusual. Consider as unusual any result that differs from the mean by more than 2 standard deviations. That is, unusual values are either less than μ - 2σ or greater than μ + 2σ.

9) According to AccuData Media Research, 36% of televisions within the Chicago city limits are tuned to "Eyewitness News" at 5:00 pm on Sunday nights. At 5:00 pm on a given Sunday, 2500 such televisions are randomly selected and checked to determine what is being watched. Would it be unusual to find that 623 of the 2500 televisions are tuned to "Eyewitness News"?

FIGURE 3.2

- **Glock handgun.** This weapon is commonly seen as a streamlined and modern handgun and is capable of holding 17 bullets in a standard-sized magazine. The gun can have different calibers, such as 9 mm, 10 mm, .40 caliber and .45 caliber. Generally speaking, the 9 mm caliber is the smallest and cheapest to purchase. This handgun is commonly used at the shooting range and is easy to maintain.
- **Sig Sauer.** A German-made handgun known for its efficient design.
- **Smith & Wesson.** This weapon is most commonly a revolver known for its reliability and American-made status.
- **Colt Python.** A popular revolver in the *Resident Evil* video game series and the *Walking Dead* TV series. While it only holds six bullets, it is valued for its accuracy and stopping power.
- **Desert Eagle.** An Israeli-made handgun that is available in a .50-caliber round. This gun was made popular because of the enormous kick it gives when fired. This overpowered and impractical handgun is also popular in the *Call of Duty* video game series.
- **FN P90.** This is a bullpup-style carbine that fires expensive ammunition. It was made popular in the movie *Stargate* and the *Call of Duty* video game series. The rifle is very recognizable due to its compact size and high magazine capacity of 50 rounds laid out across the top of the rifle. The FN pistol uses the same ammunition and was the weapon of choice by the psychiatrist who killed 13 and injured 29 in the 2009 Fort Hood shooting (Appendix B: 57).
- **AR-15.** A rifle made popular following several of the recent large school and movie theater shootings, including at Newtown, Connecticut (Appendix B: 75), and at the Aurora, Colorado movie theater attack (Appendix B: 74). It is often the subject of debate between gun enthusiasts and those looking to reduce access to firearms in the United States. It was written about in the manifesto of the El Paso attacker (Appendix B: 143).
- **Crossbow.** This weapon has been made more popular following the TV series *The Walking Dead* and its use by one of the lead characters, Darryl. It is also featured on many of the *Call of Duty* video games and is seen as a more elegant way to kill opponents with skill rather than the power of traditional weapons.
- **EOtech.** This company manufactures a high-quality set of optics and holographic weapon sites that are used in many popular TV shows, movies and video games.
- **Hollow-Point Bullets.** These used to be known as "cop-killers" because of their wound pattern and tendency to break up into smaller projectiles upon impact.
- **Tracer Rounds.** Ammunition that has a pyrotechnic charge in the base. Used to help identify distant targets, night targets or to give the operator a warning that they are running low on ammunition. They were used in the Las

Vegas shooting (Appendix B: 109) and mentioned by the Parkland attacker (Appendix B: 114) in a video recovered off his cell phone by police.

- **Airsoft**. Hobbyists who play intricate military games use these toy guns frequently. The guns are popular with teenagers and young adults.

The following is a list of common concepts and terminology that are useful for those assessing social media threats and written content as part of a violence risk assessment. This is not meant to be a comprehensive list and certainly does not reflect any expertise in chemistry or explosives.

- **C4**. This is a military-grade plastic explosive used for its relative stability. Frequent media references to this make it a commonly known explosive, even though its availability is highly restricted.
- **Radio–Controlled ("RC") Car**. These are used in the *Call of Duty* video game, where radio-controlled cars are strapped with C4 explosive and a video camera. They are available to the player to drive around and "explode" when triggered.
- **The Anarchist Cookbook**. Popular in the 1970s, the cookbook contains information about how to make bombs and illegal drugs, and includes ways to subvert the phone company. Made available on the internet, it has been downloaded and studied by several involved in bombing attacks and school assaults.
- **Pressure-Cooker Bomb**. This is a method of creating an explosive device using a pressure cooker, shrapnel and an explosive charge. It's a low-tech, low-cost method of creating an explosive device and was used for the April 2013 Boston Marathon bombing.
- **Dirty Bomb**. This is a bomb made with some kind of radioactive material designed to contaminate a larger area. The concept was made popular by many TV shows, movies and video games.
- **Pipe Bomb**. This is a small, contained explosive made out of a plumbing or PVC pipe. Similar to a pressure-cooker bomb, basic materials needed may be found at hardware stores and fireworks outlets.
- **Little Cricket**. These bombs were used during the Columbine attack (Appendix B: 20) and are made from CO_2 cartridges, explosives and fuses. They may be mentioned by those who study past attacks and seek to copycat previous assaults.

Surveillance/countersurveillance efforts are important areas to assess when looking at written content. When assessing a writing sample, social media post or email, it is important to explore if the author has stalked, observed or watched the target. When assessing surveillance/countersurveillance, the following considerations may be helpful:

- Have they taken pictures or video or been involved in observation in an unusual manner to document facilities or processes?
- Consider reviewing CCTV footage around the target for evidence of probing, stalking or surveillance by the student of concern.
- Is there is a larger attack plan with planning and methods hidden through countersurveillance?
- Have they implemented countersurveillance techniques to protect their plan?
- Have they deleted or altered social media postings to misrepresent a location or conceal memberships or contacts?
- Have they begun to use encrypted communication and media applications with unknown or overseas users?
- Have they taken security measures, such as swapping sim cards in cell phones and using "burner" phones?
- Have they asked questions about operations, security or procedures outside normal interest?
- Have they tested security procedures (false alarms)?

PERSONALITY/MENTAL STATE

A *hardened point of view* is an intractable belief that carries an ardent investment for the individual (O'Toole 2002; Sokolow et al. 2014; Van Brunt 2012, 2015a). Sokolow et al. (2014), write, "The individual begins to selectively attend to his or her environment, filtering out material or information that doesn't line up with his or her beliefs. Stances begin to harden and crystalize" (p. 7). The student holds a strong passion about their belief and subsequently filters out any data that does not support that belief. These views often include religion, politics, academic expectations, social justice or relationships (NTAC, 2019; Van Brunt, 2016; Van Brunt et al., 2017). These views are beyond a strongly held belief and contain a passion and emotion that rejects other points of view or hardened ideological positions, and they are reinforced through other personal experiences and networks (Sageman, 2007).

Drivenness and a justification for violent action occur when a student is willing to commit violence for a cause (ATAP, 2006; Deisinger, Randazzo, & Nolan, 2014; Meloy et al., 2011; Turner & Gelles, 2003; USPS, 2007). Before committing to violence, it is necessary for the individual to achieve a sense of peace and larger justification for their actions (Moghaddam, 2005). As a student moves towards violence, they experience moral disengagement and adherence to the mission where their target is depersonalized and dehumanized (O'Toole, 2002; O'Toole & Bowman, 2011; Van Brunt, 2012, 2015a). They experience a pervasive sense of anger and frustration toward the target and a driving desire for revenge (Pressman, 2009). They see violence as a natural consequence for an unjust enemy (Horgan, 2008; Pressman, 2009).

TABLE 3.3 Common Grievances and Injustices

Being teased at work for having food allergies or not wanting to eat certain foods	Anger at marginalized groups like GLBTQ and African Americans
Family members making them suffer	Rejection by a romantic interest
Peers who mistreated them	Failure to get a promotion or grade
The rich getting away with things and not being held to the same tax standards	Being fired from a job for an unjust cause or being singled out
Frustration at recent politics and feeling teased and isolated	Rejection from an academic program despite working hard
A supervisor who constantly is trying to get them fired from their job	Frustration when others fail to respect their religious beliefs about being gay
Being upset about not getting an invite after expressing interest in going to party	Upset over parking ticket, feeling singled out and targeted
Obsession with health or fear of poisoning	Not being treated fairly by others

Grievance or injustice collection is a common trait found in attackers. In their 2017 study, Gill, Silver, Horgan and Corner found just over half (56%) held a grievance against a particular person or entity. These grievances are often directed against those in power, who the attacker believes are responsible for real or imagined unfairness and difficulties. O'Toole described this individual as "a person who feels 'wronged,' 'persecuted' and 'destroyed,' blowing injustices way out of proportion, never forgiving the person they felt has wronged them" (O'Toole & Bowman, 2011, p. 186). An individual can have a grievance about almost anything. Some examples are included in Table 3.3.

Most attackers are *suicidal* (ATAP, 2006; Dunkle et al., 2008; Lankford, 2010, 2013, 2018; Meloy et al., 2014; NTAC, 2019; O'Toole, 2002; Randazzo & Plummer, 2009; Turner & Gelles, 2003; USPS, 2007; Vossekuil et al., 2002). In their most recent report, the National Threat Assessment Center (2019) found half of the attackers had shared or demonstrated behavior related to suicide or self-harm. Lankford (2018) reviewed several studies of attackers from 1974 to 2008 with 70%–90% of the attackers experiencing suicidal thoughts or behaviors prior to their attack. Often, these students have feelings of indifference towards life, hopelessness and do not care about the future. They often feel disempowered, marginalized, misunderstood and lost.

Most attackers had experienced psychological, behavioral, or developmental symptoms (NTAC, 2019). *Mental illness*, particularly related to thought disorders, depression and bipolar (Van Brunt & Pescara-Kovach, 2019), is often an aggravating factor when assessing threat. Given that half of attackers had received one or more mental health services prior to their attack, mental illness awareness is an important factor to assess, though not a replacement for a multidisciplinary threat assessment (NTAC, 2019). In their study of 115 attackers from 1990 to 2014, Gill et al. (2017) found 44% of the sample had a history of substance abuse and 41% had a diagnosed mental health disorder. At least eight of the offenders had previously tried to kill themselves, while many others regularly spoke of a desire to kill themselves.

While many risk factors for violence are associated with mental health conditions, they also occur in the absence of a diagnosis. This tendency to overstate mental illness as a causal factor is exacerbated when the media and the court of public opinion present sensationalized and unrelenting depictions of the attack where the attacker's mental illness is often given as a central cause (Van Brunt & Pescara-Kovach, 2019). In fact, those with diagnosed mental illness are more likely to be victims than perpetrators of crime (Desmarais et al., 2014; Teplin et al., 2005). So, while mental illness is a risk factor for predatory violence, like all risk factors, it should be seen in context rather than a singular factor.

The **use of substances**, particularly those classified as stimulants, impacts the student's decision-making, may increase isolation and disengagement and reduces impulse control. A history of drug or substance use has been connected to inappropriate ideation or behavior. Substances of enhanced concern are meth-amphetamines or amphetamines, cocaine or alcohol (ATAP, 2006; O'Toole & Bowman, 2011; Turner & Gelles, 2003; USPS, 2007).

A common risk factor for those who engage in predatory violence is a lack of desire/ability to understand different perspectives. A **lack of empathy and remorse for actions** is seen as an aggravating factor in a threat assessment. Most attackers were victims of bullying (NTAC, 2019), resulting in a focus on their safety, pain and feelings that increases the risk of them disregarding the feelings, pain and safety of others. The student may intimidate, act superior to others and/or display intolerance to individual differences (ATAP, 2006; Van Brunt, 2012; O'Toole, 2002; Turner & Gelles, 2003).

When students are struggling, frustrated or overwhelmed, they engage in **fantasy rehearsals** that may involve them confronting, punishing and/or destroying the fixation and focus of their perceived injustices. This may involve them writing, drawing, creating content on social media and/or perseverating on the wrongs they perceived having been done to them. O'Neill et al. (2008) stress the importance of exploring these communications: "Writings, drawings, and other forms of individual expression reflecting violent fantasy and causing a faculty member to be fearful or concerned about safety, should be evaluated contextually for any potential threat" (pp. 32–33). O'Toole (2014) writes, "Mission-oriented shootings are hardly impulsive crimes. They are well-planned and can involve days, weeks, months, even years of making preparations and fantasizing about the crime" (p. 9).

There is critical balance here between valuing self-expression, an essential developmental task for students, and seeing this content creation as leakage for an attack. As with the story of Goldilocks, it's the "just-right" porridge that becomes the goal. Overreactions to student's creative process or underreactions with the explanation, "oh, they are just being creative," are equally gigantic misses in a threat assessment process. Materials should be explored within the context of the student's motivation and intention, their background, career interests, age and social connections. Caution should be taken to guard against the assumption that violent or disturbing ideas or writings are a direct link, or smoking gun, for a future violence. Additionally, the audience for the writing is important to consider. There is less cause for alarm when a creative writing student shares violent content with a mentor for feedback. It may be more concerning when a student shares graphic threatening content with an entire class or on social media. The context is vital to understanding the potential for risk.

Feelings of isolation and hopelessness are often experienced by those who engage in predatory violence. Students may experience discrimination based on a marginalized status with little or no hope for a pathway to a better tomorrow (Sinai, 2012) or they may experience a lack of social or occupational opportunities at home and school (Schmid, 2013). They often experience longer term isolation and/or an inability to create or maintain sexual or intimate relationships with others (O'Toole, 2002; Van Brunt et al., 2017). The National Threat Assessment Center (2019) found nearly two-thirds of the attackers they studied either spoke about their sadness, depression or loneliness, or these appeared through their behaviors. In terms of threat assessment, many of these individuals confided in others about their feelings or wrote about them online or in school assignments.

A student may experience *marginalization* as they interact with the school community or larger society. These feelings of marginalization may be based on social factors, ethnic or racial differences, cultural dissimilarities or diverse gender expression (Langman, 2009; Lankford, 2013; Sue, 2010). These feelings often lead to experiences of discrimination that result in a perceived threat to those they identify with, causing a sense of moral outrage (Bhui et al., 2012; Sageman 2007). Although many students may feel marginalized, treated unfairly, discriminated against and unengaged in society, only a small number of these students move toward violence to express these frustrations, bring about change or punish others.

Fascination with violence (Mohandie, 2014; NTAC, 2019; O'Toole, 2002) is present in approximately half of those who escalate toward predatory violence. When assessing violence risk, it is important to explore whether the subject has a preoccupation or fixation on violent topics, how this may negatively impact the student and where the interest originated. This may include drawing violent pictures (as in the Freedom High averted attack [Appendix B: 71]), instructions on how to kill (as with the Colorado movie theatre shooing [Appendix B: 74] and the thwarted Bartow Middle School stabbing [Appendix B: 134]), keeping a journal or writing assignments with attack themes and following or quoting past attackers such as those at Columbine, watching videos of animals being killed, discussion or fascination with Hitler or an obsession with weapons. When these are discovered in written content, further information gathering and a more detailed assessment should be conducted and seen within the context of what is beyond a normal interest (Meloy et al., 2011; NTAC, 2019; Van Brunt, 2012, 2015a).

An example of this occurred at a college where a student had drawn a picture in a notebook during class of a partial female figure and a detailed rifle (Figure 3.3; Van Brunt & Solomon, 2019). This was reported to the campus BIT/CARE team for review and the student was asked about the drawing. He shared that he often doodled in his notebook and had taken anatomy drawing courses in the past and drew the rifle image from a Lego picture he had. He was asked to not draw pictures of guns in class, as it was potentially upsetting to other students. He said he agreed and understood why it might cause concern. The case was resolved without further intervention.

The *desire for fame* and to make a mark on the world is present in many of the predatory violence cases in the recent years. In his writing, Lankford (2016) explores 24 cases of offenders who explicitly stated that they wanted attention and fame and/or directly contacted media organizations to get it. These were often the deadliest offenders. Those struggling with frustration at being bullied or marginalized by society often seek attention to right this perceived wrong (Bhui et al., 2012; Sageman, 2007). An example of this was found on the Parkland (Appendix B: 114) attacker's cell phone. In a video explaining his coming actions, he says, "With the power of my AR, you will know who I am." (Ovalle & Nehamas, 2018). As with suicidal terrorists, mass shooters "produce martyrdom videos,

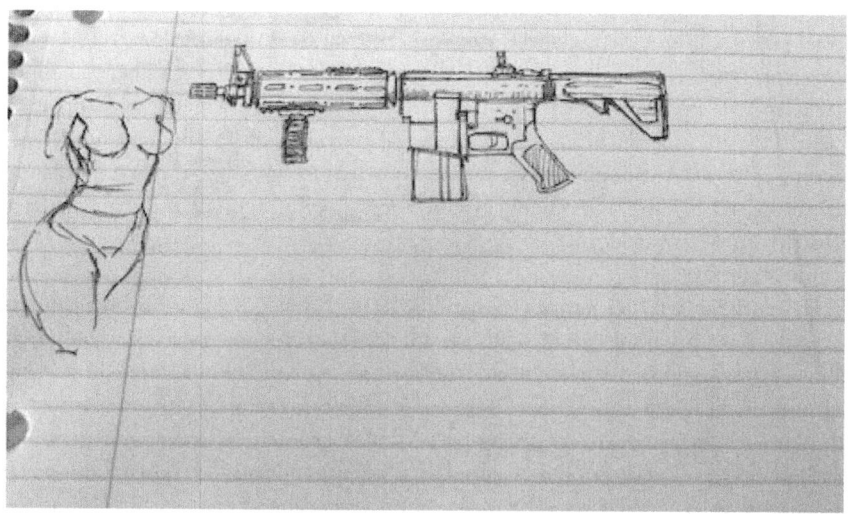

FIGURE 3.3

48

murals, calendars, key chains, posters, postcards, and pennants with the names and photos of past suicide terrorists, they show potential participants that committing a suicide attack is a path to fame and glory" (Lankford, 2018, p. 6).

On the pathway toward violence, an increasing *objectification and depersonalization* is part of the escalation (Van Brunt, 2012, 2015a). Grossman (1996) discussed these phenomena related to military training in his book, *On Killing*. He argued that soldiers are loathe to kill, yet this aversion has been overridden through sophisticated methods. In writing and social media posts, this may manifest as a negative view or dehumanization of the target. This language may be hostile, insulting, diminishing, misogynistic or focused on separating the author from their target (Van Brunt, 2016).

The Virginia Tech shooter's (Appendix B: 44) writings and the video manifesto he sent to NBC contain this objectifying language. Cho leaves us with vivid images of himself holding guns and hammers, demonstrating, prior to his attack, his desire to destroy those he held responsible (Van Brunt, 2015a). Jared Loughner attacked Giffords as a representative of the illegal system of government he ranted against (Appendix B: 67). Pekka-Eric Auvinen in 2007 (Appendix B: 47) and Matti Saari (Appendix B: 51) took part in two devastating attacks in Finland. Both wrote extensively about their disdain for humanity and their desire to destroy humanity.

In May 1998, 15-year-old Kipland ("Kip") Kinkel (Appendix B: 19) was suspended pending an expulsion hearing from Thurston High School for being in possession of a loaded, stolen handgun. He then killed his parents to "spare" them the embarrassment before returning to school. He parked two blocks away from school and hid several weapons and 1,127 rounds of ammunition under his trench coat. He shot two while entering the school and then shot another 24 students in the cafeteria. After firing 50 rounds (27 hits resulting in two deaths), Kinkel was tackled by another seven students and then was arrested by police (Curry, 2003; Hammer, 1998; Sullivan, 1998). Kinkel left some journal writings prior to the killing spree that shed light on his romantic frustrations:

> I don't understand any fucking person on this earth. Some of you are so weak, mainly, that a four-year-old could push you down. I am strong, but my head just doesn't work right. I know I should be happy with what I have, but I hate living ... I am evil. I want to kill and give pain without a cost. And there is no such thing. We kill him—we killed him a long time ago. Anyone that believes in God is a fucking sheep
>
> (Van Brunt, 2012, p. 12).

ENVIRONMENTAL FACTORS

An extreme sense of loss and hopelessness often follows a *catalyst event*. These events may include the loss of a job, death of a friend or family member, parental divorce, experiences of domestic abuse, drug use or criminal charges, failure to achieve an academic goal such as passing a critical test or losing the ability to study in a program. As with a catalyst in a chemical reaction, these perceived catastrophic events speed up and focus the attack plan. A recent example of a catalyst event can be found in the El Paso shooting (Appendix B: 143), where the attacker makes mention in his manifesto that time is running out after watching the Democratic primaries and he has come to realize the state of Texas may go Democratic. This also occurred in the loss of an adoptive parent by the Parkland (Appendix B: 114) attacker, who lost his adoptive father by heart attack in 2004 and his adoptive mother to pneumonia in the fall of 2017 and then was expelled from school. While traumatic events stress the coping skills of the attackers studied (NTAC, 2019), simply having a bad experience or series of bad experiences should not be seen as predictive of a future attack.

It is common for attackers to **experience teasing and bullying** prior to an attack. Bullying is a problem faced by students and continues to be identified as a factor in NTAC's research on targeted violence in schools, with most of the attackers in their 2019 study having been bullied, often as part of a persistent pattern which lasted for weeks, months or years. They define bullying as "unwanted, aggressive behavior among school-aged children with an intent to do physical, social, or emotional harm; which involves a real or perceived power imbalance; and is, or could be, repeated" (NATC, 2019, p. 33). This can occur in various ways, including verbal, physical, social, property and cyber. About one-third of attackers in their study engaged in bullying behavior themselves.

A particularly powerful example of how bullying impacted an individual can be found with Wellington Menezes de Oliveira (Appendix B: 68), who talked about a long history of bullying, depression and a desire for suicide in a note before his 2011 attack in Rio de Janeiro, Brazil. In a video recorded two days before the shooting, he stated, "The struggle for which many brothers died in the past, and for which I will die, is not solely because of what is known as bullying. Our fight is against cruel people, cowards, who take advantage of the kindness, the weakness of people unable to defend themselves" (Van Brunt, 2012, p. 19).

As an encompassing phrase, *free fall* captures a wide range of difficulties the attacker experiences in their community, school, work, primary support group and/or social circle. Examples of this would include chronic unemployment, a financial crisis, death of a loved one, problems adjusting to a new life circumstance such as an adjustment to a new school, dismissal from an academic program or internship, the sudden loss of a job or a sense of blocked upward mobility based on their personal characteristics such as race, ethnicity, religious beliefs or appearance (Bhui et al., 2012; Schmid, 2013; Travis, 2008). Students experiencing this increase collection of stressors often feel little hope for improvement. As problems occur in families and conflicts in the home, academic or disciplinary actions, or other personal issues, they become increasingly overwhelmed.

A *decrease in academic progress* would be an additional aggravating risk factor, particularly after a period of doing well. There are a number of other behaviors providing an understanding of the offender's behavioral background. Gill et al. (2017) write, "63% experienced long-term stress. Examples of this include academic frustration stemming from learning disorders; difficulty maintaining employment and failure in business ventures; disabling injuries from automobile and work accidents; long-term financial debts; a range of mental health issues including depression, bipolar disorder, and post-traumatic stress disorder; being a victim of sexual/physical abuse in childhood; an inability to establish appropriate social relationships; and long-lasting discord in marriages and romantic relationships" (p. 711).

As with other factors, simply experiencing difficulties in life does not turn one into a school attacker. Rather, of those who have moved forward with an attack, the vast majority have experienced social stressors with their peers and/or romantic partners. When assessing threat, BIT/CARE teams should gather information about the stressors, how the student is experiencing them and if there are additional stressors in their past that are still impacting them, and then balance this with how their current supports are functioning. Simply put, stress is manageable when the individual has the supports and scaffolding needed while returning to balance (NTAC, 2018).

An increase in *social isolation*, particularly as a result of teasing and bullying, is an additional risk factor (Sokolow et al., 2019; O'Toole, 2002; Van Brunt, 2012, 2015a, 2015b). In their study, Gill et al. (2017) found that 75% of attackers spoke about their sadness, depression or loneliness, or appeared through their observable behaviors to be experiencing these feelings. Some attackers confided in others about their feelings or wrote about them online or in school assignments. Bystanders also observed the attackers isolating themselves, withdrawing from others, appearing sad or crying.

MOVING FORWARD

This chapter has offered a detailed review of several dozen risk factors for targeted violence. As educators and BIT/Care teams are increasingly asked to assess the potential violence risk in written content such as emails, social media posts, creative fiction and other communications, an understanding of research-based risk factors is the starting place to build an assessment of threat. In parallel to the risk factors, Chapter 4 will review the protective and supportive factors that provide a counterpoint to the violence.

REFERENCES

Association of Threat Assessment Professionals (ATAP). (2006). *Risk assessment guideline elements for violence (RAGE-V): Considerations for assessing the risk of future violent behavior.* Sacramento, CA: ATAP.

Bhui, K., Hicks M., Lashley, M., & Jones, E. (2012). A public health approach to understanding and preventing violent radicalization. *BMC Medicine*, 10, 16.

Calhoun, F., & Weston, S. (2009). *Threat assessment and management strategies: Identifying the Howlers and Hunters*. Boca Raton, FL: CRC Press.

Cornell, D. (2010, January/February). Threat assessment in the college setting. *Change Magazine*, pp. 9–15. www.changemag.org.

Curry, V. (2003). Thurston High School: The effects of both distal and emotional proximity in an acute instance of school violence. *Journal of School Violence*, 2(3), 93–120.

Desmarais, S., Van Dorn, R., Johnson, L., Grimm, K., Douglas, K., & Swartz, M. (2014). Community violence perpetration and victimization among adults with mental illnesses. *American Journal of Public Health*, 104, 2342–2349.

Deisinger, E., Randazzo, M., & Nolan, J. (2014). Threat assessment and management in higher education: Enhancing the standard of care in the academy. In J.R. Meloy & J. Hoffmann (Eds.), *The international handbook of threat assessment*, (pp. 107–125). New York: Oxford University Press.

Dunkle, J.H., Silverstein, Z.B., & Warner S.L. (2008). Managing violent and other troubling students: The role of threat assessment teams on campus. *Journal of College and University Law*, 34(3), 585–636.

Fein, R., Vossekuil, B., & Holden, G. (1995). *Threat assessment: An approach to targeted violence*. Washington, DC: National Institute of Justice.

Gill, P., Silver, J., Horgan, J., & Corner, E. (2017, May). Shooting alone: The pre-attack experiences and behaviors of U.S. solo mass murderers. *Journal of Forensic Sciences*, 62(3), 710–714.

Grossman, D. (1996). *On killing: The psychological cost of learning to kill in war and society*. Lebanon, IN: Little, Brown, and Company Back Bay Books.

Grossman, D., & Siddle, B. (2000). Psychological effects of combat. In L. Kurtz (Ed.), *Encyclopedia of violence, peace and conflict*. UK: Academic Press.

Hammer, J. (1998, June 8). Kid is out of control. *Newsweek*, 131(23), 32.

Hart, S., & Logan, C. (2011). Formulation of violence risk using evidence-based assessment: The structured professional judgment approach. In P. Sturmey & M. McMurran (Eds.), *Forensic case formulation* (pp. 83–106). Chichester, England: Wiley-Blackwell.

Hart, S., Sturmey, P., Logan, C., & McMuran, M. (2011). Forensic case formulation. *International Journal of Forensic Mental Health*, 10, 118–126.

Horgan, J. (2008). From profiles to pathways and roots to routes: Perspectives from psychology on radicalization into terrorism. *Annals of American Academy of Political and Social Sciences*, 618, 80–94.

Horgan, J., Shorland, N., Abbasciano, S., & Walsh, S. (2016). Actions speak louder than words: A behavioral analysis of 183 individuals convicted for terrorist offenses in the United States from 1995 to 2012. *Journal of Forensic Sciences*, 61, 1228–1237.

Howard, P. (1999). *The owner's manual for the brain: Everyday applications from mind-brain research* (2nd ed.). Austin, TX: Bard Press.

Langman, P. (2009). Rampage school shooters: A typology. *Aggression and Violent Behaviour*, 14, 79–86.

Lankford, A. (2010). *Human killing machines: Systematic indoctrination in Iran, Nazi Germany, Al Qaeda, and Abu Ghraib*. Boston, MA: Lexington Press.

Lankford, A. (2013). *The myth of martyrdom: What really drives suicide bombers, rampage shooters, and other self-destructive killers*. New York: Palgrave Macmillan.

Lankford, A. (2016). Fame-seeking rampage shooters: Initial findings and empirical predictions. *Aggression and Violent Behavior*, 27, 122–129.

Lankford, A. (2018). Identifying potential mass shooters and suicide terrorists with warning signs of suicide, perceived victimization, and desires for attention or fame. *Journal of Personality Assessment*, 5, 1–12.

Meloy, J. (2000). *Violence risk and threat assessment: A practical guide for mental health and criminal justice professionals*. San Diego, CA: Specialized Training Services.

Meloy, J., Hoffmann, J., Guldimann, A., & James, D. (2011). The role of warning behaviors in threat assessment: An exploration and suggested typology. *Behavioural Sciences & the Law*, 30, 256–279.

Meloy, J., & O'Toole, M. (2011). The concept of leakage in threat assessment. *Behavioral Sciences and the Law*, 29(4), 513–527.

Meloy, J.R. (2006). The empirical basis and forensic application of affective and predatory violence. *Australian and New Zealand Journal of Psychiatry*, 40, 539–547.

Meloy, R., Hoffmann, J., Roshdi, K., Glaz-Ocik, J., & Guldimann, A. (2014). Warning behaviors and their configurations across various domains of targeted violence. In J.R. Meloy & J. Hoffmann (Eds.), *The international handbook of threat assessment* (pp. 39–53). New York: Oxford University Press.

Moghaddam, F. (2005). The staircase to terrorism: A psychological exploration. *American Psychologist*, 60, 161–169.

Mohandie, K. (2014). Threat assessment in schools. In J.R. Meloy & J. Hoffman (Eds.), *The international handbook of threat assessment* (pp. 126–147). New York: Oxford University Press.

National Institute of Mental Health (NIMH). (2017). Suicide prevention. Retrieved from https://www.nimh.nih.gov/health/topics/suicide-prevention/index.shtml

National Threat Assessment Center (NTAC). (2018). *Enhancing school safety using a threat assessment model: An operational guide for preventing targeted school violence*. Washington, DC: United States Secret Service, Department of Homeland Security.

National Threat Assessment Center (NTAC) (2019). *Protecting America's schools: A United States secret service analysis of targeted school violence*. Washington, DC: United States Secret Service, Department of Homeland Security.

New York Times. (2002, October 31). Gunman in Arizona wrote of plan to kill. *The New York Times*, p. 18.

O'Neill, D., Fox, J., Depue, R., & Englander, E. (2008). *Campus violence prevention and response: Best practices for Massachusetts higher education*. Boston, MA: Applied Risk Management, LLC.

O'Toole, M.E. (2002). *The school shooter: A threat assessment perspective*. Quantico, VA: FBI.

O'Toole, M.E. (2014). The mission-oriented shooter: A new type of mass killer. *Journal of Violence and Gender*, 1(1), 9–10.

O'Toole, M.E., & Bowman, A. (2011). *Dangerous instincts: How gut feelings betray*. (New York: Hudson Street Press).

Ovalle, D., & Nehamas, N. (2018). "You're all going to die." Nikolas Cruz made cellphone videos plotting Parkland attack. Retrieved on December 7, 2019 from https://www.miamiherald.com/news/local/community/broward/article212199899.html

Pavela, G. (2013). The Pavela report. *Coll Admin Publ.*, 18, 1–19.

Pollack, W., Modzeleski, W., & Rooney, G. (2008). *Prior knowledge of potential school-based violence: Information students learn may prevent a targeted attack*. Washington, DC: United States Secret Service and United States Department of Education.

Pressman, D. (2009). *Risk assessment decisions for violent political extremism*. Ottawa: Her Majesty the Queen in Right of Canada.

Randazzo, M., & Plummer, E. (2009). *Implementing behavioral threat assessment on campus: A Virginia Tech demonstration project*. Blacksburg, VA: Printed by Virginia Polytechnic Institute and State University.

Sageman, M. (2007). Radicalization of global Islamist terrorists. United States Senate Committee on Homeland Security and Governmental Affairs. Retrieved on December 7, 2019 from https://www.hsgac.senate.gov/download/062707sageman

Scalora, M., Simons, A., & Vansly, S. (2010, February). Campus safety: Assessing and managing threats. *FBI Law Enforcement Bulletin*, 79(2), 1-10.

Schmid, A.P. (2013). Radicalisation, de-radicalisation, counter-radicalisation: A conceptual discussion and literature review. *The International Centre for Counter-Terrorism-The Hague*, 4(2), 1–91. Retrieved on March 26, 2020 from https://icct.nl/publication/radicalisation-de-radicalisation-counterradicalisation-a-conceptual-discussion-and-literature-review

Sinai, J. (2012, Summer/Fall). Radicalisation into extremism and terrorism. *The Intelligencer*, 19, 22-23.

Sokolow, B., Van Brunt, B., Lewis, W., Schiemann, M., Murphy, A., & Molnar, J. (2019). *The NaBITA risk rubric*. King of Prussia, PA: The National Behavioral Intervention Team Association.

Sokolow, B.A., Lewis, W.S., Van Brunt, B., Schuster, S., & Swinton, D. (2014). *The book on BIT* (2nd ed.). Berwyn, PA: The National Behavioral Intervention Team Association.

Sue, D. (2010). *Microaggressions in everyday life: Race, gender, and sexual orientation*. Hoboken, NJ: John Wiley & Sons.

Sullivan, R. (1998). A boy's life. *Rolling Stone*, (795), 76.

Teplin, L., McClelland, G., Abram, K., & Weiner, D. (2005). Crime victimization in adults with severe mental illness: Comparison with the National Crime Victimization Survey. *Arch Genral Psychiatry*, 62, 911–921.

Travis A. (2008). MI5 report challenges views on terrorism in Britain. *Guardian*, 20, 558–579.

Turner, J., & Gelles, M. (2003). *Threat assessment: A risk management approach*. New York: Routledge.

United States Postal Service (USPS). (2007). Threat assessment team guide. Retrieved on November 30, 2019 from https://www.nalc.org/workplace-issues/resources/manuals/pub108.pdf

Van Brunt, B. (2012). *Ending campus violence: New approaches to prevention*. New York: Routledge.

Van Brunt, B. (2015a). *Harm to others: The assessment and treatment of dangerousness*. Alexander, VA: American Counseling Association.

Van Brunt, B. (2015b). Violence risk assessment of the written word (VRAW²). *Journal of Behavioral Intervention Teams (JBIT)*, 3, p. 12-25.

Van Brunt, B. (2016). Assessing threat in written communications, social media, and creative writing. *The Journal of Violence and Gender*, 3(2), p. 78-88.

Van Brunt, B., Murphy, A., & Zedginidze, A. (2017). An exploration of the risk, *Protective, and Mobilization Factors Related to Violent Extremism in College Populations*, 4(3), p. 81-101.

Van Brunt, B., & Pescara-Kovach, P. (2019). Debunking the myths: Mental illness and mass shootings. *Journal of Violence and Gender*, 6(1), p. 53-63.

Van Brunt, B., & Solomon, J. (2019). *Threat case studies*. King of Prussia, PA: The National Behavioral Intervention Team Association.

Vossekuil, B., Fein, R., Reddy, M., Borum, R., & Modzeleski, W. (2002). *The final report and findings of the safe school initiative: Implications for the prevention of school attacks in the United States*. Washington, DC: U.S. Secret Service and U.S. Department of Education.

Chapter 4

Protective Elements in Targeted Violence

In Chapter 3, we explored the risk factors that elevate our concerns when assessing individuals related to potential targeted violence. We used the analogy of a teeter-totter on a playground and described the risk factors as having the individual raised high toward the sky with their feet dangling, precariously perched on the precipice of violence. The more risk factors, the higher the teeter-totter sits, requiring extensive intervention to deescalate and bring it back to the ground. In contrast, during this chapter, we begin to bring down the teeter-totter as we consider the protective factors that add stability and support to an individual's experience making their potential for violence less concerning. Protective factors literally "ground" the individual and create a defense against elements that may incite or motivate violence.

The Centers for Disease Control and Prevention (CDC) define *protective factors* as "individual or environmental characteristics, conditions, or behaviors that reduce the effects of stressful life events. These factors also increase an individual's ability to avoid risks or hazards and promote social and emotional competence to thrive in all aspects of life, now and in the future" (Centers for Disease Control and Prevention [CDC], 2018, para. 2). The research on protective factors and targeted violence is not quite as extensive as the risk-factor research discussed in Chapter 3, but some organizations and researchers have explored the elements that pull against movement toward targeted violence (O'Toole, 2002; Van Brunt et al., 2017; National Threat Assessment Center [NTAC], 2018; Sokolow et al., 2019). A helpful table of some of the most common protective factors is provided below in Table 4.1.

Protective factors serve two purposes for our discussion of written threats. First, they provide a framework for prevention programs and initiatives related to targeted violence. By focusing efforts for individuals and groups on the enhancement of protective factors, we essentially build up their immunity to more nefarious elements that could potentially motivate targeted violence. You could also think of protective factors as though you are creating emergency exits for

TABLE 4.1 Assorted Protective Factors for Targeted Violence

Social support	Empathy to others	School engagement	Religious supports
Family support	Perspective-taking	Work engagement	Nonviolent outlets
Positive future view	Intimate relationship	Positive self-esteem	Problem-solving
No weapon access	Sense of identity	Consequence-aware	Emotional stability
Social/political safety	Housing stability	Resiliency	Lacks reactivity

individuals escalating toward violence. These factors support movement toward nonviolent attitudes and behaviors when life goes awry.

Protective factors also provide a "lens" for us to view behaviors and attitudes when we are considering and assessing threats and concerning behavior. They help us examine the complex layers of a person's experience so we can better understand underlying motivations and drivers. One of the most difficult things for individuals and teams working with those making threats or acting in scary and dangerous ways is trying to discern why they feel the way they do and recognizing how they could act in such an extreme way. When we consider the interactions between both risk factors and protective factors, it helps us better conceptualize how to support nonviolent action.

In a recent threat scenario at a university in Canada, a male student had begun messaging a female student who had an open Instagram account with pictures. He messaged her for three days without a response, becoming increasingly agitated and eventually threatening (Van Brunt & Solomon, 2019). Figure 4.1 contains a small sampling of the messenger comments he made. The perfume mention harkens back to a previous message about her smelling his perfume when he would eventually hug her.

While the case had a concerning level of risk around threats to harm others and commit suicide, there were some mitigating elements and protective factors that worked into the analysis. In terms of *mitigating elements,* the student had done this frequently with other women he found attractive, creating a lack of specificity and level of disorganization to his threat. He also was an English as a Second Language (ESL) student, that added to his lack of understanding of how this persistent, aggressive approach to would create distance rather than connection. The student also some mental illness concerns that gave an obsessive and younger developmental tone to his writing. Of note, this case is given to demonstrate some mitigating elements and protective factors, although it bears repeating that the female in this case should not be exposed to this kind of harassment and threat. In terms of *protective factors*, he has support from his parents at home, support from counseling off-campus and is building additional friend supports.

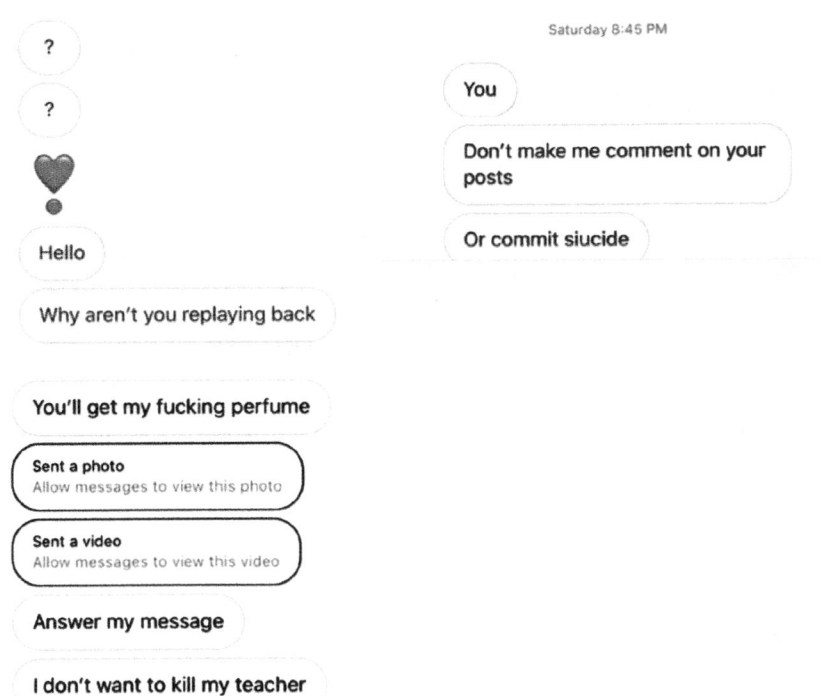

FIGURE 4.1 Canadian threat case Instagram messages.

PROTECTIVE FACTORS AND MITIGATING ELEMENTS

In this section, we introduce five protective factors from the research. In addition, we discuss the concept of mitigating elements. In Chapter 6, we will return to this concept as part of a research-informed model for the assessment of written content. Mitigating elements are closely related to the concept of protective factors. Mitigating elements consider details of the concern that lessen the severity or seriousness of the risk; specifically, here we consider the author's disposition and the context in which the writing occurred. For example, if the written piece is composed by someone who is a creative fiction author actively working on a project, this lessens our concern about targeted violence, especially when other protective factors are in place. Similar to someone writing to a specific class assignment and offering contextually appropriate themes despite their disturbing nature, we consider this a lower risk concern, particularly when other protective factors align.

To help you make the connections between mitigating elements and protective factors, we include them throughout this next section as examples of how context and disposition can be informed by an understanding of protective factors in the research. First, we highlight five protective factors representing important

FIGURE 4.2 Foundational protective factor.

attitudes and experiences that promote nonviolence. There are summarized in Figure 4.2. We will discuss each item in some detail along with related mitigating elements.

ENVIRONMENTAL AND EMOTIONAL STABILITY

In their most basic form, protective factors consider the positive influences surrounding an individual. *Environmental and emotional stability* occurs when an individual's life experiences have consistency and constancy, and their reactions to change or crisis represent a similar calm and resilience. This is an indication that there are fewer elements pulling them toward creating disruption in the status quo through violent action (Van Brunt et al., 2017). Here, the overall environment in which the person operates is positive without dramatic shifts. The person has stable employment and/or academic enrollment, and they are engaged in these professional or academic arenas. There have not been recent terminations or suspensions, and the family or home environment is generally stable and healthy. The person is not challenged by instability in their situation. They are connected and progressing toward academic or professional goals.

Of course, there are times for each of us when our life feels out of balance and off-center. This protective factor considers both the experience and our reaction to it. Are there opportunities to improve our situation? Is the instability short-term or something we have the capacity to overcome? Do we get knocked down with a blow, become upset and hurt for a time period but then return to our routine, or do we remain fixated on the blow and who or what caused it? In the heat of the moment, reactions, outbursts or frustrated communications can occur, but this is less concerning than more thoughtful communications coming out of a wound that has festered. When teams consider the context of a threat, they should consider the mitigating factor of whether the post is an *affective reaction to a specific stressor* and transient in nature. This type of reaction to short-term instability in the environment is less concerning than writing that demonstrates a build-up of frustration and resentment around regularly occurring concerns without any relief in sight.

The latter is highlighted in the following note left behind after the Campbell County High School shooting in Jacksboro, Tennessee, on November 8, 2005 (Appendix B: 33). Acting on a tip from another student that a student had brought a firearm in to school, he was brought into the office and proceeded to shoot the principal and two assistant principals. The spiral of isolation, sadness

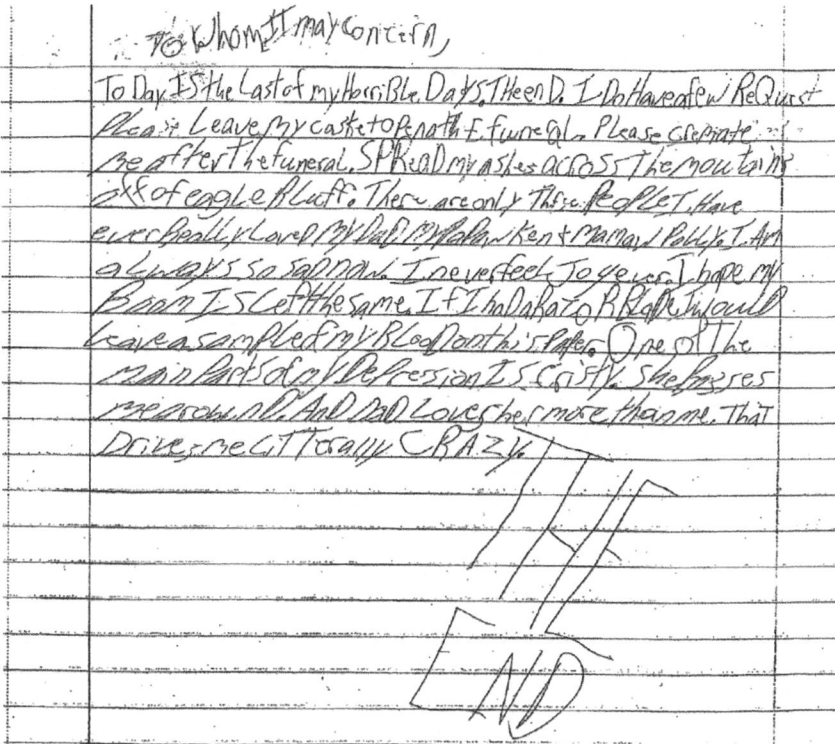

FIGURE 4.3 Campbell High School shooter's suicide note.

and depression helped create the catalyst for the attack. His note is provided in Figure 4.3.

In addition to the stability of an individual's environment, we must also consider the stability of their emotions. In Chapter 3 on risk factors, we discuss personality and mental state, specifically the need to consider suicidality and mental illness as potential aggravating factors. Emotional stability is enhanced when there is a corresponding *psychological steadiness* and well-being (Pressman, 2009). Here, individuals have a generally positive sense of themselves and their opportunities in the future. Even when more complex mental concerns discussed in the risk factors are present, a protective factor can be access to mental health support and/or treatment when needed. There are other aspects of mental health that may mitigate our concerns about threats as well. If an author is *rambling and incoherent*, this can be an indicator of a connection to mental health concerns that can be mitigated through provider treatment and support as opposed to a more intentional dangerousness. "Competent and adequate professional supervision and control will…influence the degree of risk for exposure to destabilizing factors" (Borum et al., 1999, p. 334).

59

We may also observe expression that is influenced by developmental conditions, where the writing is influenced by a lack of **emotional control or regulation**, as with an individual diagnosed with Asperger's syndrome, for example. This accidental or transient type of threat lacks the concerning intentionality of targeted violence. Last, the context of the writing can also reflect a mitigating element related to mental health where the writer is using the writing activity in a **therapeutic process**, such as journaling to avoid action, which is actually a positive indicator of emotional awareness and health.

SOCIAL HEALTH AND CONNECTION

A second protective factor relates to stability in relationships with family, friends and significant others. The person feels **socially connected in healthy and positive ways**. They feel safe in their own skin, and do not feel marginalized or discriminated against based on their identity or identity group. They are surrounded by others where they can be themselves, feel accepted and are not judged for their beliefs or circumstance. The National Threat Assessment Center (2018) identifies factors such as relationships without judgment, but also those that provide positive support and direction. For example, **positive and trusting relationships** with adults in schools is important for students. They also feel emotionally connected to those around them, which girds against a desire to harm or threaten. There are certainly times where we all experience social conflict or concerning experiences in our relationships with others. When considering someone's social experience, context matters. A person writing concerning posts in **retaliation for a social wrong** as a means of "saving face" or "gaining power" is much more of a reactionary concern to a perceived wrong as opposed to a targeted threat. By responding to this type of concern by offering new opportunities for social connections and supportive relationships instead of further isolating from the larger sense of social safety, we are able to mitigate the potential risk.

ACCESS TO NONVIOLENT OUTLETS

Having access to alternative, nonviolent courses of action is an important protective factor. When you are upset or grieved, how do you deal with those frustrations? Do you have those you can talk with about your concerns? Are you able to utilize formal and informal processes for resolving grievances, negotiating solutions or advocating for change? Any of these options represent **access to nonviolent outlets** for expressing frustrations and resolving problems. Individuals have opportunities for positive collective action on issues and concerns instead of turning to violence (United Nations Educational, Scientific and Cultural Organization, 2016). Especially when considering written threat, it's important to consider if this is someone seeking a safe space to communicate and discuss issues of concern or radical ideas about improving the way the world works.

Consider for a minute those that use social media and blogs to "troll" and agitate others, sometimes motivated by free speech or other ideological goals. In research, trolling is provocative and designed to gain a reaction (Sanfilippo et al., 2018). The more deviant trolling behaviors that mock or degrade are still done as a way to upset people and cause disruption and discord in the community. According to the same study, rarely are trolls concerned about a specific target or target group. This type of *professional agitator or troll* is less concerning, and this is actually seen as a nonviolent outlet for the person to communicate options. Another example of a mitigating element related to access to nonviolent outlets is when someone is writing a *rhetoric or opinion piece* in an effort to change attitudes and behaviors of others. They may use satire or provocative language, but this is different from written materials fixated on a target with other risk factors present.

EMPATHY AND CONNECTION

In our earlier discussion of risk factors, we identified the element of increasing objectification and depersonalization as part of the escalation toward violence. Here, the protective factor that fights against these dangerous attitudes is that of *empathy or compassion*. The empathetic or compassionate person demonstrates the ability to consider others' perspectives or others' ideals without seeing them as challenging or competitive to his or her own beliefs. This can manifest itself as tolerance and an appreciation of diverse perspectives as well. Empathy can be experienced when thinking about people who live differently than us, engaging with other cultures and confronting our own biases, as well as learning to listen to other's perspectives and collaborating with them (Priddy, 2018).

The protective factor of empathy is also a good example of how our interventions in concerning situations can potentially act to support an increase in empathy and a decrease in mistrust, deception and manipulation (Chialant et al., 2016). Several competency areas have been identified related to the development of empathy in others (Borba, 2018). These include the ability to read emotions, or emotional literacy. This can be made more difficult in writing or online. Other competencies include self-regulation and being able to keep our emotions in check, as well as moral courage and the desire to help others despite consequences. In Table 4.2, listed are many related efforts in our schools and organizations that are connected to the protective factors discussed here and have the potential to build on these important aspects of safety and wellness.

When viewing written materials, we can consider if there are messages of understanding or acceptance embedded within because this gives us a positive place to begin when intervening and demonstrates aspects of empathy. The use of another person's name in the writing can be a demonstrated connection

TABLE 4.2 Efforts Related to the Development of Protective Factors

Positive organization or school climates	Equity	Social, emotional learning and development
Cultural competence and responsiveness	Relationship skills	Trauma-informed processes and staff
Mindfulness	Whole-child initiatives	Sense of belonging
Problem-solving	Self-control/emotional regulation	Positive psychology

obviously different than name-calling or abusive language that distances them from other individuals. Even the use of words as simple as "feeling" or "understanding" can reflect empathetic responses in writing. On social media, you may see someone being considerate of others' viewpoints different from their own. You might also observe the person communicating a distinct and different point of view, but they are able to do so without breaking into contentious arguments or harmful debate. Any of these actions can be indicators of an empathetic and connected attitude towards others, which decreases our concern about violence.

POSITIVE SOCIAL AND INDIVIDUAL ACTION

The last protective factor we will discuss in this chapter relates to our two previous concepts of empathy and nonviolent outlets. Here, we see someone who is engaged in *positive social action* for the betterment of a group or community, or even at a lesser developmental place of just positive action for the sake of their own *individual consequence*. The second is fairly simple. This individual has an awareness of how their choices result in positive or negative consequences minimally for themselves or those in their circle, and thus, chooses actions to avoid harm. "I choose not to hurt someone because there could be negative consequences for me, my family, my friends." Individuals can also choose nonviolent pathways because of perceived rewards and motivators, such as continued access to participation in school or work activities (NTAC, 2018). On a higher level, positive social action includes a more inclusive and collaborative participation to improve situations, remove barriers to success, and foster positive change. This level of critical thinking, awareness of others and inclusivity truly reflects the opposite of violent action and the risk factors explored in Chapter 3. When someone feels a part of a broader community and is surrounded by positive social supports with promising opportunities for the future, this exemplifies how the protective factors guard against potential violence risks.

MOVING FORWARD

Now that we have reviewed the protective and risk factors, we will take a deeper dive into the nature of threat and how these concepts can be brought together in a more practical approach called Looking Glass in Chapter 6.

REFERENCES

Borba, M. (2018). Nine competencies for teaching empathy. *Educational Leadership*, 76(2), 22–28.

Borum, R., Fein, R., Vossekuil, B., & Berglund, J. (1999). Threat assessment: Defining an approach for evaluating risk of targeted violence. *Behavioral Sciences and the Law*, 17, 323–337.

Center for Disease Control. (2018). Protective factors. Retrieved on March 28, 2020 from https://www.cdc.gov/healthyyouth/protective/index.htm

Chialant, D., Edersheim, J., & Price, B.H. (2016). The dialectic between empathy and violence: An opportunity for intervention? *The Journal of Neuropsychiatry and Clinical Neurosciences*, 28(4), 273–285.

National Threat Assessment Center (NTAC). (2018). *Enhancing school safety using a threat assessment model: An operational guide for preventing targeted school violence.* Washington, DC: U.S. Secret Service, Department of Homeland Security.

O'Toole, M.E. (2002). *The school shooter: A threat assessment perspective.* Quantico, VA: FBI.

Pressman, D. (2009). *Risk assessment decisions for violent political extremism.* Ottawa: Her Majesty the Queen in Right of Canada.

Priddy, N. (2018). Empathy is academic: Lessons from lotus slippers. *Education Update*, 60(12), 1–2.

Sanfilippo, M.R., Fichman, P., & Yang, S. (2018). Multidimensionality of online trolling behaviors. *The Information Society*, 34(1), 27–39.

Sokolow, B., Van Brunt, B., Lewis, W., Schiemann, M., Murphy, A., & Molnar, J. (2019). *The NaBITA risk rubric.* King of Prussia, PA: The National behavioral Intervention Team Association.

United Nations Educational, Scientific and Cultural Organization. (2016). *A teachers guide to the prevention of violent extremism.* Paris, France. UNESCO (United Nations Educational, Scientific and Cultural Organization). https://en.unesco.org

Van Brunt, B., Murphy, A., & Zedginidze, A. (2017). An exploration of the risk, protective, and mobilization factors related to violent extremism in college populations *Violence and Gender*, 4(3), 81–101.

Van Brunt, B., & Solomon, J. (2019). *Threat case studies.* King of Prussia, PA: The National Behavioral Intervention Team Association.

Chapter 5

All Threats Are Not Created Equal

Threat assessment is about balance. Balancing what is potential leakage for an attack and what is trolling for attention or reaction, a passive attempt at help-seeking, an immature action or a marginalized student looking to exercise power. What is evidence of an attack plan and what is poking at others for attention, to cause chaos or express pain?

To highlight the challenge, the following is a suicidal statement made by a student on Reddit. It was made in December 2019 prior to finals at a college in the Northeast (Van Brunt and Solomon, 2019). The post was anonymous and included a screenshot from *Cowboy Bepop*, an anime series about a bounty hunter who travels through space (Figure 5.1).

The case brings to light the challenge facing educators when responding to concerning written content. What is a true threat of suicide versus seeking attention? Was this made to troll or gain reactions from the community or cause disruption and worry to the campus administrators? Was this a dare gone wrong? Or was it actually a post made by someone on the edge? How can the school do anything when the post was made anonymously?

Betterdeadafterall 🖋 -1 points · 4 days ago

I'm sorry to say but I've decided to kill myself on Wednesday by hanging myself in my closet. Might as well spend the next two days enjoying my time with friends at the pancake breakfast and enjoy a drunk night with my Discord friends on Tuesday.

I just wanted to give y'all a heads up and get you all mentally prepared for the emails you get next week about a student being hung in their closet. It won't be easy for some of you and I'm sorry. However while I have made great memories at SUNY Poly, all good things must come to an end.

See you Space Cowboy...

Reply Share ···

FIGURE 5.1 Threat of suicide by Student on Reddit.

64

When approaching these scenarios, the Goldilocks fable is useful to recall. The school should avoid a response that is either too hot or too cold. In this case, too hot would be shutting down the campus or sending an emergency alert; too cold would be assuming that since the post was anonymous, there is nothing that can be done. The "just right" approach would involve looking at the context, consulting with IT and law enforcement to see if there is a way to narrow down who made the post. Even if the identity of the poster cannot be determined, a supportive message from the school (such as in Figure 5.2) would be advisable.

Threats of suicide or harm to others should be approached in a balanced manner. BIT/CARE teams should not overact or underreact to threats, but rather approach them consistently in an evidenced-based manner. Avoiding assumptions and speculation and keeping an eye towards mitigating personal or systemic bias should be considerations in any assessment of risk. Common errors are summarized in Table 5.1.

Direct threats identifying the target of violence rarely result in an attack (Scalora et al., 2010; Turner & Gelles, 2003). Fein et al. (1995) made the clear distinction between posing a threat and making a threat. Students might write concerning material to express anger, control or intimidate others, communicate frustrations or express hopelessness and desperation. When determining risk, the social media posts or other written material should be assessed in the larger context of their occurrence. Ideally, this would involve a threat assessment interview to determine the exact nature and likelihood of the threat (Van Brunt, 2015a).

Threats should be assessed to answer the question, "Are the social media posts or other writings evidence of a larger threat or attack plan?" These pre-attack behaviors are common in most predatory violence cases and offer educators and BIT/CARE teams an opportunity to avert an attack. Threats that are expressed verbally or in a written format can represent potential leakage (behaviors or actions prior to an attack that are communicated to a third party) or simply be an impulsive expression of frustration. Meloy (2001) wrote: "...for directly communicated threats and subsequent violence: most individuals who directly communicate a threat are not subsequently violent and most individuals who do not directly communicate a threat are not subsequently violent" (p. 1213).

Jeniferra 15 points · 4 days ago ⑤

Hi - this is Jennifer Adams from SUNY Poly. I chair our Care Team and saw your post. There are a lot of people here who care and want to help or at the very least listen. I can listen. Please reach out to me and we can meet. jennifer.adams@sunypoly.edu. There are other great people on our Care Team, as well; Kaila Aimino from Adirondack, Megan Lennon from Community Standards, Katie Tynan from Title IX Sandy Mizerak from Counseling, Gary Bean from University Police, Carlie Phipps from our faculty - any of us are here for you. All of our residential team cares about you - any Resident Advisor or any of the Hall Directors can help. 7911 or 911 can get you to SUNY Poly University Police dispatch, which can get you help and/or to me. If you walk into the Wellness Center in the Campus Center and privately tell the very confidential person at the desk that you wrote the reddit post and need to talk to someone, they will get you in with one of our counselors. Please let us help. Office hours extend until 5pm every day this week, but there are other resources for after hours or not on campus, too - the Oneida County Mobile Crisis Assessment Team (MCAT) is free and available 24.7 - they will come to where you are to talk! 315-732-6228 or 844-732-6228. There is also a free 24/7 Crisis text line - text HOME to 741741 and someone will talk to you. **You are not alone in this.**

FIGURE 5.2 Campus response to threat of suicide.

TABLE 5.1 Common Errors When Assessing Threat

Written Concern	Poor Response	Good Response
Student posts threat of suicide anonymously on social media	Assume since it is anonymous that there is nothing to be done	Consult internal IT, law enforcement and the website where it was posted to identify the student
Student makes hateful, derogatory statements about another race or gender online	See this as a free speech issue and, while the school doesn't support the comments, avoid any further analysis or intervention	Assess the nature of the comment in the context of their other posts, look for additional risk factors as discussed in Chapter 3
Student writes a paper in class about a coming war following a political election that goes against their desires	See this as free speech and have no reaction, or overreact and see the student as a potential terrorist	Assess the nature of the assignment, how the student has responded in the past, consider a more detailed assessment in person
Student writes a manifesto and rap lyrics about a desire to kill those who are part of the boomer generation	Make an assumption that this is free speech or satire and avoid any further investigation	Assess the nature of the threat through a multidisciplinary team approach involving law enforcement, mental health staff and student conduct staff

If the threat is determined to be indicative of leakage related to an attack plan, the BIT/CARE team should move toward an in-person threat assessment process. This is not the same as a mental health assessment and instead focuses on determining the presence of escalating risk factors (discussed in Chapter 3) against the contextual backdrop of protective factors (discussed in Chapter 4). The book *Harm to Others: The Treatment and Assessment of Dangerousness* (Van Brunt, 2015a) offers a detailed approach to the threat assessment process through the use of the SIVRA-35. Other approaches include the RAGE-V (Association of Threat Assessment Professionals [ATAP], 2006), the HCR-20 (Hart & Logan, 2011) and MOSIAC (de Becker, 2019).

Commonly in violence risk assessment, the process involves determining the motivation and context of threat, social media post or written content where there is no evidence of a lethal attack plan. The concern is well summed up here by Calhoun and Weston (2009) as they discuss those who are seeking attention and those planning an attack: "... as a practical matter howlers can become hunters. Some howlers reach a point where something happens to propel them across the line up to take up the hunt. Something tips them across the great divide that separates howling from hunting. We call that tipping point the last straw syndrome" (p. 135). Much of the research on this topic was conducted prior to the rapid growth in social media, as discussed in Chapter 2.

An example of this occurred months prior to the attack at Chardon High School on February 27, 2012 (Appendix B: 73). On December 30, 2011, the attacker posted the following story as an update to his account:

> In a time long since, a time of repent, The Renaissance. In a quaint lonely town, sits a man with a frown. No job. No family. No crown. His luck had run out. Lost and alone. The streets were his home. His thoughts would solely consist of "why do we exist?" His only company to confide in was the vermin in the street. He longed for only one thing, the world to bow at his feet. They too should feel his secret fear. The dismal drear. His pain had made him sincere. He was better than the rest, all those ones he detests, within their castles, so vain. Selfish and conceited. They couldn't care less about the peasants they mistreated. They were in their own world, it was a joyous one too. That castle, she stood just to do all she could to keep the peasants at bay, not the enemy away. They had no enemies in their filthy orgy. And in her, the castles every story, was just another chamber of Lucifer's Laboratory. The world is a sandbox for all the wretched sinners. They simply create what they want and make themselves the winners. But the true winner, he has nothing at all. Enduring the pain of waiting for that castle to fall. Through his good deeds, the rats and the fleas. He will have for what he pleads, through the eradication of disease. So, to the castle he proceeds, like an ominous breeze through the trees. "Stay back!" The Guards screamed as they were thrown to their knees. "Oh God, have mercy, please!" The castle, she gasped and then so imprisoned her breath, to the shallow confines of her fragile chest. I'm on the lamb but I ain't no sheep. I am Death. And you have always been the sod. So repulsive and so odd. You never even deserved the presence of God, and yet, I am here. Around your cradle I plod. Came on foot, without shod. How improper, how rude. However, they shall not mind the mud on my feet if there is blood on your sheet. Now! Feel death, not just mocking you. Not just stalking you but inside of you. Wriggle and writhe. Feel smaller beneath my might. Seizure in the Pestilence that is my scythe. Die, all of you
>
> (GlobalGrind Staff, 2012, p. 1).

The story is one that has several of the risk factors discussed in Chapter 3. There is a narrowing down on the target through a fixation and focus on the castle. The castle is objectified through negative language; "every chamber is Lucifer's laboratory," conducting a "filthy orgy" and "a sandbox for the wretched sinners." The author refers to himself both as God and Death, imbibed with the power to stalk, punish and kill. He is a suffering martyr, "enduring the pain" with "no job, no family, no crown." There is a discussion of overcoming potential obstacles to a successful attack, such as overpowering the guards. The final scene invokes feelings of killing and rape with the concluding line "Die, all of you." The danger here is seeing this story as simply an artistic expression or under the protection of free speech when the story gives larger evidence of a potential attack plan (Van Brunt, 2015b). A more detailed process on how to better understand these writings is explored in Chapter 6.

Warren et al. (2014) offer a detailed and helpful model when it comes to understanding the different types of threats educators may encounter. These are summarized in Table 5.2 and include Screamers, Shockers, Shielders, Schemers and Signalers. As mentioned above, the task in front of BIT/CARE

TABLE 5.2 Five Types of Threateners (Warren et al. 2014)

Threateners	Description	Example
Screamers	The most common; reactive and emotional statements, often made in response to a wide range of provocations.	In a class, a student writes on the chalkboard a diagram with a bomb to blow up the school after the teacher challenges him to do a math problem he doesn't know how to do.
Shockers	Threats made to induce panic and fear in others. Often used to obtain dominance over others or regain lost power.	A student writes a mock version of a "modest proposal," advocating the eating of the teachers after being suspended from school for disruptive behavior.
Shielders	Self-protective statements with the intention of pushing away those who may cause harm.	After being teased and bullied at school, a student writes an open letter to the student body saying, "If this continues, you will all feel the power I have within me."
Schemers	A demand or threat made to influence others. Often thought about beforehand and made with the intent to have the target comply with their demands.	A student writes a fiction essay about how everyone should band together to rise up and take control of the school.
Signalers	Threats that are aimed at future promises to harm the target in response to actual or perceived harm.	An email is sent to the police to inform them the school isn't safe during graduation and that a well-placed explosive could end everything really quickly.

teams is to differentiate between these types of threats and ascertain the overall lethality of the violence risk.

In demonstration of a *screaming threat*, a student at a community college in southern California wrote on the back of his exam paper the following poem, "A smile indeed, Is the scariest thing, It, can come, from any need, even from anger and madness it springs. Do I smile? Indeed, yes, of course, But you'll never know if I'll hug you or gut you, and laugh at your corpse" (Van Brunt & Solomon, 2019). The student in question had a long history of being bullied, was on medication for depression and was failing his course. Upon interview, it was determined there was little direction to the threat, but steps were taken to ensure the student had access to counseling and academic support. This is categorized as a screaming threat as it was reactive to his failing the class and his increasing frustration, hopelessness and desperation.

In a classic *shocker threat*, an individual posted on the website 4chan a threat concerning an impending violent attack in the Philadelphia area in early October 2015 (Figure 5.3). The threat referenced the fatal shooting at Umpqua Community College in Oregon (Appendix B: 96). The 4chan user wrote, "On October 5, 2015, at 1:00 PM CT, a fellow robot will take up arms against a university near Philadelphia. His cries will be heard, his victims will cower in fear, and the strength of the Union will decay a little more" (Tanenbaum, 2015, p. 1). The date passed with no attack occurring, though the news coverage and widespread panic from the threat makes it an excellent example of a shocking threat.

Schemers seek to manipulate others to comply with their wishes. In the 2014 Isla Vista attack (Appendix B: 87), the attacker created a YouTube video and wrote a 141-page manifesto entitled, "My Twisted World," in which he expressed his romantic frustrations (Speer, 2014). He wrote, "All I ever wanted was to love women, and in turn to be loved by them back. Their behavior towards me has only earned my hatred, and rightfully so! I am the true victim in all of this. I am the good guy. Humanity struck at me first by condemning me to experience so much suffering. I didn't ask for this. I didn't want this. I didn't start this war. I wasn't the one who struck first. But I will finish it by striking back. I will punish

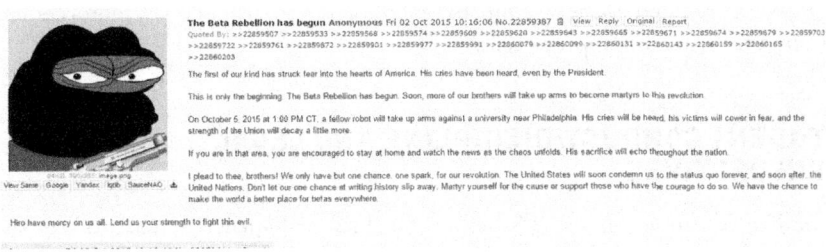

FIGURE 5.3 Threat made on 4chan (Craig, 2015).

everyone. And it will be beautiful. Finally, at long last, I can show the world my true worth" (Rodger, 2014, p. 141).

A *signaler* example can be found with the averted attack in August 2011 in Tampa, Florida (Appendix B: 71). The student in question was expelled from Freedom High School in 2009 and planned an attack that was stopped by police in August of 2011 (Teicher-Khadaroo, 2011). Police obtained a warrant and found the attacker with quantities of fuel, shrapnel, plastic tubing and timing and fusing devices for making pipe bombs, along with marijuana and marijuana cultivation equipment. The student recorded a 60-second video describing his plans for the attack on his cell phone. The text of this recording is as follows:

> For those of you retards who don't know who I am, I'm the Freedom High School shooter in Tampa, Florida. Well, I will be in a couple months. I thought I would run over my game plan with y'all. The cafeteria at Freedom. My plan is to set a bomb here at point A, here at point B, point C and point D. Then I got to get to the side entrance of the school by 7:24. The bombs blow at 7:26. I'm going to come in and advance on the courtyard where there'll probably be at least sixty people. [I'll] come through the door then shoot everybody at the front desk. Mr. Costanzo's office is right here, I've got to kill him. Mrs. Carmody is here I've got to kill her. Mr. Pears is here, I've got to make sure he doesn't die, because I like him. There's nothing I can do about it, there's nothing anybody can do about it other than wait for it to unleash. If you don't like it just find a way to find people like me and just line us up and shoot us
>
> (Pow, 2012).

On November 17, 2015, Keen University experienced a *shielding threat* after multiple Twitter threats were made against black students in the community (Van Brunt & Solomon, 2019). The student who made the threats was a black activist who was frustrated by white counter-protesters at a rally. She created a false Twitter account and made the threats (Figure 5.4; Alicea, 2015). Then she went back to the rally to make others aware of the threats (Lewis, 2016). This case demonstrates a shielding threat, as the tweets were designed to ward off potential aggression directed to her group by encouraging a stronger law enforcement reaction to the counter-protesters.

STUDENT CONDUCT/DISCIPLINE AND LEGAL PERSPECTIVES

Whether Screamer, Shocker, Schemer, Shielder or Signaler, schools often have the choice to engage in a BIT/CARE and/or a conduct response. This is where the legal issues from Chapter 1 become more prevalent. A good way to think

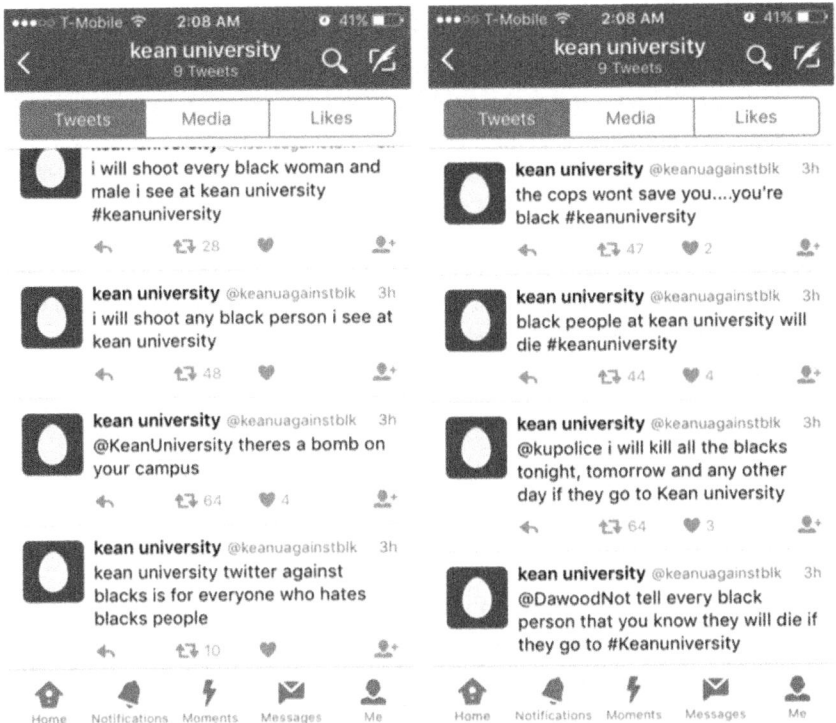

FIGURE 5.4 Threats made at Keen University.

about this is as two different trains pulling from the station. The school may have the option to have the BIT/CARE train pull from the station first, reach out to the student and gauge the student's response before having the student conduct train pull from the station and send a notice of allegation/investigation. The school may choose to have the Student Conduct Office (SCO) send notice before the BIT/CARE outreach and see how the student responds. Or, the school may choose to have both groups reach out independently at the same time.

It is important to remember that BIT/CARE, when done properly, does not engage in adverse acts towards the student. As such, the due process provisions that apply to student conduct do not apply to BIT/CARE, so long as BIT/CARE does not make the mistake of acting like conduct. BIT/CARE does not suspend, expel, remove students from classes or even recommend suspension. While there may be a set sanction for failing to comply with a mandated assessment that may include suspension, BIT/CARE is not doing the suspending; the conduct office determines the final outcome after affording the student adequate due process.

But as mentioned in Chapter 1, BIT/CARE and the SCO need to be very cognizant of what speech is protected under the First Amendment. It is equally important to remember that not all speech is protected. The three areas where this surfaces in the BIT/CARE world are:

1. Harassing speech
2. Disruptive speech
3. True threats

Harassing Speech: In order for speech to reach the level of harassment, the speech has to hit certain thresholds. Sexual harassment (sometimes referred to as "Title IX cases") provides a good insight into how this is evaluated. For the speech to lose its protections, it must be:

1. severe, and
2. persistent, or
3. pervasive, and
4. objectively offensive

Generally speaking, no one or two utterances of even the most offensive sexist, racist or misogynistic statements are going to rise to the level of "severe." Severe, as a standard, is typically reached thorough persistence or pervasiveness. The speech need only be objectively offensive, but the context of the speech will matter. Campuses will generally encounter this with social media posts or statements of sexist, sexual, racist, homophobic, etc. language showing a hardened perspective or referencing injustice collecting. It is critical that the school evaluate the language to see if it is protected. In other words, someone can post or say virtually anything once or twice and it will not rise to the level of persistence or pervasiveness. There are some other variables that need to be considered as well—notably the relationship between the speaker and recipient and the location of the speech. For example, when the speech is uttered by someone in power over the recipient, the number of times needed to be persistent may be less than if they are peers.

Where the speech is uttered is important as well. This is often referred to as a forum analysis. The more public the forum, the less restrictions a school can place on the speech. The types of fora are:

1. Public Forum—places like a street corner, the internet, etc.
2. Designated Public Forum—where you need permission to access the space (e.g., the space outside the student union where vendors can rent a table).
3. Limited Public Forum—where you need to have some affiliation with the school to gain access to the space, like reserving a classroom.
4. Private Forum—your home, and to a lesser extent, your office (your employer can limit speech in some offices).

The further down the list above, the easier it is to restrict the speech. In a public forum (like a street corner), people have a higher degree of free speech than in someone's home or office. The internet is generally considered a public forum, but a discussion group board moderated by a professor would be a limited public forum.

As of late, there has been an uptick in complaints about people saying or posting things that offend someone that will not rise to the level of harassing speech but may still be inappropriate. This is an area ripe for BIT/CARE to intervene and educate the speaker and recipient, as the SCO is unable to sanction protected speech.

Disruptive Speech: In order for speech to reach the level of disruption needed to lose protection, it must actually cause a disruption or identical speech must have recently caused a disruption. In the seminal case on this issue, Cohen v. California, 403 U.S. 15 (1971), a man was arrested for wearing a jacket that said "Fuck the Draft" in a public courthouse in the heat of the Vietnam War protest era. He was arrested under the guise that he would cause a disturbance. The Court determined the anticipation of disturbance is not sufficient. This concept is applied to schools in Tinker v. Des Moines, 393 U.S. 503 (1968) where kids wanted to wear armbands at school to protest the war. The Court reminds us that we do not "check our Constitutional rights at the schoolhouse gates." Schools would be cautioned against manufacturing the disruption as well, trying to create protest with ideas that administrators disagree with.

True Threat: In order for the speech in these cases to lose the protection of the First Amendment, the evaluation of the threat itself as well as its intent or reasonably foreseeable consequences is required. In other words, if someone issues a threat against a person or group of people, the threat itself has to be evaluated. Is it possible for this person to carry out the threat? Did they mean the threat to scare this person or group? If not, is it reasonable that the statement would cause this person or group to be actually scared? This may seem like a low subjective bar, but it is not. Schools would do well to utilize their trained BIT/CARE teams to assess the level of threat of the statement before taking any action.

Application: Let's take the Tatro v. U. of Minnesota, 800 N.W.2d 811 (2011) case as an example. Ms. Tatro was a mortuary science student at the University of Minnesota (Appendix B: 59). She was a non-traditional age student who had several social media posts that caused some concern amongst the faculty at Minnesota, resulting in her removal from the program and her then suing the institution. The posts are as follows (Bernie is the name she gave the cadaver assigned to her):

1. Nov. 12: "(I) Gets to play, I mean dissect, Bernie today. Let's see if I can have a lab void of reprimanding and having my scalpel taken away. Perhaps if I just hide it in my sleeve..."
2. Dec. 6: "...looking forward to Monday's embalming therapy as well as a rumored opportunity to aspirate. Give me room, lots of aggression to be taken out with a trocar." (NOTE: A trocar is a large needle used to drain the body of fluids and/or inject embalming fluid.)

3. Dec. 7: "Who knew embalming lab was so cathartic! I still want to stab a certain someone in the throat with a trocar though. Hmm..perhaps I will spend the evening updating my 'Death List #5' and making friends with the crematory guy. I do know the code..." (NOTE: The "code" is the entry code to the crematorium.)

4. Undated, but believed to be on Dec. 7: "Realized with great sadness that my best friend, Bernie, will no longer be with me as of Friday next week. I wish to accompany him to the retort. Now where will I go or who will I hang with when I need to gather my sanity? Bye, bye Bernie. Lock of hair in my pocket."

Taking these posts one by one and analyzing them gives insight into the free speech analysis of her statements. First and foremost, the statements are made on her personal Facebook page, a public forum, so the school's ability to regulate her speech and take action based on it is already very limited. This, however, does not stop the school from encouraging the report to the BIT and assessing for further concerns of escalations.

The first statement, "(I) Gets to play, I mean dissect, Bernie today. Let's see if I can have a lab void of reprimanding and having my scalpel taken away. Perhaps if I just hide it in my sleeve..." is fully protected but should have resulted in a BIT/CARE report to assess and monitor for further escalation. There is nothing inherently threatening or offensive about the statements, and it is not a call to disruption or lawless action. But it is interesting that she has had to have her scalpel taken away in class. The BIT/CARE team should investigate why that occurred. A quick outreach to the professor might answer this. At most, it is a possible announcement that she might violate classroom procedures by hiding her scalpel in her sleeve to avoid having it taken away. But even then, a professor who would take it away on the basis of this post and without any behavior to fall back on, especially at a public school, may risk that being viewed as taking an adverse act on the basis of her free speech. Similar to the disruptive speech analysis, it cannot be the anticipation of the act. Further, at this point her speech may even appear to be sarcastic in nature. At best, this is a good time to ensure the BIT/CARE team is aware.

The second statement, "...looking forward to Monday's embalming therapy as well as a rumored opportunity to aspirate. Give me room, lots of aggression to be taken out with a trocar," may seem on its face to potentially be threatening, but to whom? Bernie? This is protected speech and is not a true threat. There may be a disruptive element to this, as it could be upsetting to other class members that she refers to embalming as "therapy" and comments on her own aggression. Additionally, it may be a professional practice issue for future conversations related to medical professionalism. In terms of intervention, at most, a soft outreach would be appropriate, but if she was non-responsive to the outreach, any consequence would track back to the protected speech.

The third statement, "Who knew embalming lab was so cathartic! I still want to stab a certain someone in the throat with a trocar though. Hmm..perhaps I will spend the evening updating my 'Death List #5' and making friends with the crematory guy. I do know the code…" is the first statement where any adverse action may be considered. But here, the true threat test is critical. Who is the "certain someone?" If she does have access to this person and she has access to the trocar and there is reason to believe that she has a motive to harm them or make them apprehensive of the harm, then this statement might cross the direct threat test. When the "Death List #5" and crematory references are added, it adds to the level of threat. The specificity of the threat escalates it as well. Her writing style is still satirical, so the protections may still be in place, but it is certainly less likely now, as the Court agreed. Though, remember here, this is a criminal analysis, which may be different from the student code of conduct and discipline violations in the academic setting.

If the "certain someone" is her ex-boyfriend who lives and works in Florida, the threat, while intended to cause him apprehension, would not reasonably do so, as she has no access to him. If it is a person in her program or in that class, the nature of the threat is dramatically increased, and the protections for the speech are dramatically reduced. For BIT/CARE, this is a definitive escalation of risk. For the student conduct officer or assistant principal, this is an actionable threat. For her academic program, there may be an academic or professionalism issue with her access to the crematorium. All of these issues need to be addressed with sufficient due process and an awareness that four separate processes and analyses are occurring simultaneously.

The last statement, "Realized with great sadness that my best friend, Bernie, will no longer be with me as of Friday next week. I wish to accompany him to the retort. Now where will I go or who will I hang with when I need to gather my sanity? Bye, bye Bernie. Lock of hair in my pocket," has elements of protected and unprotected speech. Ms. Tatro's sadness on losing her "best friend" Bernie is concerning but could still be viewed as sarcasm. Her desire to "accompany him to the retort" may be considered suicidal ideation or, again, sarcasm. The same applies to her need to "hang with him to gather my sanity." From a BIT/CARE's perspective, this would result in face-to-face assessment to see whether she is suicidal or deteriorating, especially when coupled with progressive nature of her previous posts. From a student conduct officer or assistant principal perspective, these statements are not actionable.

However, the last part of that statement, "Lock of hair in my pocket," is potentially actionable on several fronts. Taking hair from a cadaver is a violation of law in every state and thus, also a violation of the student conduct code. While it is not necessarily a confession, it warrants an investigation. The academic program will also want to look into it as a violation of professional and program standards and could, on an interim measure, ban her from class or access to the cadaver until the matter is investigated.

75

These last two posts are excellent examples of when a school needs to make a decision on what process should occur first. The lower-hanging fruit, if you will, is going to be the conduct related to the removal of the lock of hair. It bears noting that a decision on the academic professionalism matter would receive the least scrutiny from the courts. In the actual case, Ms. Tatro was disciplined, she sued and the courts all the way up to the State Supreme Court upheld the university's response, especially to the last two postings. In an interesting footnote to the case, Ms. Tatro appealed to the U.S. Supreme Court from the State Supreme Court, but she passed away while the appeal was under consideration, rendering her appeal moot (Levine, 2012).

Over the last few years, posts on social media have received less and less protections for consideration of harassment and threat, and the trend is seemingly continuing in that direction. That said, schools would be wise to consider the step-by-step analysis proposed and if choosing to act, make sure that appropriate due process is given for any interim and/or final actions. Schools would also be encouraged to understand the multi-departmental approaches to these cases from a psychological, legal and student conduct/discipline perspective. Overreliance on any one process limits the effectiveness of the assessment and intervention. These concepts are discussed in more detail in Chapters 7, 8, and 9.

LAW ENFORCEMENT AND THREAT ASSESSMENT PERSPECTIVES

As discussed in earlier chapters, law enforcement (LE) is typically limited in its response to threats. They assess threats through a lens of the criminal code; is this an arrestable offense or not? This translates to a limited approach that does not always attend to the early warning signs and red flags. Some agencies, such as larger metropolitan LE, may have threat assessment units or assigned detectives, though they are rarely focused on early concerns. Instead, they view each case by asking, "Can an arrest be made? If not, what safety measures can be put in place to prevent the act of violence?"

Collaboration is critical to any threat assessment process. Historically, LE has conducted investigations in a bubble. While law enforcement agencies have become better at sharing intelligence or information with other agencies, they often fall short in working outside of LE, especially in conducting threat assessment investigations, which can create silos. LE must "look beyond the call." LE must train line staff, frontline supervisors and detectives to look beyond the call and reach out to partners in the community such as schools, workplaces and colleges/universities to share information.

Advanced Analysis: In terms of gathering online data while conducing threat investigations, LE can't always count on their own resources to provide the staffing and technology. This means local LE should request assistance from countywide teams such as "High Tech Crime Units," Homeland Security, the Federal Bureau of Investigation or create in-house specialized positions. Most agencies will not have the capability or level of expertise within their own department. In addition to specialized units, it is essential to train local patrol officers on the basic principles of open-source internet searches to support investigations of threat or self-harm. This includes training on open-source social media searches, as well as reaching out to specialized units such as High Tech Crimes or Fusion Centers with higher risk cases. Following the terrorist attacks of 9/11, the United States began to look for ways to bring together local law enforcement, private sector interests and government law enforcement to work collaboratively on intelligence sharing and threat assessment (Homeland Security, 2019). Educators and administrators should talk with their school resource officers, chiefs of police and local law enforcement to better understand how to refer and work collaboratively with these groups.

The Problem with a Miss: Law enforcement cannot afford to be wrong when it comes to targeted violence. They must think beyond what is easily observable and look beyond the call. This means taking those few extra steps in the investigative phase. A simple checklist, such as the one in Table 5.3, details some of the initial actions taken by patrol officers or detectives when the call has elements of self-harm or harm to others. Along with basic LE actions such as checking criminal history, officers should be proactive and look at conducting consent or probation/parole searches, access to transportation, access to weapons (red flag laws), online environment and neighbors, as well as look for behaviors of concern. If an officer believes that a person is on the pathway to violence or suicide, the case should be handled expeditiously, bringing in specialized resources such as threat-trained detectives and/or federal expertise. LE no longer can show up to a call and have a "failure of imagination" of what might or could happen if there is no follow through.

Managing the Volume: Law enforcement manages a very large volume of calls and, as mentioned above, they have very little room to have an off day or miss an important piece of an assessment. For smaller agencies, especially campus based LE, this volume can be burdensome and overwhelming. One part of the overall strategy to ease this triage is instilling a vertical training methodology where all patrol staff, detectives and frontline supervisors have a baseline of training in threat assessment. LE should provide threat assessment training for all employees, based on a Structured Professional Judgment (SPJ) model (Hart & Logan, 2011; Mohandie, 2014; Van Brunt, 2012, 2015a) and by using a consistent risk rubric to reduce bias (O'Toole, 2002, 2014; Sokolow et al., 2019). LE can be more efficient in assessing risk in a large volume of cases by understanding the lower risk of transient threats and allotting additional time to those calls that involve substantive threats.

TABLE 5.3 Beyond the Call Checklist*

Area of Concern	Checklist
Weapons and Firearms	■ Conduct search of person/room ■ Assess room safety/protective sweep ■ Registered firearms ■ Online firearms presence, i.e., posting range visits to social media ■ Access to firearms (firearms stored in home, other locations) ■ Access to weapons of any kind (explain)_____ _____ ■ Are there temporary prohibitions from buying guns or ammunition (e.g. California GVRO and 'red flag laws')? ■ Search warrant related to weapons (if applicable)
Suicide	■ Level 1: No thoughts of suicide or treatment history ■ Level 2: Vague thoughts of suicide with no plan and/or past treatment history of therapy or inpatient admissions ■ Level 3*: Currently suicidal with plan and access; limited past treatment history and/or single inpatient admissions ■ Level 4*: Currently suicidal with plan and access, extensive past treatment history for chronic suicide attempts *Screen for inpatient psychiatric admission
Medical Information	■ Is the subject under a doctor's care? ■ Prescribed medications ■ Non-prescribed medications ■ Assess substance use (type, last use, overdose history) ■ Chronic illness
Behaviors of Concern	■ Have they become increasingly isolated from supportive others? ■ Have they recently attempted to purchase weapons or research the purchase of weapons or para-attack materials (load-bearing tactical clothes, bulletproof vests, kneepads, gloves, face coverings)? ■ Is the subject stockpiling ammunition? ■ Has the subject drastically changed appearance? ■ If the subject reached out to an extremist group, have they been rejected by that group as "too extreme"? ■ Has the subject been surveilling a potential target? Rehearsing or practicing violent activities? ■ Does the subject mention a desire for fame and attention to gain meaning for their mistreatment and frustrations with the world?

continued...

TABLE 5.3 continued...

Area of Concern	Checklist
Threat	■ Have they recently lost an important dating/intimate relationship? ■ Does the subject feel enraged or frustrated by the lack of willingness of others to date them or find them attractive? ■ Does the subject show an unusual and increasingly intense interest in violence, mass shootings, school shootings, terrorism or the end of the world? ■ Is the subject feeling overwhelmed by hopelessness or desperation? Do they feel as if nothing will ever change? ■ Has there been a direct threat on a specific person with a time or location mentioned or implied? ■ Is there a theme of seeing things in an "us vs. them" manner with the subject lacking empathy and perspective-taking? This may go hand-in-hand with a sense of moral outrage.
Current Domestic Violence	■ Level 1: No physical violence ■ Level 2: Pushing, shoving, grabbing with no bruising or marks (no medical attention) ■ Level 3: Cuts, bruises, bites and/or punching without weapon/shod foot and requiring medical treatment ■ Level 4: Weapon/shod foot used to cause cuts, bruises and/or minor broken bones requiring medical treatment ■ Level 5: Life-threatening injuries requiring immediate medical attention (stabbing, gunshot, broken bones, fall from height) Additional Questions: Assess for direct threat of violence in their current relationship such as: *"I'll kill you," "You won't survive the week if you pull this kind of thing one more time," "Maybe I'll kill myself and just take you with me."* Have they made social media posts or written notes containing a direct threat of violence? Assess for an indirect threat of violence in their current relationship such as: *"If you go out tonight, I will make sure you regret it," "Don't disrespect me that way, or you will not like what happens next," "If you aren't going to be with me, I'll be damned if I will let you be with anyone else."* Have they made social media posts or written notes containing a threat?
Law Enforcement History	■ Wants/warrants/probation status ■ Local agency contacts/non-custodial ■ Probation or consent search of: __Residence __Residence hall __Office __School locker __Vehicle ■ Criminal history ■ Orders of protection (temporary restraining order [TRO], emergency protection order [EPO], restraining order [RO], Trespass) ■ Previous clery warnings issued at school or college about the individual

* This checklist is provided as a starting place for the development of a checklist for a patrol officer. There are additional areas that should be explored.

One of the methods we strongly suggest is developing a patrol checklist to use in the field. This follows the concept behind the book, *The Checklist Manifesto* (Gawande, 2011). This checklist process allows officers to have a structured process for assessing the risk in targeted violence investigations. A checklist offers a compass and map when moving through an investigation process, reducing fears and mitigating legal risk of being capricious and arbitrary in these types of investigations. A patrol checklist guides law enforcement through an evidence-based process, increases consistency and ensures clues aren't missed in the rush of an investigation process fraught with time and political pressures.

PSYCHOLOGICAL AND EDUCATIONAL PERSPECTIVES

From a psychological perspective, there are a number of reasons why students make threats. They may be made to obtain a reaction to perceived injustices, as a blind strike back at those who have caused harm in their lives, from intense suicidal or self-harm feelings, as symptoms of a serious mental health disorder, as an attempt at processing their rage and frustration regarding being teased or bullied or as leakage concerning an actual attack plan. Understanding the range of threats helps the BIT/CARE team address potential bias and stay focused on an accurate assessment of the risk.

An important consideration when assessing threat is the academic context under which the writing was shared. An essay about self-injury with disturbing content as part of an assignment where the teacher asks the students to "Write about one of the hardest challenges you have overcome in your life" should be somewhat expected. The writing in Figure 5.5 is taken from an essay written by a college student in Massachusetts about their self-injury. While it is certainly upsetting, but it could be argued the student was asked to share this exact kind of material (Van Brunt & Solomon, 2019).

Likewise, there are times where a student's mental illness is clearly in the forefront of the writing. When a student is experiencing reality-testing difficulties

I pulled my utility blade from the plastic. My heart is racing with the adrenaline pulsing through my veins. My brain is craving the high that slices in my skin will bring. I hold the blade tightly. It's twice the size of the pencil sharpener razors I'd used in the past. My brain asks if I'm in to deep again as I rip my shorts from my body. Rubbing the scarred skin I feel the thin raised white lines. A smile pulls at my lips as I put the blade to my skin. Ripping it across a dozen times the angry red lines start to drip. I lean back letting my head res against the door. Taking shaky breaths while the endorphins fill my up. The rivers flowing down my thigh bring goose bumps to skin. The sticky crimson reaches the white tile floors. I immerse myself in the feeling, shutting my eyes as I ride out my high.

FIGURE 5.5 Essay from student on self-injury.

"A study in character, values, courage, nobility, honesty, and, selflessness. "A mind is a terrible thing to waist!" & "he's come a long way, baby!", (remember these quotes?) who embodies the very best in our wonderful society, and in us higher minded people!..." By John Kennedy Tool " (World famous auther). Visit Twitter website @freddythefreel1 briefing package. Nine photos on homepage, half typed info. to counter twitters character limit. Subliminal suggestion & conspiracy tactics, collectively in effect. Respectfully,... (Machiavellianism, narcissism, psychopathy,... watch out for these behaviorally manifested characteristics, (unless, via introspection, I'm unique). I'm the founder of this civilian counter intelligence tactic, your being made aware of the "mentality war" that's came about over the last 35 years. I'd like to keep struggling if life is tolerable, informing people about our "mutual enemies", the self alleged, "baser nature" my "intelligence" sponsored self alleged "baser nature" "own me" and who knows who else. This is only one of three major characteristics, another is "TAKEOVER" COLLECTIVELY, by a secret criminal organization within the u.s. intelligence community, (and international), using the criminally minded. The third is, alians UNDER ALL u.s.military bases, allegation was noted in the "Dulce book" (classified information leaks), I dont remember what chapter, proceed to my twitter website for better understanding. Your going to need oil prospecting technology, a form of radar to detect geological density under the surface. Possibly start at runways. Regards once again, Earl. P.S. The personality characteristics mentioned at the onset of this message, think, look around! DO NOT let any one take your photograph if required to look into the lens of their camera untill you've read page three on website. Last, a collection via money gram, or Western Union money would be spent informing citizens.

FIGURE 5.6 Mental illness written threat.

related to schizophrenia or bipolar disorder, the BIT/CARE team may be faced with sorting through rambling, psychotic speech to assess the risk. It is important to remember that individuals with mental illness are far more likely to be the victim that the perpetrator of an attack (Van Brunt & Pescara-Kovach, 2019). An example of this type of case is provided in Figure 5.6. This was a student from a Washington, DC, university who had posted some concerning and rambling content to the administration that raised concern around potential threat and violence (Van Brunt & Solomon, 2019).

Betterdeadafterall 5 points · 1 day ago
UPDATE: Thanks for the comments and messages. I know i didn't respond to them but they were appreciated. I'm sorry to end this scare with an anticlimax but I have decided to postpone my suicide for now due to unavoidable circumstances. I'll be taking my noose down. When will I try again? I don't know but probably not this week anymore. So the school can now stop worrying about bad press and students can sleep soundly tonight. I want to do it so badly and still do but due to things I don't want to disclose, I kinda can't right now.

Whether if I end up dead or alive in a month I probably won't see any of you anymore regardless. My mental breakdown and borderline catatonic depression lead to me bombing all my finals and half assing my report papers. Now to clear things up, finals is not the motivator to kill myself. But rather it's a large cluster of reasons that I don't want to disclose here.

But anyways, thank you for the supportive comments. You'll probably never know who I am or ever see me but I'll miss you all. I hope you all will sleep well tonight knowing theres no suicide tonight. Goodbye.

FIGURE 5.7

UPDATE ON THE REDDIT CASE

For those interested in the outcome of the case which started this chapter, the post found in Figure 5.7 was made prior to the deadline for the suicide. In addition to the school's post, there were dozens of supportive posts made by those inside and outside the college community.

MOVING FORWARD

In the next chapter, we will offer an approach to rating the risk of violence as it relates to written content. This approach is based on an expert system model, which focuses on drawing the best practices of evidenced-based research into a model that is useful for members of a BIT/CARE team to address the potential for violence. This is a practical method that seeks an approach that provides clarity when balancing the challenges outlined in the first part of this book.

REFERENCES

Alicea, J. (2015). Kean community on high alert after threats on twitter. Retrieved on December 13, 2019 from http://kutower.com/2015/11/18/kean-community-threatened-after-peaceful-rally-on-campus-last-night/

Association of Threat Assessment Professionals (ATAP). (2006). *Risk assessment guideline elements for violence (RAGE-V): Considerations for assessing the risk of future violent behavior.* Sacramento, CA: ATAP.

Calhoun, F., & Weston, S. (2009). *Threat assessment and management strategies: Identifying the Howlers and Hunters.* Boca Raton, FL: CRC Press.

Craig, D. (2015). Origin of a threat: What is the 'Beta Uprising?' Retrieved on December 13, 2019 from https://www.phillyvoice.com/what-beta-uprising/

Cohen v. California, 403 U.S. 15, 1971.

De Becker, G. (2019). www.mosaicmethod.com

Fein, R., Vossekuil, B., & Holden, G. (1995). *Threat assessment: An approach to targeted violence.* Research in action. Washington, DC: National Institute of Justice.

Gawande, A. (2011). *The checklist manifesto.* New York: Picador Paper.

GlobalGrind Staff. (2012). "Die, all of you": T. J. Lane, alleged gunmen in high school shooting, writes chilling letter (details). GlobalGrind. Retrieved on December 13, 2019 from https://globalgrind.com/1796904/tj-lane-alleged-gunmen-chardon-high-school-shooting-letter-die-all-you-details/

Hart, S., & Logan, C. (2011). Formulation of violence risk using evidence-based assessment: The structured professional judgment approach. In P. Sturmey & M. McMurran (Eds.), *Forensic case formulation* (pp. 83–106). Chichester, England: Wiley-Blackwell.

Homeland Security. (2019). Fusion centers. Retrieved on March 6, 2020 from https://www.dhs.gov/fusion-centers

Levine, R. (2012). Tatro vs. The University of Minnesota. Retrieved on March 19, 2020 from https://www.aclu-mn.org/en/cases/tatro-v-university-minnesota

Lewis, T. (2016). Black Kean University Grad jailed for tweeting racist threats. Retrieved on December 13, 2019 from https://www.essence.com/news/black-kean-university-grad-jailed-tweeting-racist-threats/

Meloy, J.R. (2001). Communicated threats and violence toward public and private targets: Discerning differences between those who stalk and attack. *Journal of Forensic Science* 46, 1211–1213.

Mohandie, K. (2014). Threat assessment in schools. In J.R. Meloy & J. Hoffman (Eds.), *The international handbook of threat assessment* (pp. 126–147). New York: Oxford University Press.

O'Toole M.E. (2002). *The school shooter: A threat assessment perspective.* Quantico, VA: FBI.

O'Toole, M.E. (2014). The mission-oriented shooter: A new type of mass killer. *Journal of Violence and Gender*, 1(1), 9–10.

Pow, H. (2012). You don't even know ****ing terror yet. *Daily Mail Online.* Retrieved on December 13, 2019 from https://www.dailymail.co.uk/news/article-2235785/Jared-Cano-case-Cell-phone-video-shows-Florida-student-planned-blow-school-foiled-2011-attack.html

Rodger, E. (2014). My twisted world. Retrieved on December 13, 2019 from https://www.documentcloud.org/documents/1173808-elliot-rodger-manifesto.html

Scalora, M., Simons, A., & Vansly, S. (2010, February). Campus safety: Assessing and managing threats. *FBI Law Enforcement Bulletin*, 79(2), 1-10.

Sokolow, B., Van Brunt, B., Lewis, W., Schiemann, M., Murphy, A., & Molnar, J. (2019). *The NaBITA risk rubric.* King of Prussia, PA: The National Behavioral Intervention Team Association.

Speer, R. (2014, May 28). A selfie-era killer: Social media and Elliot Rodger. *The New York Post.* Retrieved from http://nypost.com/2014/05/28/a-selfie-era-killer-social-media-and-elliot-rodger/

Tanenbaum, M. (2015). FBI, ATF: Threat of violence against "University near Philadelphia" on Monday. Retrieved December 13, 2019 from https://www.phillyvoice.com/fbi-atf-threat-violence-university-philadelphia/

Tatro v. U. of Minnesota, 800 N.W.2d 811, 2011.

Teicher-Khadaroo, S. (2011, August 19). Columbine lessons may have prevented Tampa school shooting. *The Christian Science Monitor.* Retrieved on June 14th from https://www.csmonitor.com/USA/Education/2009/0420/p02s04-usgn.html

Tinker v. Des Moines, 393 U.S. 503, 1968.

Turner, J., & Gelles, M. (2003). *Threat assessment: A risk management approach.* New York: Routledge.

Van Brunt, B. (2012). *Ending campus violence: New approaches to prevention.* New York: Routledge.

Van Brunt, B. (2015a). *Harm to others: The assessment and treatment of dangerousness.* Alexander, VA.: American Counseling Association.

Van Brunt, B. (2015b). Violence risk assessment of the written word (VRAW^2). *Journal of Behavioral Intervention Teams (JBIT)*, 3, 12–25.

Van Brunt, B., & Pescara-Kovach, P. (2019). Debunking the myths: Mental illness and mass shootings. *Journal of Violence and Gender*, 6(1), 53–63.

Van Brunt, B., & Solomon, J. (2019). *Threat case studies.* King of Prussia, PA: The National Behavioral Intervention Team Association.

Warren, L., Mullen, P., & McEwan, T. (2014). Explicit threats of violence. In J. R. Meloy & J. Hoffmann (Eds.), *The international handbook of threat assessment* (pp. 18–38). New York: Oxford University Press.

PART II

ASSESSMENT AND INTERVENTION

Chapter 6

Assessing the Violence Risk of the Written Word

Having a research-informed process to assess written material on social media, emails or creative content and essays allows teams to be consistent in their approach, avoid bias-informed decision-making and will serve to reduce legal liability for school districts, colleges and universities. To develop this new expert system, Looking Glass, named after the character in the comic book and HBO Series *Watchmen,* we analyzed over 200 cases (Appendix B) with written content to develop a consistent, informed system for K-12, college and university BIT/ CARE teams. These cases provided a knowledge base for the expert system to better inform intervention decisions and highlight "hotspots" of interest for a more formal, in-person threat assessment interview.

The concept of an expert system was first developed by Edward Feigenbaum at Stanford in the 1970s. These systems are designed to take accumulated experience and design a set of rules for applying knowledge to a particular task or scenario. When analyzing written threat and social media posts, the process outlined in this chapter will be useful for teams looking to apply current research and case examples to new content they come across to better gauge intervention efforts. The intervention process itself also borrows from the Structured Professional Judgement Model (SPJ) (Hart and Logan, 2011; Van Brunt, 2015b), which works to identify risk factors, apply them to a particular case, develop a formulation of risk and plan for interventions based on the expressed risk. This combination of modeling between expert systems and SPJ allows for non-clinical staff on BIT/ CARE teams to bring the research and knowledge base to the forefront of the decision-making process. This is different from a psychological test or assessment, which is more limited to clinical staff and is targeted to specific populations.

The system outlined is built upon other research (Smith, 2007; Van Brunt, 2015b, 2016) that sought to provide a more detailed risk assessment of concerning written content. The Violence Risk Assessment of the Written Word (VRAW^2) is explained in Van Brunt's article and VRAW^2 scores are provided for each of the cases in Appendix A for comparison to Looking Glass. This new approach helps teams better guide their intervention processes in order to not over- or under-react to potential violence risk, bring research to bear on new threats, limit bias in decision-making and develop multidisciplinary intervention plans. In this chapter, we will outline the development of Looking Glass, a summary of the escalating elements, mitigating elements, a suggested scoring guide and an intervention checklist. Each of the tabletop exercises in Appendix A have VRAW^2 and Looking Glass scoring examples at the end of each example. This offers a comparison of the two measures.

OVERVIEW OF LOOKING GLASS

Cases were collected based on the presence of written material, social media content or leakage that occurred prior to the attack. In some instances, these attacks were thwarted; in others, the attack occurred. There were no efforts made to separate cases based on K-12, college, university or workplace, as the central thread for the research is the presence of written leakage behavior prior to the attack. This research methodology is different from others, where the location of the attack, age of the attacker and/or number of people killed were used to divide research subsets. This approach is limiting, as there is no single profile for an attacker, and adopting a more open-ended, qualitative methodology provided more detail to inform the expert system.

Looking Glass is made up of two sides, escalating and mitigating elements. The *escalating elements* represent an increased acceleration in the overall dangerousness based on the qualities of the written content. The *mitigating elements* serve to lessen the concern and reduce the overall risk of dangerousness of the situation. These elements can then be observed in combination to help better inform an in-person threat assessment as outlined in *Harm to Others* (O'Toole, 2002; Turner & Gelles, 2003; United States Postal Service [USPS], 2007; Hart and Logan, 2011; Douglas et al., 2014; Van Brunt, 2015a) and fuel intervention efforts (Hart & Logan, 2011; Schiemann & Molnar, 2019).

An internet search was conducted for incidents that contained leakage related to social media content or writing created by the attacker prior to the attack. This was conducted through an internet search using key terms, "social media threat," "Snapchat threat," "Facebook threat," "Instagram threat," "Twitter threat" and "school shooting." Cases that were placed in the *active attacks* catalog include those where an attack took place or was imminent. Imminent cases involve those with a clear plan of attack or substantive threat of attack and where the perpetrator obtained weapons in order to complete the attack. In some cases, the attack was thwarted in the late stages of planning, and in some the attacker was already beginning the attack when it was thwarted, but in either case, the threat was substantive and had a high probability of completion. The secondary category of cases included those with writing that was intended to troll, related to an attack that was *non-imminent* or the threat was transient in nature.

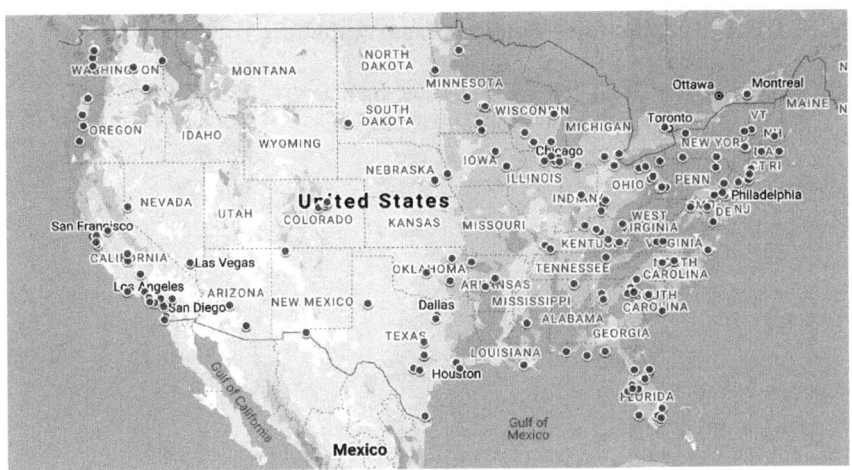

FIGURE 6.1 Threats and Attacks across the United States.

The authors reviewed 206 cases, 113 (55%) active attacks and 93 (45%) non-imminent threats. Out of the 113 active attacks, 79% (89 out of 113) involved people being shot, injured or killed (including just the attacker killed). In terms of location of the attacks or threats for all 206 cases, 16% (32) incidents were at colleges or universities, 61% (126) at K-12 settings, 7% (15) at a workplace, 2% (4) at Walmart, 2% (4) at a law enforcement/naval base, 1% (3) at a place of worship and 11% (22) at other locations. A summary of the United States incidents is included in Figure 6.1.

As part of this naturalistic inquiry, some cases involving workplace violence were included in the tally. Additionally, 17 cases were included that lacked written or social media content, but the case details were useful for contextual analysis. They either had verbal threats or no leakage prior to the attack (Table 6.1).

When examining the remaining 189 cases for the manner in which written content was shared, 5% (10) involved essays, creative writing, speech, story or poem, 3% (6) involved graffiti, 8% (16) were journal entries, 20% (37) involved letters or emails, 7% (13) involved manifestos, 7% (13) were notes or notebooks, photos and plans, 46% (87) were over social media, 5% (9) were over text and 8% (15) involved videos. Of the total number of cases reviewed, 92% (189) of cases had some form of leakage or communication, with 42% (87) occurring through social media. Keep in mind, many cases involve multiple types of leakage and the numbers above reflect that. Of note, 6% (13) had detailed manifestos (Appendix B: 8, 9, 16, 44, 61, 70, 71, 84, 87, 93, 94, 96, 138).

When examining the cases in Appendix B, there are several important findings we wanted to highlight. While this is a limited sample, and the methodology is challenging when attempting to gather more information given legal issues related to the case or when the attacker has been killed, this kind of exploration

TABLE 6.1 Specific Case Findings from Appendix B

[206] Details from Cases	[113] Active, Imminent, Substantive (%)	[93] Trolling, Non-Imminent, Transient (%)
People shot, injured or killed (or attacker killed)	79	0
Author dies by suicide (includes killed by police)	42	0
Author was killed in "suicide by cop"	4	0
Written or verbal suicidal content (author suicide)	32	0
Written or verbal suicidal content (author lives)	31	1
Commits suicide with no suicidal communication	9	0
References a previous attack	41	12
References fame-seeking or larger purpose for attack	27	4
Experiences isolation or hopelessness	45	2
Experiences or perseverates on an injustice or grievance	61	15
Displays hardened, black-or-white thinking	41	12
Graphic or violent descriptions in writing	24	16
Target detail (person, school, place) in their writing	42	63
Weapon detail (guns, bulletproof vests, etc.) in their writing	24	17
Details about the attack plan/location in their writing	26	23

towards social media and written content cases proves useful for BIT/CARE teams as they approach these assessments.

First, references to *"suicide"* and then *"hopelessness and isolation"* show a large disparity between *active, imminent, substantive attacks* (63% and 45%) and *trolling, non-imminent, transient cases* (1% and 2%). **When assessing written threat and** *social media, suicide and feelings of hopelessness and isolation should be seen as a critical aggravating element in the assessment.*

Second, the target detail element has occurred at a higher rate than expected for *trolling, non-imminent, transient* or attention-seeking cases. *Fixation* is described towards a group (e.g., women, immigrants, pro-life advocates), while *focus* narrows to smaller groups (e.g., a women's aerobics class, immigrants looking for work at the Home Depot, the Women's March in San Diego). When this was broken down further for *trolling, non-imminent, transient cases*, we found 76% of cases occurred with a fixation (K-12, college, Walmart, hospitals) and 24% of cases occurred with a focus (on specific people or groups of people at a location). *When assessing written threat and social media, specific mentions of people or small groups (focus) should be seen as a more significant aggravating element.*

Third, there was also a large difference in cases that include perseveration on past grievances or injustices and those that contain hardened, either/or thinking between *active, imminent, substantive attacks* (61% and 41%) and *trolling, non-imminent, transient cases* (15% and 12%). *When assessing written threat and social media, expressing perseveration on past grievances and injustices in a hardened, passionate and inflexible way should be seen as a more significant aggravating element.*

Fourth, there was a 30% higher difference in those cases that referenced previous shootings between those *active, imminent, substantive attacks* (43%) and *trolling, non-imminent, transient cases* (12%). *Mentions of previous attackers should be seen as a significant aggravating element when assessing written threat and social media content.*

Fifth, when assessing mitigating factors, we found 25% (23 out of 93) of the *trolling, non-imminent, transient cases* contained a transient, retaliatory expression. Here, the author attempts to save face or gain back lost reputation through eliciting a reaction from their readers. Similarly, written content by an author who has a history of sharing written material designed to enflame and enrage others into a reaction occurred in 32% (30 out of 93) of the cases involving *trolling, non-imminent, transient cases*. *When assessing written threat and social media, a tendency towards trolling, being a constant agitator and posting material to save face or draw a reaction from others should add a mitigating element to the assessment.*

Finally, those with elements of poor thinking, being young, having a developmental mental health disorder or not understanding the consequences of their actions also show a tendency to occur more in the *trolling, non-imminent, transient cases*, with 32% (30 out of 93) of the cases displaying this. *Being young, not thinking through the consequences of actions or having poor critical-thinking skills are mitigating elements in the assessment.*

91

TABLE 6.2 Review of Escalating Elements When assessing Written Content

		Escalating Element Name	Escalation Element Description
AUTHOR QUALITIES	1.	Suicidal Content	This element reflects details in the story, email or social media post that indicate direct or indirect suicidal references.
	2.	Isolation and Hopelessness	The writing sample has elements of isolation, loneliness and/or marginalization from the larger societal group.
	3.	Fame-/Meaning-Seeking	The writing sample or social media post has a tone of seeking larger status as an all-powerful figure, a martyr or someone who is smarter and more knowledgeable than the rest of the population.
	4.	Injustice/Grievance Collecting	Righting a wrong, striving for power. Here, the writer gives evidence of being wronged by others.
TONE	5.	Hardened, Black/White Thinking	The writer expresses a hardened quality to the writing that reflects an either/or way of thinking; they reject other points of view or ideological positions in a passionate, fueled, emotional manner.
	6.	Graphic and Violent Descriptions	The writer uses graphic and shocking language to describe a potential attack or the traits of their targets. This could include vivid adjectives, threatening tones, torture or descriptions of blood and gore.
CONTENT	7.	Target Detail	The author narrows their fixation and focus onto a more specific individual or group target. There often is an overall negative tone in references to their target's intelligence, appearance, gender, religion or status.
	8.	Weapon Detail	The writer includes details of the brandishing of weapons on social media and/or a specific discussion of what weapons might be used in an attack.
	9.	Threat Plan Detail	The writing sample includes a detailed threat plan with the time or date of the attack, lists of items to acquire (such as bulletproof vests and high-capacity clips) or schematics of the attack site.
	10.	Previous Attack Detail	The writing sample includes references to previous attacks that occurred. This could also include comments about certain dates (such as Hitler's birthday, April 20) or references to studying past attacks.

The cases in Appendix B add a practical layer to the existing research supporting risk and protective elements that have been outlined in Chapters 3 and 4. Moving forward in this chapter, we outline 10 escalating elements from the research and cases that present a heightened quality to the overall threat assessment. Four of these are related to author qualities, two address tonal qualities in the writing sample and four involve content details. These are outlined in Table 6.2 and further explained in the following section.

We then review the mitigating elements (Table 6.5) that should be taken into account to balance the escalating elements. These elements include an understanding of the motivating and dispositional qualities of the author as well as the contextual details of the social media content or written material. A new approach to bringing these together will them be explored at the conclusion of the chapter.

ESCALATING ELEMENTS: AUTHOR QUALITIES, TONE AND CONTENT DETAILS

A clear example of all four of these qualities can be found from the October 15, 2015, attack at Umpqua Community College (Appendix B: 96). The attacker left a detailed manifesto (Figure 6.2) that details his feelings of isolation, hopelessness and a sense of collecting grievances and injustices. He praises other attackers actions: Elliot Rodgers (Appendix B: 87), Vester Flanagan (Appendix B: 95), the Columbine attackers (Appendix B: 20), Adam Lanza (Appendix B: 75) and Seung Cho (Appendix B: 44). Near the end of the manifesto, the attacker discusses his desire to die a martyr's death, echoing the Virginia Tech attacker's words (Figure 6.3).

My Story

I have always been the most hated person in the world. Ever since I arrived in this world, I have been under siege from it. Under attack from morons and idiots. I write this manifesto so that others will know of my story and perhaps find some solace in it, some kind of inspiration for their own lives. It will contain various sections dealing with my life. It will be divided into sections based on different things. My whole life has been one lonely enterprise. One loss after another. And here I am , 26, with no friends, no job, no girlfriend, a virgin. I long ago realized that society likes to deny people like me these things. People who are elite, people who stand with the gods. People like Elliot Rodger, Vester Flanagan, The Columbine kids, Adam Lanza and Seung Cho.

FIGURE 6.2 Excerpt from Umpqua Attacker's Manifesto.

For the Vestor Flanagans, Elliot Rodgers, Seung Cho, Adam Lanzas of the world, I do this. For all those who never took me seriously this is for you. For all those who haven't made their stand I do this. I am the martyr for all those like me. To quote Seung Cho, "Today I die like Jesus Christ".

FIGURE 6.3 Excerpt from Umpqua Attacker's Manifesto.

AUTHOR QUALITIES (1–4)

1. **Suicidal Content:** This element reflects details in the story, email or social media post that indicate direct or indirect suicidal references. The writer makes direct reference or alludes to dying by their own hand or entering into circumstances where they would be killed. This may be an idea or thought or an actively described plan. Suicidality is present in the vast majority of campus attacks and is a primary risk factor in all existing threat assessment approaches and research (Turner & Gelles, 2003; White & Meloy, 2007; Langman 2009, 2015; Newman & Fox, 2009; Meloy et al., 2011; Van Brunt, 2012, 2015a; Lankford, 2013, 2018; National Threat Assessment Center [NTAC], 2018). The element is present in 63% (71) of the 113 cases involving an active attack (Appendix B: 1, 2, 3, 4, 5, 7, 8, 11, 15, 17, 18, 20, 21, 22, 23, 24, 26, 28, 32, 33, 35, 36, 37, 39, 40, 42, 43, 44, 47, 49, 53, 55, 56, 58, 61, 65, 66, 67, 68, 74, 75, 77, 80, 81, 83, 85, 86, 87, 89, 90, 92, 93, 94, 95, 96, 100, 101, 103, 107, 108, 112, 113, 114, 115, 129, 130, 133, 134, 143, 144, 167).

   An example of this language is found in the El Paso attacker's manifesto (Appendix B: 143), where he writes, "My death is likely inevitable. If I'm not killed by the police, then I'll probably be gunned down by one of the invaders. Capture in this case is far worse than dying during the shooting because I'll get the death penalty anyway. Worse still is that I would live knowing that my family despises me. This is why I'm not going to surrender even if I run out of ammo. If I'm captured, it will be because I was subdued somehow." (El Paso, 2019, p. 4). On September 27, 2006, at the Platte Canyon High School in Bailey, Colorado, the attacker took six female students hostage and killed one before committing suicide (Appendix B: 40). He wrote in his suicide note: "Please forgive me for the terrible things you have heard or are about to hear. Suicide is sometimes an embarrassment to family members, so for this I truly apologize for any hurt I may cause all of you. To me suicide is a final release from an empty and painful life that has never had any meaning for me. I'm tired of living, and for the past 15 years I'm tired of living in pain. Constant pain" (Van Brunt, 2012, pp. 25–26).

2. **Isolation and Hopelessness:** The writing sample has elements of isolation, loneliness and marginalization from the larger societal group. There is an overall quality of sadness and isolation, and a lack of options or any choices that lead to a positive outcome. The author writes in a manner that indicates there is no better way to resolve the conflict or find a way out. This may be stated directly, indirectly hinted at through the writing's tone or as part of the fiction narrative. This isolation and hopelessness for a better future is another central risk factor for targeted violence (Turner & Gelles, 2003; White & Meloy, 2007; Langman 2009, 2015; Newman & Fox, 2009; Meloy

et al., 2011; Van Brunt 2012, 2015a; Lankford, 2013, 2018; NTAC, 2018). The element is present in 45% (55) of the 113 cases that involved an active attack (Appendix B: 1, 2, 4, 5, 10, 11, 14, 15, 16, 17, 18, 19, 21, 23, 26, 32, 33, 34, 35, 36, 37, 39, 40, 41, 43, 44, 46, 47, 67, 68, 70, 73, 74, 75, 77, 80, 81, 83, 86, 87, 93, 95, 96, 101, 107, 112, 113, 114, 116, 136, 141).

In the months leading up to the Chardon High School shooting on February 27, 2012, the attacker posted a story on Facebook (Appendix B: 73). He was reported to have been bullied and isolated at school, and in his story, the protagonist waits outside a castle, isolated and alone, planning his revenge, "In a quaint lonely town, sits a man with a frown. No job. No family. No crown. His luck had run out. Lost and alone. The streets were his home. His thoughts would solely consist of 'why do we exist?' His only company to confide in was the vermin in the street" (GlobalGrind, 2012, p. 1). On May 23, 2014, an attacker killed others in the Isla Vista massacre (Appendix B: 87). In his video confession, the attacker recounts, "All you popular kids, you've never accepted me, and now you will all pay for it. And girls, all I ever wanted was to love you, and to be loved by you. I've wanted a girlfriend, I've wanted sex, I've wanted love, affection, adoration. You think I'm unworthy of it. That's a crime that can never be forgiven" (Langman, 2014, p. 1). Another example of this is the discussion board post made years prior to the 2017 attack at Aztec High School (Appendix B: 112). This is included in Figure 6.4.

3. **Fame-/Meaning-Seeking:** The creator of the writing sample or social media post has a tone of seeking larger status as an all-powerful figure, a martyr or someone who is smarter and more knowledgeable than the rest of the population (Lankford, 2013, 2016, 2018). The author may have "found an answer" that others are too dumb or cowardly to consider, and the author or protagonist in the story is forced into a hero's journey that others are not worthy of following. They may see themselves as a glorified avenger, dark knight or punisher to make things right. They are willing to give their life for the larger glory, to find honor and fame in the afterlife or to better carry out their overall message. The attacker sees their actions as pure and blessed and their enemies as flawed and corrupt (Moghaddam, 2005). They may have a higher purpose to the attack and a message they want to impart. In the cases that involved an active attack, 27% (30 out of 113) had themes of fame-seeking or reference a larger purpose/meaning for the attack (Appendix B: 7, 12, 20, 36, 43, 44, 47, 56, 57, 61, 67, 70, 85, 87, 88, 91, 94, 95, 96, 107, 109, 114, 115, 128, 134, 135, 136, 138, 140, 143).

On the evening of June 17, 2015, a shooting took place at Emanuel African Methodist Episcopal Church in downtown Charleston, South Carolina. The shooter posted a manifesto he wrote before the attack describing some of his pre-attack planning. He wrote, "I have no choice. I am not in

Stuck in a Rural Redneck town
Posted by Demetrius Alcala on September 2, 2014 at 4:32am in Advice

I don't want to be lame or anything but I should probably come out about all this.

In this town (flora vista)..

#1. I have no education. I dropped out of AHS back in ~10, then was forced to attend again and dropped out again in ~12. I had a 3.5 GPA but the culture there was backwards as hell, as if it was stuck in the 1950s. Nothing but savages and douchebags. I never motivated myself to get a GED, I need the forced classes and structure of school, but couldn't deal with all the methheads, roughnecks and rednecks.

#2. I have no job, I tried to apply at a few places, Wendys, General Dollar, and Dairy Queen. All rejected lol And besides, I don't have the strength to deal with those people, I can be a hard worker, but I got real bad social anxiety, hate and fear of all these people. Plus I don't got a phone to keep in touch with the boss if they force me to go in for overtime. I got a nocturnal schedule anyways. No car though, nor a license.

#3. I have no friends here. All my friends are digital not, only time in life that I had a social life were the times I didn't live in the four corners. I tried a lot during my childhood in this area. But let me just put it this way- one of my friends and their little brothers and sisters, stealthily stole my Plyastation 1 I had since the 90s, along with dozens of games - all which could be worth thousands of dollars nowadays.

During high school, the other borrowed my N64 and games over the summer, promising to return them once school started again, and guess what the jackass did? He sold it to a guy in denver for $200. Didn't even give me any of the dough. Then threatened to kick my ass when I defended myself from some hicks.

The others talked crap behind my back.. There was a time though around 4/20/12 when I got high with a few people out in the hills. One of the kids lived a few houses down and when I dropped out didn't even stop over to say hello.

I may not seem the type, but I've been somewhat outgoing, friendly, a joker. I wasn't that kid who actively avoided people all the time and dressed in all black and listened to goth music. I went in, did my damned work, made straight A's then went home to a crap abusive family and did more work and surfed the net.

My point? I tried to socialize in this shit town but to no avail.

#4. Major Depression, large amounts of anger and hatred, lots of boredom.. I used to cure it through bong hits and video games but I cant even find those enjoyable anymore.

FIGURE 6.4 Aztec High Attacker Online Post.

the position to, alone, go into the ghetto and fight. I chose Charleston because it is most historic city in my state, and at one time had the highest ratio of blacks to Whites in the country. We have no skinheads, no real KKK, no one doing anything but talking on the Internet. Well someone has to have the bravery to take it to the real world, and I guess that has to be me" (Bernstein et al., 2015, p. 1). Similar themes occurred in Christchurch (Appendix B: 138), Norway (Appendix B: 70) and El Paso (Appendix B: 143). In 2015, a disgruntled TV anchor from Roanoke, Virginia, shot and killed a reporter and cameraman during a live broadcast (Appendix B: 95). He had been fired from the station and expressed frustrations about being mistreated as a gay, black man. His desire for fame can be seen from the pubic nature of his attack and his explanations immediately after the shooting on his Twitter page (Figure 6.5). Prior to committing suicide and while being chased by police, he sent a 23-page fax explaining his motives for the attack.

FIGURE 6.5 Live TV shooting Attacker's Twitter Page.

4. **Injustice/Grievance Collecting:** The writing sample contains language about the author's frustration with past negative treatment, real or perceived. O'Toole described this individual as "a person who feels 'wronged,' 'persecuted' and 'destroyed,' blowing injustices way out of proportion, never forgiving the person they felt has wronged them" (O'Toole & Bowman, 2011, p. 186). They narrow in on certain causes, groups or individuals they have been mistreated by in past business relationships, academic progress, social interactions, relationship disappointments or administrative job actions (Calhoun & Weston, 2009; Van Brunt 2015a, 2016). There is an overall tone that some series of past embarrassments or negative interactions have risen to a tipping point where a rant or action is demanded. ASIS International and Society for Human Resource Management published "Workplace Violence Prevention and Intervention" (2011), a set of standards for security and human resource personnel to prevent or intervene in potentially dangerous scenarios. This concept is described as, "chronic, unsubstantiated complaints about persecution or injustice; a victim mindset" (p. 22). The element is present in 61% (69) of the 113 cases that involved an active attack (Appendix B: 3, 4, 5, 7, 8, 9, 10, 11, 12, 13, 14, 15, 16, 21, 24, 25,

FIGURE 6.6 Vent Misogynistic Posts.

26, 28, 32, 34, 41, 43, 44, 53, 54, 56, 57, 60, 61, 65, 66, 67, 73, 76, 80, 81, 87, 89, 90, 91, 92, 94, 95, 96, 100, 108, 111, 112, 114, 135, 138, 143). The vast majority of themes in these cases were to obtain revenge, primarily for past bullying. Other perseverations were academic, anti-government, anti-women and regarding immigration/race.

In May of 1998, a student was suspended pending expulsion from Thurston High School for bringing a gun to school (Appendix B: 13). He returned to school and shot 24 people, killing two. Prior to the attack, he wrote in his journal, "I don't understand any fucking person on this earth. Some of you are so weak, mainly, that a four-year-old could push you down. I am strong, but my head just doesn't work right. I know I should be happy with what I have, but I hate living. I am evil. I want to kill and give pain without a cost. And there is no such thing. We kill him—we killed him a long time ago. Anyone that believes in God is a fucking sheep" (Van Brunt 2012, p. 12). In a community college outside of Detroit, a student shared numerous angry posts about women around campus (Van Brunt & Solomon, 2019). He was seen as threatening to several women on campus and was brought in through the conduct process. Examples of his perceptions about past wrongs are found in Figure 6.6 (note: racist, triggering language).

TONE QUALITIES (5–6)

5. **Hardened, black/white thinking:** The writing sample should be explored for the presence of a hardened quality to the writing that reflects an either/or ("black/white") way of thinking (Glasl, 1999; Turner & Gelles,

2003; Van Brunt, 2012, 2015a, 2016). The author's views are hardened and inflexible, where they only see one side of the story. These views are beyond a strongly held belief and contain a passion and emotion that rejects other points of view or hardened ideological positions, and they are reinforced through other personal experiences and networks (Sageman, 2007). In the active attack cases, 41% (46 out of 113) of the cases had examples of hardened and inflexible thoughts (Appendix B: 3, 5, 7, 9, 12, 14, 16, 20, 22, 24, 28, 32, 34, 38, 43, 44, 47, 53, 54, 56, 57, 61, 67, 68, 70, 75, 79, 81, 83, 85, 87, 91, 94, 96, 106, 111, 113, 114, 116, 126, 135, 136, 138, 140, 143, 192).

In the Virginia Tech shooting (Appendix B: 44), the attacker expressed his views on white, entitled and privileged students, "Only if you could be the victim of your reprehensible and wicked crimes, you Christian Nazis, you would have brute-restrained your animal urges to fuck me. You could be at home right now eating your fucking caviar and your fucking cognac, had you not ravenously raped my soul" (Langman, 2014, p. 1). In the 2007 Jokela School Shooting in Tuusula, Finland (Appendix B: 47), the attacker writes, "Of course there is a final solution too: death of entire human race. It would solve every problem of humanity. The faster human race is wiped out from this planet, the better... no one should be left alive. I have no mercy for the scum of earth, the pathetic human race." Examples from this case are included in Figure 6.7.

6. **Graphic and Violent Descriptions:** The writer uses graphic and shocking language to describe a potential attack or the traits of their targets. This could include vivid adjectives, threatening tones, torture or descriptions of blood and gore (Van Brunt, 2015a, 2015b, 2016). In a 2008 report to the Massachusetts Department of Higher Education by O'Neill, Fox, Depue and Englander, they write, "Writings, drawings, and other forms of individual expression reflecting violent fantasy and causing a faculty member to be fearful or concerned about safety, should be evaluated contextually for any potential threat" (pp. 32–33). This graphic language often gives evidence of fantasy rehearsal that gives rise to moral disengagement. There is little empathy for those outside their specific group (Pressman, 2009). In the cases that involved an active attack, 24% (27 out of 113) used graphic language (Appendix B: 10, 13, 15, 16, 20, 28, 44, 46, 51, 71, 76, 80, 81, 86, 87, 90, 91, 93, 96, 107, 114, 116, 134, 136, 138, 143, 161). Examples of this kind of language are highlighted in Table 6.3.

As with each of the elements in this list, a singular focus on one element, say, graphic or vulgar language, can give rise to an overreaction fueled by bias; the bias here being individuals who use vulgar language or graphic descriptions are at a higher risk for targeted violence. One only has to look to author Stephen King, filmmaker Quentin Tarantino and rapper Eminem

"Of course there is a final solution too: death of entire human race. It would solve every problem of humanity. The faster human race is wiped out from this planet, the better... no one should be left alive. I have no mercy for the scum of earth, the pathetic human race." -Pekka

Expand

#mass shooting   #columbine   #shooting   #sc

381 notes

#pekka eric auvinen

1,317 notes

FIGURE 6.7 Threats online from Jokela School Shooting.

to see the use of gratuitously offensive language and content should not be used as a sole source to establish risk.

CONTENT QUALITIES (7–10)

7. **Target Detail:** The more detail shared about the specificity of a target, the higher the level of risk. As the author begins to narrow their fixation and focus on to a more specific target, they will often mention this in writing and social media posts (Turner & Gelles, 2003; Van Brunt, 2012). There is often an overall tone in the writing sample that includes negative references to the target's intelligence, appearance, gender, religion or status. The author may mention a past grievance or wrong that was done to them and identify the person, organization or group that is to be held responsible. In writing samples, emphasis techniques such as the use of capital letters, quotes, references to past attackers and events, color or font changes, parenthetical inserts, underlining or emoji use may occur (Van Brunt, 2015b). Repetition of phrases and further narrowing in on an individual's or location's schedule, personal characteristics or geographic characteristics also

TABLE 6.3 Specific Examples of Graphic Violence

Cases	Examples of Graphic Content
13	"It's my first murder, I'm at the point of no return. I look at his body on the floor, Killing a bastard that deserves to die, Ain't nothing like it in the world"
16	"On Saturday of last week, I made my first kill. The date was April 12, 1997 about 4:30 p.m. The victim was a loved one. My dear dog Sparkle. I will never forget the howl she made. it sounded almost human. We laughed and hit her hard. I picked up the book bag, which was now soaked in her blood, and drug her across the ground dropped into the woods. A hole developed in the bag and the dog stuck her head out, fully engulfed in flames."
44	"To you sadistic snobs, I may be nothing but a piece of dog shit. You have vandalized my heart, raped my soul, and torched my conscious again and again. You thought it was one pathetic, void life that you were extinguishing. Thanks to you, I die, like Jesus Christ, to inspire generations of the Weak and Defenseless people — my Brothers, Sisters, and Children — that you fuck."
51	From a video: "You will die next," followed by firing four shots in the direction of the camera
76	"As he had said it he cut the restraints making him fall into the pit of spikes. There were screams coming out of the pit, as David was being cut and stabbed by the many points causing him to thrash about. His thrashing caused him to cut and shred his flesh. He was stuck in a loop of thrashing and getting cut." "The person posted there was asleep so he got up behind her and stabbed her in the back of the neck with a long knife. While he did that he wrapped her head in plastic wrap, so no blood would go any ware. After he killed her he picked up the keys and locked all the doors in the gym."
80	"Today I will bring a god dam pistol and rifle to shoot you and see how you like it when someone making fun of you. Once I kill you your life will be noting but nightmare and bad dreams."
87	"I will cut them, flay them, strip all the skin off their flesh, and pour boiling water all over them while they are still alive, as well as any other form of torture I could possibly think of. When they are dead, I will behead them and keep their heads in a bag."
107	"I'm going to destroy Victoria's head. She'll be completely beyond recognition."
138	"I will wipe you the fuck out with precision the likes of which has never been seen before on this Earth, mark my fucking words... I will shit fury all over you and you will drown in it. You're fucking dead, kiddo."

demonstrate an increased level of risk. When assessing the written or social media content, the disorganization of the threat or broadness of scope on multiple targets should be seen as a mitigation to the overall risk. There were 42% (47 of the 113) of active attack cases that included details concerning the target (Appendix B: 3, 7, 8, 15, 16, 20, 22, 23, 24, 28, 29, 38, 39, 43, 46, 47, 52, 55, 67, 71, 74, 77, 79, 80, 81, 83, 85, 86, 87, 90, 92, 93, 100, 107, 108, 114, 115, 116, 133, 134, 136, 137, 138, 140, 144, 161, 167).

One of the attackers at Columbine (Appendix B: 20) gave an example of emphasis with the narrowing of the target to the students at their high school and the use of capitalization to stress their point here: "You all better fucking hide in your houses because I'm comin [sic] for EVERYONE soon, and I WILL be armed to the fuckin [sic] teeth and I WILL shoot to kill and I WILL fuckin [sic] KILL EVERYTHING!" (Langman, 2014, p. 2). In 2014, the Isla Vista attacker (Appendix B: 87) wrote, "The first people I would have to kill are my two housemates, to secure the entire apartment for myself as my personal torture and killing chamber."

Another example involved a nursing student shooting and killing several professors at Arizona College of Nursing in 2002. In a particularly horrific attack, he killed a nursing professor in her office before finding two other professors in front of a class as they were administering an examination (Appendix B: 24). Prior to the attack, he bragged to classmates that he received a concealed weapon permit and noted that he had failed a class in nursing and had to retake it. A year-and-a-half before the attack, he threatened to "end it all" and to "put something under the college." He left a letter to be found after the attack entitled, "From the Dead," explaining his motives and targets. This is included in Figure 6.8. and Figure 6.9.

Ms. Amari,

Greetings from the dead. You have received this letter after a rather horrendous event. To be perfectly honest with you, I do not know what forces are compelling me to write this. I do not know how it will be taken. Will you read it in it's entirety or will you toss it in the circular file? Will you view me as lunatic or merely a person who just became too weary of life? I have thought about this letter for several weeks. Several weeks have passed and I haven't decided whether to write it and revise or do I subscribe to the Jack Kerouac method and write as the thoughts arrive for a more honest work? Maybe I shall do some of both.

Introductions are in order. I am, or more accurately was, Robert Stewart Flores. Think of me as Bob as I dislike the formality of Robert. I was born in Los Angeles in 1961. I have two older sisters and one younger brother. The winds of circumstances and time

FIGURE 6.8 From the Dead Intro.

treatment it will not change my future. People will want to know why I did this? Why the innocent lives?

To the sociologist, it wasn't the Maryland sniper. I have been thinking about this for awhile. To the psychiatrist, it's not about unresolved childhood issues. It is not about anger because I don't feel anything right now. To Ellen Goodman, it is not about gun control. I have had guns for a long time and it was my trade in the military. I do not have gun magazines. A waiting period or owner registration would not have stopped me. I have a concealed carry permit but I have never brought a gun to the University, (until now). I was a boyscout. I cross the street at the crosswalk. It is not about revenge as I have always thought that revenge was a waste of time and energy. I guess what it is about is that it is a reckoning. A settling of accounts. The University is filled with too many people who are filled with hubris. They feel untouchable. Students are not given respect nor regard. It is unfortunate but the only force that seems to get any attention from the University is economic force.

FIGURE 6.9 From the Dead Conclusion.

8. **Weapons Detail:** There should be an assessment of knowledge and content related to weapons and protective tactical gear mentioned in the sample. This may include bulletproof vests and high-capacity clips. The specific mentioning of these items gives evidence of a more detailed, organized attack plan. Meloy et al. (2011) refers to this as identification warning behavior: "any behavior that indicates a psychological desire to be a 'pseudo-commando' (Dietz, 1986; Knoll, 2010), have a 'warrior mentality' (Hempel et al., 1999), closely associate with weapons or other military or law enforcement paraphernalia, identify with previous attackers or assassins, or identify as an agent to advance a particular cause or belief system" (p. 265). In the active attack cases, 24% (27 out of 113) had examples of weapons detail (Appendix B: 15, 20, 35, 36, 44, 47, 52, 70, 71, 77, 80, 81, 83, 86, 87, 100, 107, 114, 115, 126, 130, 134, 135, 140, 143, 144, 161). Examples from these cases are provided in Table 6.4.

Prior to his attack in Oslo, Norway, the attacker spent a massive amount of time and energy acquiring the weapons he needed to carry out the attack and documented this process through his manifesto/journal (Appendix B: 70). He wrote, "I have now sent an application for a Ruger Mini 14 semi-automatic rifle (5.56). It is the most 'army like' rifle allowed in Norway, although it is considered a 'poor man's' AR-15. I envy our European American brothers as the gun laws in Europe sucks ass in comparison. However, the EUSSR borders to Turkey and the Middle East so acquiring illegal arms isn't exactly rocket science providing you are motivated enough. In any case; I would rather have preferred a Ruger Mini 30, but I already own a 7.62 bolt rifle and it is likely that the police wouldn't grant me a similar caliber. On the

TABLE 6.4 Specific Examples of Weapons Mentions

Cases	Examples of Weapons Mentions
15	"I have thought to myself, what kind of damage can a 12-gauge slug do to a human's internal organs or their head?"
36	"Well, today I gave Arlene a complete makeover. I turned her into Eric's shotgun. I sawed off the barrel and stock of the shotgun with a hacksaw. It took a lot less time than I thought it would. I taped the butt of the shotgun with duct tape. Now I just have to test her."
44	"All the shit you've given me, right back at you with hollow points."
81	"I bought my Stevens 320. It was not the initial gun I was expecting, but I think it will work better. I like the pistol grip."
114	"My goal is at least 20 people with an AR15 and a couple tracer rounds that I think I can do it and get done."
143	"Main gun: AK47 (WASR 10) – I realized pretty quickly that this isn't a great choice since it's the civilian version of the ak47. It's not designed to shoot rounds quickly, so it overheats massively after about 100 shots fired in quick succession. I'll have to use a heat-resistant glove to get around this. 8m3 bullet: This bullet, unlike pretty much any other 7.62×39 bullet, actually fragments like a pistol hollow point when shot out of an ak47 at the cost of penetration. Penetration is still reasonable, but not nearly as high as a normal ak47 bullet. The ak47 is definitely a bad choice without this bullet design, and may still be with it."

application form I stated: 'hunting deer.' It would have been tempting to just write the truth; 'executing category A and B cultural Marxists/multiculturalist traitors' just to see their reaction" (Brevick, 2011, p. 1,423).

9. **Threat Plan Detail:** The writing samples and social media posts have high amount of detail regarding the target, overcoming obstacles, enacting countermeasures, the date or time of the attack and acquiring items such as bolt-cutters or chains. The author may reference schematics, steps to dismantle cameras, combat elbow and knee pads, night vision goggles or distraction devices like homemade flashbangs or smoke. These pre-attack planning behaviors are well documented in the threat assessment literature (Deisinger et a 2008; Meloy et al., 2011; Van Brunt, 2012, 2015a, 2015b; Meloy et al., 2014; Deisinger and Scalora 2016; MSD, 2019). In the active attack cases, 16% (29 out of 113) had created content that included planning details for an attack (Appendix B: 2, 3, 16, 20, 22, 23, 35, 36, 55, 56, 71, 74, 77, 79, 81, 85, 86, 87, 90, 93, 107, 112, 114, 115, 134, 137, 140, 161, 167).

An example of this can be found in journal of the student who carried out the attack at Arapahoe High School in 2013 (Appendix B: 81). This is included in Figure 6.10. The attacker also wrote in his journal, "I intend on going as follows: I walk through the asshole in the north side of the trophy

Thursday, December 12, 2013, I went to Cabela's and I bought a sling, ammo belts, and of course, ammo. It included 5 sabot slugs! I think I'll need more. Luckily, I'll take off tomorrow.

[...]

Friday, December 13, 2013, today is going to be fun. I dropped ▓▓ off at school today, and went to Walmart, bought some ammo. I then dressed my weapons, loaded my belts, got my backpack ready. I then went to Brunswick, bowled, got some mountain dew (I bought it for the glass bottles). I'm going to make some Molotov cocktails-shaken, not stirred. Update 45 minutes I built my Molotov cocktails, and I think they look great. I only had oil for three,

FIGURE 6.10 Arapahoe Attacker Journal.

hall, waltz in shooting everyone in my way to the [redacted] (shouldn't be too many, it's not far, I go to the [redacted], to kill [redacted]. From there, there are classrooms in the [redacted] where I will do something I have wanted to do for a while-mass murder and be in a place of power where I and I alone are judge, jury and executioner."

In a more recent attack at Stoneman Douglas High School in Parkland, Florida (Appendix B: 114), the attacker recorded a video on his cell phone that was recovered by police. He said, "Alright, so here's the plan. I'm going to go take an Uber in the afternoon before 2:40. From there I will go to the school campus, walk up the stairs, load my bag, and get my AR and shoot people down at the main courtyard. Await and people will die."

Similarly, the attacker from the Aurora, Colorado, movie theatre shooting (Appendix B: 74) wrote a pro/con list in his journal as he planned his attack. This is included in Figure 6.11.

10. **Previous Attack Detail:** The writing sample includes references to previous attacks that occurred. This could also include comments about certain dates (such as Hitler's birthday, April 20) or other attack details such as "chaining the doors," referencing Virginia Tech's attacker. They may include studying past attacks or developing plans to kill more people than other attackers. In the cases involving an active attack, 41% (46 out of 113) referenced previous attack details (Appendix B: 4, 5, 6, 7, 10, 11, 13, 17, 20, 22, 23, 24, 28, 29, 32, 36, 38, 39, 44, 46, 47, 49, 51, 52, 55, 68, 70, 75, 77, 83, 85, 86, 90, 93, 94, 95, 96, 106, 107, 112, 116, 137, 138, 141, 143, 167). In the active attack cases when past attacks were referenced, 57% of the time it was Columbine, 11% Virginia Tech, and then a mix of Oklahoma City, Sandy Hook and others.

The types of references may be veiled such as "those kids in Colorado," or more direct as listed in the Umpqua Community College case in Roseburg, Oregon (Appendix B: 96), where the attacker wrote, "For the Vestor Flanagans, Elliot Rodgers, Seung Cho, Adam Lanzas of the world, I do this.

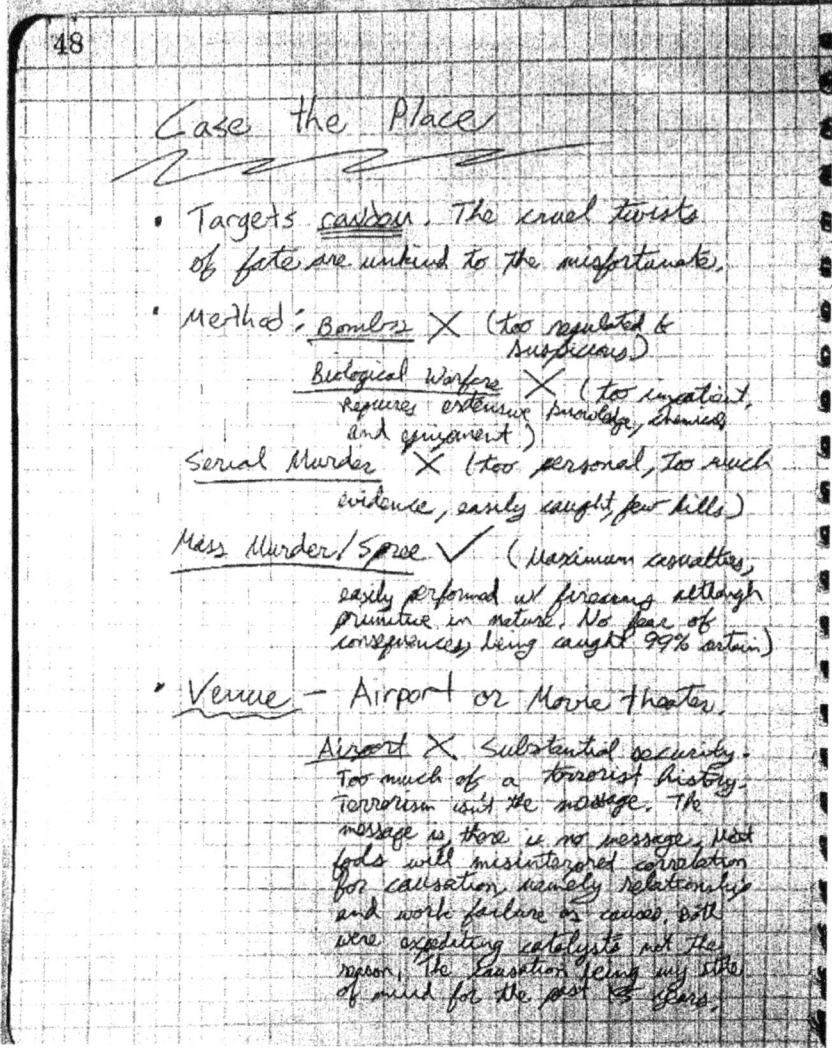

FIGURE 6.11 Aurora Movie Theatre Attacker's Journal.

For all those who never took me seriously this is for you. For all those who haven't made their stand I do this. I am the martyr for all those like me. To quote Seung Cho, 'Today I die like Jesus Christ.'" The attacker in El Paso (Appendix B: 143) began his manifesto with, "In general, I support the Christchurch shooter and his manifesto."

These 10 escalating elements offer administrators, police, counselors and instructors a detailed overview of the research related to analyzing written content.

While no expert system is perfect, this is offered as a starting place to assist school officials in sorting through the large numbers of threats and concerning written content by making use of a research-informed rubric. The VRAW^2, mentioned earlier in this chapter, is another example of a way to organize and sort through written and social media content. This new Looking Glass approach should be seen as an improvement on the VRAW^2, as it will allow for a more accessible system to be taught to BIT/CARE teams and the various departments charged with assessing threat.

MITIGATING ELEMENTS

While understanding that those red flags, warning signs and disturbing themes in a writing sample or social media post may increase the overall concern, there is an additional set of mitigating elements that should be taken into account prior to offering any risk analysis. *Mitigating elements* consider details of the concern that lessen the severity or seriousness of the risk, and these are discussed in more detail in Chapter 4 as they apply to violence risk and threat assessment. When assessing risk related to written or social media threat, we must explore the context in the analysis of the threat. This provides the BIT/CARE team attempting to assess the level of risk a sense of mitigating elements. These elements are outlined in Table 6.5 and further explained in the following section.

AUTHOR DISPOSITION

1. **Trolling:** The post was made by someone who has a long history of posting or writing material designed to enflame and enrage others. The purpose of the post or writing is to cause distress and to troll others into a reaction. In terms of cases that involved non-imminent attack, 32% (30 out of 93) involved trolling, attention-seeking and writing designed to get a reaction from others (Appendix B: 64, 98, 99, 117, 119, 121, 124, 125, 127, 131, 139, 145, 150, 154, 157, 158, 160, 170, 174, 175, 176, 178, 179, 189, 197, 201, 202, 203, 204, 206).
2. **Developmental Delay:** The writing was made by someone developmentally or mentally young, who may have a processing/expressive disorder or was transitioning to a new school or location, and the writing or social media post had a juvenile, poorly thought-out quality. There is a transitory nature to any threat that might be made. In a review of cases that involved non-imminent attacks, 32% (45 out of 93) had elements of poor thinking, being young, having a developmental mental health disorder or not understanding the consequences of their actions (Appendix B: 27, 30, 45, 48, 50, 72, 78, 82, 84, 102, 117, 118, 121, 122, 123, 131, 132, 139, 142, 149, 153, 154, 157, 158, 163, 164, 165, 166, 169, 170, 174, 178, 180, 184, 188, 189, 190, 193, 197, 198, 200, 202, 203, 204, 206).

107

TABLE 6.5 Review of Mitigating Elements When assessing Written Content

		Mitigating Element Name	Mitigating Element Description
AUTHOR DISPOSITION	1.	Trolling	The purpose of the post or writing is to cause distress and to troll others into a reaction.
	2.	Developmental Delay	The writing was made by someone developmentally or mentally young, who may have a processing/expressive disorder or was transitioning to a new school or location, and the writing or social media post had a juvenile, poorly thought-out quality.
	3.	Tangential, Rambling or Incoherent	The writing sample was influenced by a serious mental illness that disturbs thought, logic and organization.
	4.	International, Non-Native Language	The author does not have a mastery of the English language and may have made comments that, when taken out of context, sound more substantive in terms of threat.
	5.	Creative Author	The story or social media posts were related to the author's desire to be an author, artist or musician. The content of the writing or social media post, when taken out of an artistic process, looks more concerning.
CONTEXTUAL DETAILS	6.	Writing for Class	The writing sample or social media post was part of a class or group assignment. When the content is seen from this context, it may still be disturbing, but lessens the level of concern.
	7.	Therapeutic Journal	The writing or social media post is part of a larger therapeutic process (either with a professional or alone). The writing is designed to express frustration and allow the author to learn and grow to better handle frustration, impulse control and get a better handle on concerning thoughts.
	8.	Rhetoric or Opinion Piece	The writing is designed, in a nonviolent way, to bring about change through debate and rhetoric. The piece may be satire or the speech more common on more extreme radio and talk shows.
	9.	Retaliatory Expression	The writing is designed to create a reaction from the reader or viewer of the social media content. It does not contain ultimatums, but rather is written for the author to save face or gain back lost reputation.
	10.	Affective/Reactive	The writing occurs in reaction to an emotional frustration or event. If there are threats in the sample, they are vague, disorganized and transient in nature.

3. **Tangential, Rambling or Incoherent:** The writing sample was influenced by a serious mental illness that disturbs thought, logic and organization. While there may be concerning material in the writing, the larger context is part of a rambling, inconsistent thought process. There were no cases in the subject pool that matched this type. Many times, these cases are often triaged by mental health admissions or seen as transitory in nature.

4. **International, Non-Native Language:** The author does not have a mastery of the English language and may have made comments that, when taken out of context, sound more substantive in terms of threat. There may be a lack of awareness around cultural norms, sharing of personal information or expectations of privacy. Only one case (Appendix B: 69) matched a student with an ESL background lacking an awareness of cultural norms. This occurred at the University of Central Arkansas in 2011 where a foreign student became upset when another student in her orchestra class asked her to move seats. She wrote on Facebook "My current wish is to take gun and shoot all my classmates, enjoying their blood and scary" (Van Brunt, 2015a, p. 6).

5. **Creative Author:** The story or social media posts were related to the author's desire to be an author, artist or musician. The content of the writing or social media post, when taken out of an artistic process, looks more concerning. When the larger context is understood (author is creative), it helps move the threat to more of a transient state. In a review of cases that involved non-imminent attacks, 4% (4 out of 93) had authors who were connected to artistic expression (Appendix B: 27, 31, 45, 82).

CONTEXTUAL DETAILS

6. **Writing for Class:** The writing sample or social media post was part of a class or group assignment. When the content is seen from this context, it may still be disturbing, but lessens the level of concern. In a review of cases that involved non-imminent attacks, 4% (4 out of 93) had authors who were writing for a class assignment (Appendix B: 27, 45, 63, 82).

7. **Therapeutic journal:** The writing or social media post is part of a larger therapeutic process (either with a professional or alone). The writing is designed to express frustration and allow the author to learn and grow to better handle frustration, impulse control and get a better handle on concerning thoughts. When assessing this content in non-imminent attack cases, 3% (3 out of 93) had writers who wrote their content for a therapeutic journal (Appendix B: 56, 63, 163).

8. **Rhetoric or Opinion Piece:** The writing is designed, in a nonviolent way, to bring about change through debate and rhetoric. The piece may be satire or the speech more common on more extreme radio and talk shows. The

109

larger context of this style of persuasive communication helps mitigate the risk associated with the social media post or writing. When assessing this content in non-imminent attack cases, 9% (8 out of 93) had writers who seemed motivated by rhetoric and harmful debate to troll others (Appendix B: 63, 97, 98, 104, 145, 150, 162, 201).

9. **Retaliatory Expression:** The writing is designed to create a reaction from the reader or viewer of the social media content. It does not contain ultimatums, but rather is written for the author to save face or gain back lost reputation. This type of communication is described as ***howling*** in Chapters 1 and 5. In a review of cases that involved non-imminent attacks, 25% (23 out of 93) had content made in a retaliatory stance to threaten, save face or hurt others' reputation (Appendix B: 48, 64, 78, 110, 120, 122, 123, 132, 147, 155, 156, 157, 160, 164, 172, 181, 182, 183, 194, 195, 198, 199, 200).

10. **Affective/Reactive:** The writing occurs in reaction to an emotional frustration or event. If there are threats in the sample, they are vague, disorganized and transient in nature. They are a loud "bark" with very little evidence of "bite." This commonly is a social media post following a specific stressor to the person. They are often followed by attempts to take it down or apologize. In a review of non-imminent cases, 16% (15 out of 93) were made in a direct reaction to an emotional frustration resulting in a transient, vague or disorganized threat (Appendix B: 48, 59, 64, 69, 78, 102, 105, 145, 147, 155, 156, 159, 160, 164, 168).

SCORING GUIDE

For BIT/CARE teams or others conducting assessments of written threat content, a scoring scheme can be helpful to categorize and prioritize various interventions. The challenge with any scoring guide where numbers are used to represent corresponding risk levels exists in the overreliance on the numbers, overemphasis on cut-off scores and the use of the tool to take punitive action, rather than develop a tailored, advocacy-based intervention approach such as those outlined in Hart's work in the SPJ Model and the HCR-20 (Hart & Logan, 2011; Douglas et al., 2014).

For Looking Glass scoring, elements should be scored 0 if the item is not present in the writing sample or social media post and 2 if it is clearly present. Scores of 1 are given if the element is vague or poorly defined. The use of examples for each item are provided in Appendix K. The overall score can then be used to make a decision about requiring a mandated violence risk or threat assessment and put interventions into place.

The Looking Glass score is obtained by subtracting the mitigating elements from the escalating elements. This provides a range from -20 to +20. Future discussion and research related to interventions based on the scoring would need to be explored. Overall, scores of -20 would indicate an ideal where there are no escalating elements and all the protective elements. Scores of +20 would indicate a perfect negative score, with all of the escalating elements and none of the protective ones. As an expert system, Looking Glass should be used in combination with other assessment tools, such as the NaBITA Risk Rubric for initial triage, and threat assessment tools such as the SIVRA-35, HCR-20, WAVR-21 or ATAP's RAGE-V.

Table 6.6 is provided as an initial intervention guide to offer some suggestions for risk levels based on the NaBITA Risk Rubric's scores of Mild, Moderate, Elevated and Critical (Appendix J). As with the scoring outlined in the case studies in Appendix A, there is also an application of the Sample Intervention guide outlined in Table 6.6. Chapter 10 provides a detailed description and case examples of intervention from a case management perspective.

As you look to apply this material, Appendix A offers three cases studies across K-12 and college settings. For each case, scoring examples with Looking Glass and VRAW^2 are provided to help the reader better understand the practical application. Both Looking Glass and VRAW^2 are expert systems, not psychological tests or assessments. This allows the research related to violence to be more available in everyday threat analysis. When schools, colleges and universities consider bringing in a violence risk expert each time a threat or concerning writing occurs, administrators will start to push back on the cost and time delay. If the process developed to assess written and social media content is 1) costly, 2) time-intensive or 3) overly confusing, the result will be an increase in subjective and instinct-based decisions.

As with any threat or violence risk assessment, there is no substitute for a face-to-face evaluation with a well-trained and experienced professional. All assessments by a BIT/CARE team will increase in accuracy when bias is mitigated and subjectivity is reduced. As a cautionary reminder, dangerousness and violence from a student, faculty member or staff member is difficult, if not impossible, to accurately predict. Information in this book should not be seen as legal or psychological advice, as a guarantee or offering any assurance that violence will be prevented.

MOVING FORWARD

This marks the point in the book where the reader should have a better understanding of social media and the new generation, violence risk and protective factors and the importance of understanding threat from various perspectives. The Looking Glass approach is shared to help the reader more easily operationalize and put the research into practice. The following chapters will further explain the importance of a multidisciplinary team and how to intervene once the assessment is made.

TABLE 6.6 Sample Intervention Guide for Looking Glass

Score	Risk	General Summary	Suggested Interventions
-20 to -5	MILD	Very low risk related to the sample. Typically, contextual factors have reduced any risk that may have bene been present, and this likely a very transient threat.	• Possibly no direct action • Provide guidance and education to referral source • Reach out to student; assess situation and determine needs • Connect with teachers, school support resources, etc. for support and to gather more information • Provide resources to student as appropriate
-4 to 2	MODERATE	Elements of concern present in the writing content or post. Consider further threat assessment and information gathering to better assess the risk. It would be unlikely that suspension or separation would occur at that stage.	• Consider the voluntary use of violence risk or threat assessment • Hold individualized meeting with student and parent/guardian to identify a safety plan • Discuss how to reduce triggers, increase protective factors and review/adjust plan regularly • Use bullying protocols (if needed) • Refer for student discipline and/or behavior management process; address emerging behaviors under an academic disruption/discipline policy • Engage in skill-building for social and emotional learning, conflict management, interpersonal conflict resolution, problem-solving
3 to 9	ELEVATED	A higher level of concern that should trigger a required, in-person violence or threat assessment process. It is more likely that a suspension or separation would occur pending a mandated evaluation.	• Evaluate the need to assess immediate safety through welfare/safety check with in-house counseling staff, SRO or police • Meet with student and parent/guardian to assess and plan • Coordinate a mandated assessment with BIT/CARE staff trained in violence and/or threat assessment. • Referral to support services such as counseling, ADA/504, IEP • Coordinate transitions at beginning and end of in-school or out-of-school suspensions with school discipline. • Coordinate with school resource officer, local law enforcement, etc. to discuss plan for safety, community, response, etc.

continued...

TABLE 6.6 continued...

Score	Risk	General Summary	Suggested Interventions
10 to 20	CRITICAL	Highest level of concern indicating many of the elements in the writing sample match previous attackers' writings. Likely removal of student from campus, coordination with police around arrest and mental health around involuntary admission.	• Immediate wellness check/initiate evaluation for involuntary hold/initiate suicide protocols • Required contact with parent/emergency contact • Evaluate need for emergency notification to school community or to specific impacted parties • Initiate mandated assessment once immediate safety has been established • Determine and share process of assessment and action planning with parent/guardian • Coordinate with necessary parties (school resource officer, local law enforcement, FUSION center, discipline, legal and/or threat consult, etc.) to create plan for safety, response, interventions, suspension, etc. • Connect with off-campus resources as appropriate, such as case manager, child protective services, juvenile justice • Provide guidance, support, and safety planning to impacted parties, such as teachers and other students

REFERENCES

ASIS International and the Society for Human Resource Management. (2011). Workplace violence prevention and intervention: American national standard. Retrieved on March 28, 2020 from www.asisonline.org/guidelines/published.htm

Bernstein, L., Horwitz, S., & Holley, P. (2015). Dylann Roof's racist manifesto: 'I have no choice', *Washington Post*. Retrieved on March 28, 2020, from https://www.washingtonpost.com/national/health-science/authorities-investigate-whether-racist-manifesto-was-written-by-sc-gunman/2015/06/20/f0bd3052-1762-11e5-9ddc-e3353542100c_story.html

Brevick, A. (2011). 2083—A European Declaration of Independence. Retrieved on March 14, 2020, from https://publicintelligence.net/anders-behring-breiviks-complete-manifesto-2083-a-european-declaration-of-independence/

Calhoun, F., & Weston, S. (2009). *Threat assessment and management strategies: Identifying the howlers and hunters*. Boca Raton, FL: CRC Press.

Deisinger, G., Randazzo, M., O'Neill, D., & Savage, J. (2008). *The handbook for campus threat assessment and management teams*. New York: Applied Risk Management, LLC.

Deisinger, E., & Scalora, M. (2016). Threat assessment and management in higher education in the United States: A review of the 10 years since the mass casualty incident at Virginia Tech. *Journal of Threat Assessment and Management*, 3(3–4), 186–199.

Dietz, P. (1986). Mass, serial, and sensational homicides. *Bulletin of the New York Academy of Medicine*, 62, 477–491.

Douglas, K.S., Shaffer, C., Blanchard, A.J.E., Guy, L.S., Reeves, K., & Weir, J. (2014). *HCR-20 violence risk assessment scheme: Overview and annotated bibliography*. HCR-20 Violence Risk Assessment White Paper Series #1. Burnaby, Canada: Mental Health, Law, and Policy Institute, Simon Fraser University.

El Paso Attacker. (2019). The Innocent Truth. Retrieved on March 16, 2020 from https://drudgereport.com/flashtx.htm

Glasl, F. (1999). *Confronting conflict*. Stroud, UK: Hawthorn Press.

GlobalGrind Staff. (2012). "Die, all of you": T. J. Lane, alleged gunmen in high school shooting, writes chilling letter (details). GlobalGrind. Retrieved on December 13, 2019 from https://globalgrind.com/1796904/tj-lane-alleged-gunmen-chardon-high-school-shooting-letter-die-all-you-details/

Hart, S., & Logan, C. (2011). Formulation of violence risk using evidence-based assessment: The structured professional judgment approach. *Forensic case formulation*. Sturmey, P. and McMurran, M. eds., 83–106. Chichester, England: Wiley-Blackwell.

Hempel, A., Meloy, J.R., & Richards, T. (1999). Offender and offense characteristics of a nonrandom sample of mass murderers. *Journal of American Academy of Psychiatry Law*, 27, 213–225.

Knoll, J. (2010). The "pseudocommando" mass murderer: Part I, the psychology of revenge and obliteration. *Journal of American Academy of Psychiatry Law*, 38, 87–94.

Langman, P. (2009). Rampage School Shooters: A typology. *Aggression Violent Behaviour*, 14, 79–86.

Langman, P. (2014). Seung Hui Cho's "Manifesto". Retrieved on March 14, 2020 from https://schoolshooters.info/sites/default/files/cho_manifesto_1.1.pdf

Langman, P. (2015). *School shooters: Understanding high school, college, and adult perpetrators*. New York: Rowman & Littlefield.

Lankford, A. (2013). *The myth of Martyrdom: What really drives suicide bombers, rampage shooters, and other self destructive killers*. New York: Palgrave Macmillan.

Lankford, A. (2016). Fame-seeking rampage shooters: Initial findings and empirical predictions. *Aggression and Violent Behavior*, 27, 122–129.

Lankford, A. (2018). Identifying potential mass shooters and suicide terrorists with warning signs of suicide, perceived victimization, and desires for attention or fame. *Journal of Personality Assessment*, 5, 1–12.

Meloy, J., Hoffmann, J., Guldimann, A., & James, D. (2011). The role of warning behaviors in threat assessment: An exploration and suggested typology. *Behavioral Science Law*, 30, 256–279.

Meloy, R., Hoffmann, J., Roshdi, K. et al. (2014). Warning behaviors and their configurations across various domains of targeted violence. *The international handbook of threat assessment* Meloy, J.R. and Hoffmann, J. eds., 39–53. New York: Oxford University Press.

Moghaddam, F. (2005). The staircase to terrorism: A psychological exploration. *American Psychology*, 60, 161–169.

MSD Public Safety Commission. (2018). Cruz's Cell Phone Content and Internet Searches. Retrieved on December 26, 2019 from http://www.fdle.state.fl.us/MSDHS/Meetings/November-Meeting-Documents/Nov-14-1045-am-Cruz-Cell-Phone-and-Internet-John-S.aspx

MSD Public Safety Commission. (2019). Initial Report Submitted to the Governor, Speaker of the House of Representatives and Senate President. Retrieved on June 13, 2020 from http://www.fdle.state.fl.us/msdhs/commissionreport.pdf

National Threat Assessment Center (NTAC). (2018). *Enhancing school safety using a threat assessment model: An operational guide for preventing targeted school violence.* Washington, DC: United States Secret Service, Department of Homeland Security.

Newman, K. S., & Fox, C. (2009). Repeat tragedy: Rampage shootings in American high school and college settings 2002–2008. *American Behavioral Scientist*, 52, 1286–1308.

O'Toole, M. E. (2002). *The school shooter: A threat assessment perspective.* Quantico, VA: FBI.

O'Toole M. E. & Bowman A. (2011). *Dangerous instincts: How gut feelings betray.* New York: Hudson Street Press.

Pressman, D. (2009). *Risk assessment decisions for violent political extremism.* Ottawa, Canada: Her Majesty the Queen in Right of Canada.

Sageman, M. (2007). Radicalization of global Islamist terrorists. United States Senate Committee on Homeland Security and Governmental Affairs. Retrieved on December 7, 2019 from https://www.hsgac.senate.gov/download/062707sageman

Schiemann, M., & Molnar, J. (2019). *A practical guide to case management in higher education.* PA, King of Prussia: The National Behavioral Intervention Team Association.

Smith, S. (2007). From violent words to violent deeds? Assessing risk from threatening communications. *Dissertation Abstract International*, 68, 1945B.

Turner J. & Gelles M. (2003). *Threat assessment: A risk management approach.* New York: Routledge.

United States Postal Service (USPS). (2007). Threat Assessment Team Guide. Retrieved on November 30, 2019 from https://www.nalc.org/workplace-issues/resources/manuals/pub108.pdf

Van Brunt, B. (2012). *Ending campus violence: New approaches to prevention.* New York: Routledge.

Van Brunt, B. (2015a). *Harm to others: The assessment and treatment of dangerousness.* Alexander, VA: American Counseling Association.

Van Brunt, B. (2015b). Violence risk assessment of the Written Word (VRAW²). *Journal of Behavioral Intervention Teams (JBIT)*, 3, 12–25.

Van Brunt, B. (2016). Assessing threat in written communications, social media, and creative writing. *The Journal of Violence and Gender*, 3(2), 78–88.

Van Brunt, B. & Solomon, J. (2019). *Threat case studies.* PA, King of Prussia: The National Behavioral Intervention Team Association.

White, S.G. & Meloy, J.R. (2007). *WAVR-21—Workplace assessment of violence risk: A structured professional judgment guide* (3rd ed.). San Diego, CA: Specialized Training Services, Inc. Retrieved from http://www.wavr21.com.

Chapter 7

The Team Approach to Risk[1]

As the familiar adage reminds us, "two heads are better than one." This is never truer than when assessing and managing a risk of violence. Appropriately, many schools have adopted team-based approaches for responding to incidents of concern. Educators confronted with difficult and challenging scenarios involving potential risk of violence can turn to their campus team for support and assistance. In Chapter 1, you were introduced briefly to this type of multidisciplinary approach to threat assessment and behavioral intervention, including specifically the use of behavioral intervention teams (BITs), campus assessment response evaluation (CARE) teams and threat assessment teams in the review, assessment and management of threats. This type of effort is recognized nationally as a research-based best practice for the prevention of violence by entities such as the United States Secret Service (National Threat Assessment Center [NTAC], 2018). In this chapter, we will explain the differences in BIT/CARE teams and threat assessment teams (TAT). Then, we will further detail the purpose and functions of each team and how they are a critical piece of how educators identify and respond to concerns. The chapter will also describe other concepts of threat assessment and threat management as well as mental health assessment and violence risk assessment. Understanding these foundational terms is important, as Chapters 8–10 consider these concepts in action in our different school communities. Figure 7.1 outlines some of the advantages of using a team approach to address concerns and threats.

There are a variety of reasons to report an incident of concern to a team and not try to respond and manage it in isolation. When we individually review a distressing or disturbing piece of writing, our analysis or interpretation of the meaning, words and nature of the content is influenced by our own individual experiences, perceptions and biases. Consider this quote posted alongside someone holding a handgun in a recent social media post: "When it comes to my

---

1. Special thanks to Dr. Amy Murphy, Ph.D. for her contributions to this chapter.

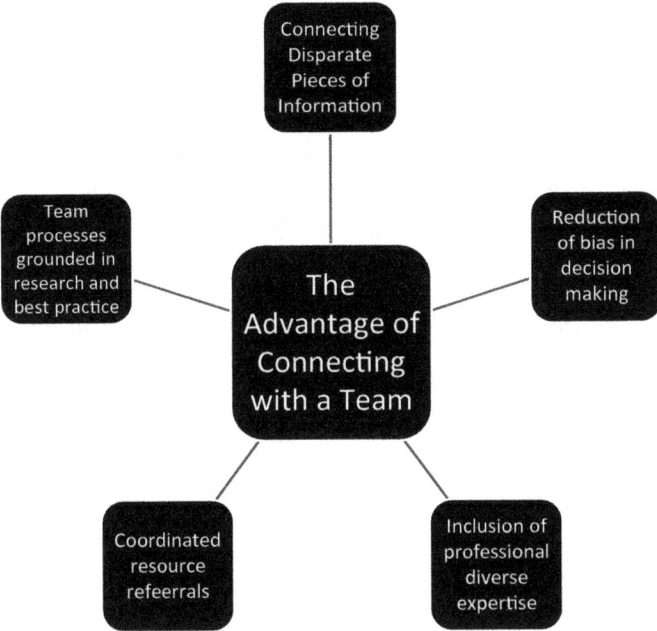

FIGURE 7.1 Team Diversity.

right to keep and bear arms, I have little desire to debate. However, I'm more than happy to educate." Is this person threatening violence, or are they simply advocating for second amendment rights? This quote might be commonly displayed in some communities on bumper stickers or t-shirts, but in others, it might immediately raise alarm. With a collaborative team-based approach, more information is gathered instead of following an initial emotional response. The team provides a more balanced and complete view of information related to situations of concern, especially when combined with objective, research-based assessment tools and followed by coordinated interventions (Figure 7.2).

When our consideration of how to respond to a threat of violence occurs in isolation, we also miss the opportunity to gather more comprehensive information from others across our school and campus communities, and we miss out on

FIGURE 7.2 Three Phases of BIT.

a collaborative approach to the response and management of the concern. Think of the many units, departments, classrooms and agencies interacting with members of your community. How many nuggets of information do we gather each day with those we work with and serve? This data can exist in isolation if there are not systems in place to intentionally compile information together to create a more complete picture of the context in which a situation occurs. A multidisciplinary team with the capacity to gather reports from across your campus or school community and then seek other related data from various pockets is just such a system. This type of team can also provide an objective risk assessment and create a response, intervention and management plan for those involved.

TYPES OF TEAMS

The terms "behavioral intervention team," "CARE team" and "threat assessment team" are sometimes used interchangeably, but it is important to understand the historical evolution of each type of team and the typical scope of functionality of each. Let's start by considering what threat assessment is. Prior to the 1990s, violent crimes occurred and law enforcement investigated the crime. As the nature of crime evolved, the Secret Service and other law enforcement agencies began to conduct investigations based on threats and behaviors of individuals that could harm others in order to prevent targeted violence (Borum et al., 1999). This activity was called "threat assessment." As you learned in Chapter 3, targeted violence is a process of thinking and includes attack-related behaviors all stemming from various interactions among the person of concern, their experiences and the potential target of violence. With these principles in mind, threat assessment developed as "a fact-based method of assessment/investigation that does not rely on profiles, but focuses on an individual's patterns of thinking and behavior to determine whether, and to what extent, they are moving toward an attack" (Borum et al., 1999, p. 335). Threat assessment teams are often focused on determining if an individual can safely continue in a specific environment or if the behavior has crossed a threshold requiring criminal action or hospitalization. Thus, teams are often coordinated via law enforcement or security units.

Behavioral intervention teams (BITs) and CARE teams, in comparison, developed following incidents of targeted violence in the closed communities of schools and workplaces. A school or university is considered a closed community because we interact with a regularly occurring population either because of their enrollment in courses or employment at the school. While some community colleges and other educational institutions may argue that they have fairly transient students, the population in schools is still more defined and limited than the population in a shopping center or movie theater, for example. This closed community lends itself to the expanded scope of behavioral intervention compared to threat assessment, which begins with an intentional cultivation of reporting from the community about behaviors of concern. BITs educate about the types of behaviors to report and how to report to a centralized reporting mechanism (Sokolow et al., 2014). As we discussed earlier in the chapter, this helps to eliminate silos of information that are not connected when a culture of reporting and collaboration does not exist. For the purposes of this book, this would mean educating for reports of written concern, including those identified in written submissions, emails or on social media (Van Brunt, 2015b).

To summarize, BITs are "small groups of school officials who meet regularly to collect and review concerning information about at-risk community members and develop plans to assist them" (Van Brunt et al., 2018, p. 4). There are typically three phases of BIT operations: 1) gathering data, 2) applying a rubric/analysis and 3) intervention (Sokolow et al., 2014). First, the BIT gathers data on incidents of concern by cultivating a culture of reporting and accessing various pockets of information on concerns. Second, the BIT performs an analysis of the information gathered related to the report by using an objective risk rubric and the various perspectives of the team. Third, the BIT selects interventions to coordinate in order to manage the nature of the concern. The three phases cycle as the situation evolves, with additional data gathered as the interventions are deployed, and the level of risk is adjusted accordingly. The term "CARE team" has evolved in popularity more recently to help highlight the preventative, nonpunitive focus of the team's work (Van Brunt et al., 2018; Schiemann & Molnar, 2019).

DIVERSITY ON THE TEAM

A key element of the team functioning is the diversity of perspectives that are found on a multidisciplinary team. A diverse team should be diverse in terms of position, as outlined in Chapter 7 and through examples in this chapter; however, diversity on the team goes beyond having law enforcement, counseling and student conduct working together. Diversity issues related to socioeconomic status, political affiliations, age, sexual orientation, race, language and the like should also be part of the team selection. This diversity allows the team to draw from varied perspectives when assessing threat, reaching marginalized and closed communities that may be resistant to report forward to a centralized authority group on campus and providing tailored outreach and intervention efforts with a higher likelihood of success. Several of these areas are outlined for the reader in Table 7.1.

Including a diverse range of individuals may be an easier task at a large university with a broader range of staff to choose from for the core and inner circle members of BIT/CARE. At smaller colleges and a number of K-12 schools (where the core group is three people), this may be next to impossible. In these cases, it is critical for these teams to take higher-level cases to a district-wide team for further discussion. Having a monthly meeting of the core members or the team chairs of all the schools discuss cases and trends will aid in adding a

TABLE 7.1 Team Diversity

Area of concern	Rationale
Socioeconomic Status	Here the team should strive to reduce bias in decision-making related to wealth, privilege and money. A team that is financially privileged may be out of touch with issues of food insecurity, access to transportation and other services. This may be a simple as attending to how someone dresses and the inequality this may unintentionally raise.
Political Affiliation	How team members define their politics can create potential for blind spots when assessing student behavior. Creating a team with varied points of view in the political arena creates an opportunity to get out in front of blind spots and bias.
Sexual Orientation	Having someone on the team with direct knowledge about living in an often marginalized and closed community (a community with its own language and codes) can provide insight for the rest of the team when balancing assessments and intervention.
Age/Generation	Team members often lean on their experiences to better inform their decisions. By embracing generational diversity on the team, the BIT/CARE increases its ability to assess and intervene with a wide range of students.
Race/Ethnicity	As with sexual orientation, those with a race or ethnicity different than that of the majority population often experience microaggressions, judgments and restricted access to services.
Language	Some students we encounter speak multiple languages. English may not be their native tongue, and this brings the potential for misunderstanding, further marginalization and inequality.

diversity of perspective. For high schools with college programs, partnering with that college's team can prove to be a valuable resource for both schools' teams. Even if a high school does not have an early college program, getting to know your local college or university's team and sharing cases (with names redacted) and trends can prove instrumental for team growth in diversity of opinion, experience and process. Any way that teams can get creative in this area is critical

Teams are most effective when they are able to balance diverse perspectives. This does not mean open hostility and arguing, but rather a fostering of the devil's advocate or red-team positions. Along with fostering rich and deep conversations within the team, the chair is a critical position in terms of selecting team membership, encouraging open and frank discussions, keeping out in front of potential "hotspots" among team members and fully exploring each case.

In the assessment process, nurturing an awareness of rival, plausible hypotheses and exploring what additional data may be needed to develop a fuller understanding of the risk is critical. Good intelligence and a willingness to imaginatively explore additional outcomes are also important. In his book *The Like Switch*, Schafer (2015) explores the importance of imagination in the risk assessment process. Before reading any further in this book, take out a piece of paper and complete the following exercise. For five minutes, write down all the things you could do with a paper clip.

The usefulness of the exercise is to come up with as many examples as possible. For each of us, it would be reasonable to assume we would come up with somewhere between one and two dozen examples, like holding paper together, picking a lock, making a chain, pressing a small reset switch and the like. If the exercise was repeated with a group of people working together, more examples could be generated if the group took the first minute to discuss the different qualities of paper clips (there could be 1 or 1,000,000, they can be metal or plastic, the metal could be melted down to make other things, etc.) and then generated double or triple the amount of ideas. The point here is found in the importance of thinking outside of the box. Teams work better than individuals as they have more ideas and perspectives. There are also times when we become restricted as an individual or a group by our perspective; for example, if someone said, "Hey, no one told us we could work together!" We become restricted by our own internal rules and expectations. By nurturing a diverse team, the process of analysis becomes more broadly defined.

THREE PHASE PROCESS OF BIT/CARE

Another important characteristic of behavioral intervention is the focus on prevention and early identification of concerns (Sokolow et al., 2014; Schiemann & Van Brunt, 2018). Threat assessment often does not begin until a threat actually emerges. With behavioral intervention, there is an intentional effort to seek reporting on concerns well before the nature of the threat becomes more direct or specific. This early level of risk is discussed in Chapter 3, where you see concerns identified as developing when someone is experiencing situational stressors but generally demonstrating coping skills. For example, a teacher or faculty member might receive an email from a student discussing troubling personal situations and how they are coping. BITs could also be notified about mild risks associated with predatory violence such as empowering thoughts when someone begins to demonstrate hardened perspectives and rejects alternative perspectives, even though there is no threat of violence. This might occur when a staff member notices a social media post of a student disgruntled about instructor feedback and grading on a recent assignment and continuing with a narrative of why the instructor was wrong. At face, these incidents are not necessarily high-risk, but by considering other contextual elements associated with each, the team has an opportunity to engage with each student and offer appropriate supports and resources to keep either situation from escalating further. With early identification, BITs have an opportunity to intervene well before an elevated threat emerges. If we wait too long, teams are left with limited intervention options, such as law enforcement and serious disciplinary outcomes, instead of more expanded interventions and support at lower levels of risk.

In addition to this prevention-based philosophy, BITs also have the capacity to perform threat assessments (Sokolow et al., 2014; Van Brunt, 2015a). BITs use an objective, research-based risk rubric to evaluate each reported incident and establish a level of risk associated with the concern. As mentioned in Chapter 3, the National Behavioral Intervention Team Association (NaBITA) (Sokolow et al., 2019) created a risk rubric useful for K-12 schools, colleges and universities to better understand the escalation spectrum of both affective and predatory violence (Appendix J). The team also has the functionality to perform more advanced threat assessments when the nature of the risk requires it. For example, in Chapter 6, a tool to assess the violence risk of the written word was introduced (Van Brunt, 2015b). BITs would use this tool to perform a complete risk assessment of any type of writing included with reports of concern. After the BIT has analyzed the concern, they then can identify corresponding interventions to mitigate the risks specific to the situation. These can include coordinated referrals to other resources, involvement of family or parents, referrals to disciplinary or conduct processes, case management efforts and even additional advanced assessment.

What types of advanced assessments might occur? There are two primary types of assessments that a BIT could deploy when the level of risk requires it: *mental health assessments* or *violence risk/threat assessments*. These are two distinct types of assessments used in the work of behavioral intervention. It is important to understand the different process and outcomes associated with both. Table 7.2 outlines several differences between these assessments.

A *mental health assessment* or psychological assessment is solely focused on the diagnosis of a mental health problem and identification of treatment options, including recommendations or requirements for hospitalization. A BIT might refer a student to a psychologist or psychiatrist in order to complete a mental health assessment. The second type of assessment is a *violence risk assessment* or threat assessment. Any member of the team can be trained in various techniques and tools to perform this type of assessment, which is focused on determining dangerousness or lethality of an individual to harm, kill or destroy a person, system or location. These tools include the Structured Interview of Violence Risk Assessment (SIVRA-35) (Van Brunt, 2012), the Historical Clinical Risk Manageement-20 (HCR-20) (Douglas et al., 2014) or the Workplace Assessment of Violence Risk-21 (WAVR-21) (White & Meloy, 2007). The risk factors identified in Chapter 3 are the foundation of violence risk or threat assessments and help a BIT to identify the level of intervention and threat management needed for each situation.

This brings us to our final concept of *threat management*. After the team has completed the analysis and assessment of the reported situation, they create a collaborative plan of interventions and risk management activities to reduce the

TABLE 7.2 Types of Assessments

Mental Health or Psychological Assessments	Violence Risk or Threat Assessments
Goal to identify and diagnose mental health problems and recommend treatment options.	Goal to determine dangerousness or lethality of an individual to harm, kill or destroy a person, system or location.
Regulated training and requirement for state oversight through licensure and national oversight through ethical codes	Growing area of practice coming from research in workplace violence, criminology, law enforcement and psychology. No regulated training or licensure at the time of this publication.
Focused on diagnosis, an assessment for inpatient care (voluntary or involuntary*), medication referral and treatment planning. *several states (including Texas and California) use law enforcement in this process rather than licensed clinical staff.	Focused on gathering background and contextual information, assessing risk factors, determine threat type (transient/substantive), assessing protective factors and creating an assessment of violence risk.
Formalized report, testing summary letter; goal is to improve decision-making and developing treatment goals. A useful support to a violence risk assessment, but often misused to replace a violence or threat assessment.	Provides decision-making guidance related to future violence risk. Summarizes risk of dangerousness with an analysis of risk factors and supportive factors; ongoing management and continuous assessment to mitigate risk over time.

risks of violence. Threat management is both the initial deployment of interventions and the long-term management of the concern. These activities may include ongoing monitoring and interactions with individuals of concern; identification of mental health, academic or personal support referrals; the separation of a student from the school community temporarily or permanently; safety-planning for individuals being targeted or impacted by the concerns; and stimulating the growth of protective elements like those identified in Chapter 4. Threat management activities are coordinated by the team but may include those who are not regular members of the team. Chapter 10 will explore the case management of dangerousness in more detail.

When risks of violence are present, it is in the best interest of the school community and individual educators to refer to and collaborate with a BIT with the capacity to gather data, perform comprehensive analysis and threat assessment of the concern and deploy coordinated interventions. When we act alone to respond to situations of concern, we lose the power of the multidisciplinary team to consider the full context of concerning incidents.

OVERALL TEAM MEMBERSHIP

To help better conceptualize a BIT/CARE team, it is useful to review the typical team membership in college/university settings and in K-12 schools. According to the 2018 NaBITA survey, the average BIT membership size is eight people (Schiemann & Van Brunt, 2018). The positions identified first are the members who attend every team meeting, usually with a well-trained back up within their functional area who can attend or assist when needed. Then, there are other positions who may attend every meeting or may just attend as needed when cases require their specific area of expertise. This second group of members will vary from school to school based on the specific needs and makeup of their campus community.

PRIMARY TEAM MEMBERSHIP

Team Chair

BIT teams should have a designated chair to provide leadership to the group, coordinate day-to-day operations and consider the long-term support and development of the team. The primary functions of the chair include vision and planning, community buy-in and support, team training and transitions, team meetings and processes and reporting and assessment (Schiemann & Molnar, 2019). As it relates to the assessment of written threats, a critical role of the chair is ensuring the team uses a consistent risk rubric in each case it reviews to mitigate bias in decision-making (Randazzo & Plummer, 2009; Van Brunt, 2012, 2015a). The consistent application of an evidenced-based rubric also ensures the team's assessments match its interventions and sets important cut-off scores to trigger parental notification and require an in-person assessment based on the level of risk present in the written or social media content (Cornell, 2010; Sokolow et al., 2019).

In their 2018 guidance, the Department of Homeland Security and the Secret Service make team leadership a requirement in either a part-time or full-time capacity, stating: "The team needs to have a specifically designated leader. The position is usually occupied by a senior administrator within the school" (NTAC, 2018, p. 3). In higher education, this is most often a Dean of Students or similar position. In K-12 schools, usually a principal chairs an individual school team, or a district administrator chairs a multi-school team. These positions work well in the chair capacity because they often have authority to compel mandated assessments when necessary, and they have the scope of knowledge and experience to understand various aspects of the student experience. Because of the considerable workload required of a team chair, it does require a position who can spend an adequate amount of time focused on BIT issues. While the suggested positions do have an extensive scope of responsibility outside of the BIT, when paired with good support positions and engaged team members, the combination is set up for effectiveness and success.

Counseling

BIT/CARE teams require membership expertise in mental health care and treatment. This position provides general insight into mental health-related behaviors as well as specific information and coordination for those cases either currently participating in counseling services or for those cases where there is a need to offer counseling services as part of an intervention. The counseling member is also trained in more advanced violence risk and threat assessment tools and can participate as needed in these mandated assessment activities. When possible in higher education, this position is a licensed administrator from the college's counseling center staff, such as the Director or an Associate/Assistant Director who has access to the center's complete client load. Licensed counseling positions on the team may come from a variety of clinical perspectives: psychologists, licensed mental health counselors, marriage and family therapists, licensed social workers or addiction specialists. If the college or university does not staff licensed counselors, then the position would be filled by a faculty or staff member with a background in psychology, a community member who can consult and work with the team or local community mental health specialists. Given that 75% of the cases that come to a typical team involve mental health issues (Schiemann & Molnar, 2019), it is critical to have some expertise in this area. In K-12 schools, the position is typically occupied by the school counselor or Director of Counseling and supplemented with regular or as needed involvement from a licensed school psychologist.

Because of the unique aspect of having both licensed and non-licensed counseling staff in these roles, it is critical to clarify two issues related to this membership: 1) is the member licensed to practice mental health care in the state, and 2) is the member hired by the school to provide mental health treatment? If the answer to both of these questions is yes, this team member has a higher level of confidentiality that shifts how they share information with the team about clients. Most other team members use privacy standards established by the Family Education Rights and Privacy Act (FERPA) (20 USC § 1232g; 34 CFR § 99). Confidentiality in a client/provider relationship requires either a specific release of information or meeting certain exceptions in order to share information outside of the professional relationship. FERPA-protected information can be shared regularly with other team members under the legitimate educational interest aspect of the statute (FERPA, 2020). This means psychologists, psychiatrists and professional clinicians will more often than not be bound by confidentiality unless an information release is in place, but school counselors or non-licensed academic/personal counselors or advisors are able to communicate more freely.

When it comes to the risk assessments completed by the team, the counseling staff are often the only team members who have extensive knowledge and coursework in differential diagnosis. To this end, diagnoses should be avoided in BIT/CARE documentation, but rather focus on behavioral descriptions of the concerns shared with the team. Unless everyone on the team has a license and can

TABLE 7.3 Behavioral Language for Diagnostic Terms

Diagnostic term	How to Document on the BIT/CARE
Asperger's/Autism Spectrum Disorder	• The student has difficulty attending to and understanding social cues when talking to other students about dating. • The student has a sensitivity to light and loud noises in the classroom. • The student asks off-topic questions and becomes frustrated when they are not answered immediately.
Schizophrenia	• The student talks often about odd and strange topics that other students and staff have difficulty understanding. • The student mumbles to themselves and often talks out loud in response to voices that only they can hear. • The student does not seem to be caring for themselves in the areas of hygiene and dress; they wear strange objects such as a white feather or are wrapped in tinfoil.
Depression	• The student is often tearful and distracted in class. They do not respond to redirection. • The student talks about "not wanting to be alive anymore" to other students and has shown self-inflicted cuts to others in class. • The student often falls asleep in class, expresses feelings of hopelessness and has lack of appetite. They are socially isolated from others.

discuss diagnostic criteria, this language should be avoided. A brief table of examples is provided in Table 7.3.

Student Conduct/Discipline

While the BIT/CARE team approaches cases from a perspective of support and care as opposed to a punitive mindset, there is still the need to coordinate team activities with a progressive and educational discipline or conduct process. In fact, one of the most common mistakes a team makes is skipping standard disciplinary actions for BIT cases, thinking they are being thoughtful and supportive. Unfortunately, this can create inconsistent standards across the educational community, and the team loses the opportunity to reset expectations and document patterns of concerning behaviors. In higher education, this position on the team is most often filled by the Director of Student Conduct, and in K-12 schools, this is usually the Assistant Principal responsible for discipline. This position is able to share information on conduct history of cases and information about reoccurring behaviors. They are also able to inform the team about typical conduct processes related to the presenting behaviors and coordinate with the team as these processes occur. This can mean coordinating when a student is going to be suspended or selecting disciplinary conditions that complement the team's selected interventions. The student conduct or discipline team member should also be trained in mandated assessment processes and advanced threat assessment tools in order to support the team when this need arises.

Law Enforcement

BIT/CARE teams should include representation from on-campus, sworn law enforcement for the college or school. For schools that do not have sworn law enforcement, campus safety, security or local law enforcement may be a reasonable substitute. This individual is the expert on criminal offenses and processes. They are able to consider the criminal nature of behaviors as well as share information related to criminal history or police contact/reports with the team. They should be trained in advanced threat-assessment tools and be able to participate as needed in violence risk and threat assessments. This position should also act as a liaison with other local, state or federal law enforcement agencies. In higher education, this is often the Chief or Assistant Chief of the campus law enforcement unit. In K-12, it may be a School Resource Officer.

Case Manager

More frequently in higher education and K-12, teams are using case manager positions to support the work of the team by providing flexible and creative support to the various cases through intervention activities, monitoring and coordinating access to care and resources and providing holistic oversight to the case. Approximately 40% of teams now include case management membership (Schiemann & Van Brunt, 2018). This can be either a clinical or non-clinical case manager. Non-clinical case managers are the most frequent and often work closely with the chair of the team to support the team functions as a primary aspect of their job responsibilities. Clinical case managers may also be members of the team, but they are often representing a counseling or health unit and serving similar roles to those described under the counseling member section. Case managers are uniquely situated to interact directly with students of concern, build relationships with them and provide longer-term management of at-risk situations. These positions are also well-suited to be trained in violence risk and threat assessment tools.

SECONDARY TEAM MEMBERSHIP

Residential Life/Housing

For campuses with residential populations, it is common for the team to include a member from Housing or Residence Life. This is usually a Director or Associate Director position with broad responsibilities, including the ability to access information across housing units related to student incidents and information. This can include incident reports, room conditions, roommate impressions, room changes or even maintenance requests. In addition to sharing information gathered from

127

housing staff interactions with students, they are also critical in coordinating interventions through Resident Advisors (RAs) or professional housing staff. Sometimes professional housing staff are also responsible for hall-based conduct processes, which adds a layer of similar coordination like those discussed in the student conduct/discipline membership.

504/Disability Services

It is critical that BIT/CARE teams have regular access and communication with disability support resources in the college or school. This may mean regular membership, or it may be as needed consultation. In higher education, this member is usually the Director of Disability Support Services, and in K-12, it will be the Special Education Coordinator. Many BIT/CARE cases involve indicators that an individual may qualify for disability accommodations. In some cases, there may already be accommodations or individual education plans (IEPs) in place for those being discussed in team meetings. These members can share accommodation-related disability information and effectively arrange accommodations for those who are qualified, as well as consult on disability issues and the rights of individuals with disabilities.

Title IX

Incidents of sexual violence, including sexual assault, dating or domestic violence, stalking and other forms of sexual harassment, often have overlapping concerns with BIT/CARE teams. All higher education and K-12 schools should have a designated Title IX Coordinator responding to these types of concerns. It is common for the Coordinator or a Deputy Coordinator to work alongside the BIT as needed. This allows coordination of support and interventions being offered to both reporting and responding parties. This can include information about no-contact orders and other supports and resources. Individuals involved in these processes are often experiencing distress and need support. The standard processes BITs use to consider other elements of student behavior and history in determining an overall risk rating for a student of concern can be important in the prevention of future violence from students exhibiting patterns of behavioral concern. Similar to student conduct/discipline members, Title IX processes should continue separate and apart from the BIT, but the two components can and should inform one another in relation to interventions, the use of support resources and risk assessments.

OTHER TEAM MEMBERS

Depending on the needs of the team, membership can also include a variety of other positions and roles, including academic affairs, health services, human resources, general counsel, student activities, athletics and academic advising. Ideally, teams should consist of between five and ten individuals, based on national standards (Van Brunt et al., 2018).

MOVING FORWARD

Now that the importance of a team approach to BIT and CARE work has been established in this chapter, the next step is to better understand the common processes related to building team cohesion, developing and nurturing open communication through regular meetings, mitigation of bias and quality documentation. Teams should address legal risk by ensuring interventions match the level of the assessment, careful analysis of community impact and avoidance of one-size-fits-all zero-tolerance policies.

REFERENCES

Borum, R., Fein, R., Vossekuil, B., & Berglund, J. (1999). Threat assessment: Defining an approach for evaluating risk of targeted violence. *Behavioral Sciences and the Law*, 17, 323–337.

Cornell, D. (2010, January/February). Threat assessment in the college setting, *Change Magazine*, 9-15, www.changemag.org).

Douglas, K.S., Shaffer, C., Blanchard, A.J.E., Guy, L.S., Reeves, K., & Weir, J. (2014). *HCR-20 violence risk assessment scheme: Overview and annotated bibliography.* HCR-20 Violence Risk Assessment White Paper Series #1. Burnaby, Canada: Mental Health, Law, and Policy Institute, Simon Fraser University.

Family Educational Rights and Privacy Act (FERPA). (2020) 20 USC § 1232g, 34 CFR § 99.

National Threat Assessment Center (NTAC). (2018). *Enhancing school safety using a threat assessment model: An operational guide for preventing targeted school violence.* Washington, DC: United States Secret Service, Department of Homeland Security.

Randazzo, M. & Plummer, E. (2009). *Implementing behavioral threat assessment on campus: A Virginia Tech Demonstration Project.* Blacksburg, VA: Printed by Virginia Polytechnic Institute and State University.

Schafer, J. (2015). *The Like Switch: An Ex-FBI Agent's guide to influencing, attracting, and winning people over.* New York: Atria Books.

Schiemann, M., & Molnar, J. (2019). *A practical guide to case management in higher education.* PA, King of Prussia: The National Behavioral Intervention Team Association

Schiemann, M. & Van Brunt, B. (2018). *Summary and analysis of 2018 NaBITA survey data.* Berwyn, PA: National Behavioral Intervention Team Association.

Sokolow, B.A., Lewis, W.S., Van Brunt, B., Schuster, S., & Swinton, D. (2014). *The book on BIT* (2 ed.). Berwyn, PA: The National Behavioral Intervention Team Association.

Sokolow, B., Van Brunt, B., Lewis, W., Schiemann, M., Murphy, A. & Molnar, J. (2019). *The NaBITA risk Rubric.* PA, King of Prussia: The National Behavioral Intervention Team Association.

Van Brunt, B. (2012). *Ending campus violence: New approaches to prevention.* New York: Routledge.

Van Brunt, B. (2015a). *Harm to others: The assessment and treatment of dangerousness.* Alexander, VA: American Counseling Association

Van Brunt, B. (2015b). Violence risk assessment of the Written Word (VRAW^2). *Journal of Behavioral Intervention Teams (JBIT)*, 3, 12–25.

Van Brunt, B., Schiemann, M., Pescara-Kovach, L., Murphy, A., & Halligan-Avery, E. (2018). Standards for behavioral intervention teams. *Journal of Behavioral Intervention Teams (JBIT)*, 6, 29–41.

White, S.G. & Meloy, J.R. (2007). *WAVR-21—Workplace assessment of violence risk: A structured professional judgment guide* (3rd ed.). San Diego, CA: Specialized Training Services, Inc. Retrieved from http://www.wavr21.com.

Chapter 8

Functional Team Concepts in BIT/CARE Interventions

Behavioral intervention teams (BIT), CARE teams and threat assessment teams consist of groups of professionals, including student affairs, faculty, law enforcement, administrators and teachers, who meet regularly to train and review at-risk cases. The team collects concerns from the greater community, applies an evidenced-based risk rubric to estimate the level of risk and then moves to develop interventions based on the level of risk assessed. These teams have been in existence for several decades at colleges and universities and became more formalized following the Virginia Tech attack in 2006 (Appendix B: 44). BIT/CARE teams that are effective begin their work with a focus on prevention rather than just reaction. A common response to violence in our colleges and universities is known as the "Bunker Mentality." The concept was originally identified by Calhoun and Weston (2009) as having two parts. First is the idea of fortifying educational institutions, which is typically not a proactive approach, and the second is zero-tolerance policies, which espouse that the mere removal of a student from a school would make it safer. Both approaches have proved to be not as successful as implementing BIT, CARE and threat assessment teams.

In this chapter, we will review several areas that are central to BIT intervention, such as holding regular meetings, providing quality documentation, encouraging rich and deep team conversations, matching the interventions to the student, diversity in assessment, bias mitigation and managing community impact. These core concepts in team development and function are critical to have in place prior to developing interventions. As you may recall from the previous chapter, BIT function relies on a three-phase process of gathering data, applying a risk rubric and moving towards intervention. This is a cyclical process that, upon applying the intervention, starts again with the gathering of data related to the effectiveness of the intervention and the assessment of behavioral change on an evidenced-based rubric. The following sections walk you through some essential foundational steps for the BIT/CARE team to be the most effective.

HOLD REGULAR, ONGOING MEETINGS

Teams meet either weekly or twice a month around 83% of the time across the country (Schiemann & Van Brunt, 2018). This meeting frequency is important for several reasons. BIT/CARE teams are tasked with keeping individuals and those in the school safe. By meeting as needed or monthly, there isn't enough time to build collaborative trust with team members, review cases carefully and thoughtfully assign a risk rating. If there are not cases pressing, the team should explore their marketing and advertising strategies to rule out the problem that the community may be hesitant to share information with the team. If the marketing and advertising are working well, then any down-time at meetings can be used to run tabletop scenarios, build team cohesion, discuss training issues related to mental illness, assessment and law enforcement and to review national cases.

This can require an adjustment in a K-12 model, as these schools are used to meeting only when an issue comes up or when a timeline related to an Individualized Education Plan (IEP) or other metric requires a meeting. The idea of forming a standing committee and building a talented and well-trained group of individuals to review cases from a multidisciplinary approach is the current best practice suggested by the National Threat Assessment Center (NTAC) (2019), the Federal Commission on School Safety (2018) and the U.S. Secret Service. Simply meeting when there is a crisis and turfing this to the school psychologist or School Resource Officer (SRO) is not a safe or legally defensible process.

QUALITY DOCUMENTATION

Many have heard the phrase, "if you don't write it down, it didn't happen." Providing clear documentation related to the gathering of information, application of the rubric and deployment of an intervention plan ensures the violence risk assessment process is effective, mitigates decision-making bias and provides legal protection for colleges, universities and K-12 school districts. Consider the following: a math teacher asks a student to complete a long-division assignment. The student does so and reports the answer as 48. The teacher says, "That is correct. How did you arrive at this answer?" The student responds, "I'm not sure, it just felt right to me." You can have the correct answer, but you fall short if there is not documentation to support how this answer was obtained.

The issue of missing or poor documentation recently came up in an audit of 642 threat assessments over three school years, from September 2015 through June 2018 (O'Matz, 2019).

Auditors reviewed a sample of 60 threat assessments out of 642 entered into a district educational management database over three school years. Of these sample cases, 23% had no documentation and 65% had documentation that was

TABLE 8.1 Dos and Don'ts for BIT/CARE Documentation

Dos	Don'ts
Do… keep notes around 4-5 sentences with a focus on what the incident was, what the team did to address it and what the future plan is.	Don't… make notes overly brief (e.g., "student was discussed at the meeting") or overly lengthy (e.g., two pages of detailed summary).
Do… document in clear, objective language about the case.	Don't… use a passionate or angry tone or subjective feelings in the notes.
Do… be sure to include a risk rating (the NaBITA risk rubric uses mild, moderate, elevated and critical) to establish a triage and move towards more information gathering and intervention.	Don't… use the risk rubric only on more serious cases or just those involving threat. Each case that comes to the BIT/CARE team must have a risk level to set up the next intervention steps.
Do… involve multiple departments in the information gathering, assessment and intervention planning.	Don't… task a single department to intervene in a vacuum with overarching team consult and involvement. Most cases will involve communication and actions from numerous departments.
Do… keep descriptions limited to behaviors, not diagnoses. Use quotes if the student mentions specific diagnosis issues.	Don't… use overly technical or diagnostic language related to mental illness.
Do… use a secure, searchable electronic database for BIT/CARE records and violence risk assessment documentation.	Don't… use paper systems, as they lack searchability and often have legibility problems.

"substantially incomplete." This concern is in line with physical security and lack of threat assessment documentation highlighted in the Marjory Stoneman Douglas High School Public Safety Commission Report (MSD, 2019). Table 8.1 provides guidance on how to write proper notes within an electronic, searchable and secure database.

ENCOURAGING RICH AND DEEP TEAM CONVERSATIONS

As BIT/CARE and threat teams were being developed, there was a transition from a single dean or administrator making decisions about a student's risk to a team approach. This movement allowed colleges, universities and K-12 schools to better address a wide range of perspectives and better explore the full nature of the threat or violence risk. This process is improved when the team chair encourages discussions from various team members to ensure all potential aspects of the risk are explored. Table 8.2 includes some considerations for the team to deepen their conversations about potential risk. The team should also follow a monthly

TABLE 8.2 Ways to Foster Better Team Communication

1. Encourage a willingness to suspend criticism and judgement around alternative perspectives, and allow these viewpoints to be expressed and explored.

2. Hold a retreat at the beginning of each semester/school year to explore the differences on the team in terms of communication styles, personality, willingness to share and cultural perspectives.

3. Identify team members who may be unwilling to share directly and check in with them on each case to encourage them to share their perspective. Encourage more vocal team members to pause and listen to other's perspectives.

4. Leave your position at the door. This means each team member has the same opportunity to share ideas and have difficult conversations without the fear of reprisal or negative consequences outside of the meeting (this works best when facilitated by the team chair and others with more power in the meeting).

5. Create training opportunities to work through tabletop exercises and hypothetical scenarios to test out team assessment and intervention skills. Consider having team members "switch roles" and roleplay to better understand other perspectives (for example, have housing staff play the role of police or the SRO and counseling play the role of conduct/assistant principle in a scenario).

training schedule to discuss a variety of topics including threat assessment, mental illness, disability accommodations, conduct and law enforcement actions (no contact orders, interim suspension, due process, arrest and court process), stress and burnout prevention and Title IX.

There are numerous assessment tools used to enhance understanding and foster community on teams. These include the Myers-Briggs Type Indicator (www.myersbriggs.org), the Keirsey Temperament Sorter (www.keirsey.com) and the Gallup StrengthsFinder 2.0 Assessment (Clifton et al., 2006; Rath, 2007; Rath & Conchie, 2009). These are discussed in detail in *The Guide to Leadership and Management in Higher Education: Managing Across Generations* (Fitch and Van Brunt, 2016). Businesses, individuals and groups have used these approaches to better understand how we communicate and make decisions in our lives. BIT/CARE teams using these methods should tread carefully to avoid conveying the idea that they are requiring personality tests for the team or these are being used to put them into boxes. As with any tool, maintaining a keen eye to appropriate application and utilization is critical.

Teams work best when they consider all elements of the case in front of them without coming to a conclusion too early and without proper assessment. Consider the following case where a student shares a story entitled "The Angel of Darkness" with her professor. Part of the concern is the professor's first name is Susan and resembles one of the characters in the story. The story is a rambling, poorly constructed account of a person in jail who is rescued by Susan, only to watch Susan attack her and then kill her brother. The student tells the professor

> "Ohh I know, you don't want any trouble but, you see I do!" She started to slowly walk around me. She placed both her hands around my neck. "You are so beautiful . I hate for something bad to happen to you. Maybe you should leave my stuff alone! Hey I just wanted to be nice! I did nothing wrong I am sorry If I rubbed you the wrong way. She grew furious her eyes bugged out of her head, the tips of her ears turned red and her eyes burned with furry. She grabbed me by the collar of my shirt and hit me with the burning hot wood that was used to heat up the stove.
>
> Dizziness over through my body. I felt nothing. I feel a burning sensation in my legs and upper back. AHHH!! I screamed in agonizing pain. AHHH I screamed again as she hit me again. Please stop Please stop I said begging her to stop. My brother came rushing to my aid. What did you do to my sister he yelled. Lilly came down stairs and saw me bleeding.she came rushing to push Susan off of me. Susan was stronger than her though. Susan would not budge. Lilly Tried with all her force but, she was too weak to move Susan. Susan laughed at her. Susan laughed and enjoyed the idea of torturing us. Lilly was right Susan is an angel of darkness. She was a demon from hell. And now I might die because I didn't listen to her. Ahhh I screamed again as she hit me one more time. This time I heard a blood curdling scream. I look to my right to see Lilly lying on the ground with blood all over her chest. Damn it you bastard I yelled at susan Why do you like to tourcher us. We did nothing leave lilly alone. Lllly . Lilly I scream NO !! Lllly please!! Stay with me Lilly !! Please stay with me!! Lilly !! No!!!!!! I heard another blood curdling scream this time it was my brother. I saw my brother cold lifeless body on the ground. Stiff. Cold. Tears started to form in my eyes to the point I could not see, JAvier Javier !! NOOOO!!! Javier!!!!.
>
> I guess i'm the lonely indian at last.

FIGURE 8.1 "The Angel of Darkness" Excerpt.

she wrote this for a journalism class. Upon follow-up with the BIT, the professor shares the student has talked about increasingly odd and seemingly fabricated stories about her brother being killed, escaping the country and her desire to join a foreign army. The story starts with the Susan character helping the narrator out of jail after a 10-year stay for stealing medication her brother needed to live. The unfolding of the narrator leaving jail is an odd journey and ends with Susan beating the narrator close to death and killing her brother. The conclusion of the story is included in Figure 8.1.

Cases like these often divide teams in terms of their analysis. Some may start with the idea that this was just creative writing and not any kind of actual plan. Others might argue that the character sharing the name Susan and the student sharing the story with her was potentially threatening, given the graphic killing scene at the end. Further, the story was not required for any class and seems to be a spontaneous creation by the student. Some may recall previous cases such as the attack at Virginia Tech (Appendix B: 44) or at the University of Alabama at Huntsville (Appendix B: 60), where both attackers wrote similar disjointed stories alluding to killings. While this story lacks any direct threat or time imperative, it does raise concern about the student's level of insight, motivation and potential mental illness issues. A team chair would do well to balance these many perspectives on the team and proceed with an evidenced-based process as outlined in Chapter 6.

MATCH THE INTERVENTION TO THE STUDENT

When setting up interventions with students based on the seriousness of a violence risk analysis, these assessments should be matched to the student in question. It isn't enough to simply identify an intervention, such as a referral to counseling, connection to activities or assistance with academic goals, but rather the intervention has to be created with the goal of the student feeling connected to the resource, sometimes called a "warm hand-off" or a "sticky referral." Consideration should be given to the student's demeanor, schedule, age, home-life, previous experience with help, gender, sexual orientation, life experience, ethnicity and race. While interventions will not always match directly to the student's experience or characteristics, nor should this be a goal, considerations around the student's buy-in to the intervention are essential.

Likewise, matching a student with a BIT/CARE team member for assessment or follow-up should not be steered through an on-call list or having them meet with whoever is up next on the team to do an intervention. Considerations must be given to ensure that not only that the correct level of intervention is chosen, but to assure a high likelihood that the student will follow through with the recommendation. Assigning a student to an assessment, case manager, academic support or counseling should not be seen as merely a box to be checked.

An example of this comes in working with a trans-male or trans-female student. While colleges, universities and K-12 schools can be among the most inclusive, diversity-appreciative environments in our society, transgender individuals often find many campus doors closed to them on the basis of their gender identity. Very often these are physical doors, such as to restrooms, locker and shower facilities and residence halls. Transgender individuals must also cope with less physical yet equally limiting obstacles that can make otherwise inclusive campuses feel unwelcoming. These include language in institutional materials that does not recognize anything beyond the traditional gender binary, lack of trans-inclusive policies, little to no educational and awareness efforts for campus constituents and exclusion from broader diversity efforts. When working with a transgender student through an intervention process, staff should understand that they have higher suicide and substance abuse rates than other populations and may have been ostracized or rejected by their families. BIT/CARE members involved in the intervention should promote an understanding of gender diversity by using appropriate terminology and common vocabulary and understanding the differences between gender identity and sexual orientation.

Another example would be student veterans in a college population. Veterans are returning from active duty to the classroom in record numbers (Wallis, 2012). Overall, educational institutions have welcomed these students, who come with guaranteed tuition funding and the focus and motivation needed to succeed academically, with open arms. However, many student veterans, most notably those who have seen active combat, arrive on college campuses with

135

TABLE 8.3 Dos and Don'ts When Helping Veterans

Dos	Don'ts
Do...ask about their service and ways you could be helpful to them in their adjustment to college.	Don't...pry into the details of their service and ask more questions when they seem uncomfortable.
Do...take into account their potential past experiences and be aware of how you address them in a crisis.	Don't...assume all veterans or active-duty military have PTSD and treat them with "kid gloves."
Do...look for opportunities to refer or connect veterans and active-duty military with others who may have served.	Don't...avoid helping, talking or automatically referring them to veteran staff because you haven't served.
Do...listen to what they say will be helpful for them and respond accordingly.	Don't...tell them how they should feel or assume their political affiliation or attitudes about past military conflicts.
Do...set limits about acceptable behaviors in the office related to threats, physical violence or yelling.	Don't...give veterans or active-duty military a "free pass" for bad behavior and avoid using panic alarms and police involvement if the behaviors warrant.

mental health challenges that can hinder their success. When combined with the stress of college, these mental health issues can become crises that can disrupt the learning environment and pose risks to both the veterans and others. Institutions need to address mental health from a proactive and preventative standpoint, and also be ready to respond when concerns become crises.

While some veteran students may be at a higher risk for mental illness or classroom disruptions (Haiken, 2013), most do very well in the college environment. Assumptions about their service past or that they may be a danger to others based on their service and potential access to weapons should be avoided. Treating each student based on their behavior and understanding their unique experiences is the key to successful interventions. In their book, Van Brunt & Murphy (2018, p. 23–24) offer a chart of how to intervene well with veterans. It's included here in Table 8.3.

BIAS MITIGATION

In keeping with a theme of diversity in assessment and team construction from Chapter 7, addressing individual bias is another essential part of assessment. Our bias is informed by our personal experience and makes up how we see the world. To this end, we cannot remove bias, but rather seek to mitigate it. This process begins when we first acknowledge that we each see the world through our lens of experience. An individual's bias can either be implicit or explicit. Common *explicit biases* are related to issues of religion, politics, social justice and race/ethnicity. These biases are known to us and are commonly acknowledged during the assessment of risk and selection of interventions. *Implicit biases* are not known to the individual and, as such, are harder to be aware of and mitigate.

One method to mitigate bias is through team training. This should include the use of tabletop exercises, practice assessments and preparation for assessing and managing future written-content cases. A set of practice exercises is available in Appendix A. When assessing written threat, there are often assumptions that should be guarded against. These include:

1. Assuming writing with graphic depictions of violence means the student is likely to act upon these descriptions. The student may be interested in creating violent content for sale, as part of a therapeutic process or to simply get a reaction out of someone at the school. While written depictions of violence would be a risk factor as they relate to fantasy rehearsal, they should not be seen a direct link.

2. Conversely, assuming that writing with graphic depictions of violence means the student is not likely to act upon these descriptions. This may be leakage prior to an attack where the student is sharing a dark and potentially hopeless and desperate worldview. The key to this assessment is balancing the risk and protective factors.

3. When a student posts content on social media, assuming students from a particular background, ethnicity, social status, religion, neighborhood or financial background are more likely to commit violence. There is no single profile for school shooter, rather a combination of risk factors escalating the potential for violence.

4. Assuming violent or threatening content in a fiction story should be disregarded if the content was related somehow to the assignment. No information or content should ever be discarded, but rather each data point in the case should be seen in combination with other risk and protective factors.

CULTURAL INTELLIGENCE

Jacques Whitfield

The conversations around diversity and inclusion have become more comprehensive and multidimensional in the twenty-first century. High-performing organizations in both the public and private sector have embraced a philosophy of cultural intelligence as an effective means of promoting diversity, inclusion and equity for their respective organizations. Cultural intelligence or cultural quotient (CQ) is having the capacity to relate and work effectively with different groups of people and across cultures (including Big-C "Culture" and little-c "culture"). Originally, the term cultural intelligence and the abbreviation "CQ" were developed by the research done by Early and Ang (2003) and Early and Mosakowski's work (2004). Cultural intelligence differs from other philosophies and approaches to promoting diversity and inclusion. It articulates core competencies and skillsets that organizations have the ability to cultivate and develop among team members and leaders through the staff development process to promote greater diversity and inclusion within those organizations.

Cultural intelligence goes beyond cultural awareness and political correctness. The essence of cultural intelligence is maximum self-awareness and situational awareness, which gives the ability to discern and articulate those attributes and characteristics that unite groups of people, and those attributes and characteristics that distinguish and differentiate groups of people. Furthermore, cultural intelligence requires the ability to suspend judgment while assessing and evaluating any given cultural situation. It is a recognition that there no one dominant worldview, but rather multiple worldviews that each deserve equal acknowledgment, respect and recognition. Cultural intelligence doesn't require "agreement" with any particular worldview, only "acknowledgment" and recognition of various worldviews.

High-performing organizations have adopted cultural-intelligence staff-development tools to operationalize diversity and inclusion strategies. These strategies have been found to be far more effective and more engaging at sustaining diversity and inclusion initiatives. Moreover, these strategies have also found to be less combative and disruptive within organizations because it doesn't require agreement with any one dominant worldview. Rather, it is an understanding that all worldviews are worthy of acknowledgement. This mutual respect and acknowledgment builds bridges between different groups of people as opposed to creating division.

Through awareness, open conversations and continual training, a BIT/CARE team and those conducting violence risk assessments for that team should address potential bias that could negatively impact decision-making. The following example from the Title IX area of practice can help the reader to better understand how implicit bias can impact our decision-making.

A group of seven male and female students sat in a common area in a college campus suite watching television and drinking. A male (Matt) and female (Sarah) got up from the couch and walked over to his bedroom. They went inside and had sex before returning to the rest of the group. The next morning, the female student came to the Title IX office to report a sexual assault. She said, "I don't remember last night and had blacked out. My friend told me I had sex with Matt. I don't remember what happened and I wouldn't have consented to this." The Title IX coordinator begins an investigation.

As part of this investigation, the Title IX investigator meets with the five students who were present when Sarah and Matt left the group to establish a timeline.

The investigator asked the first witness, "Can you tell me when Matt and Sarah left the main room where everyone was watching television?"

The student replied, "Yes, they left the room at 7:52 and returned at 8:07." Although surprised by the level of detail, the investigator nodded and continued with their questions.

After the interview was complete, the second student was brought in and the investigator asked, "Can you tell me when they left the main room where everyone was watching television?"

The student replied, "7:52 and Matt and Sarah were back at 8:07." The investigator looked puzzled again and completed the interview.

A third student was brought in and was asked the same question by the investigator. They offered the same answer, "7:52 and 8:07." This time the investigator said, "I've interviewed two of your friends who were there that night and they both gave the same exact times you did. Did you three get together and compare stories?"

The third student responded, "Oh yes. We were very concerned about this interview and how serious this all was. So, we talked to each other to make sure we were giving you accurate information." The interview was satisfied and continued with the fourth student.

The same question was asked and the fourth student gave the same answer. The interviewer said, "Hey, I have to ask. I know you all got together to make sure your memory lined up and the timeline was accurate, but I have to ask — how could you all be so specific about the time? I don't know exactly where I was last night during those times."

The fourth student says, "Oh, we looked up the TV schedule online to figure out when the commercial breaks were. Matt and Sarah left during the last commercial break of the sitcom we'd been watching, and they came back after the first commercial break of the new show we started at 8pm."

Most people who read this example find themselves imagining the students were working in cahoots to come up with a cover story or were making up times to seem more aware of what was going on prior to the alleged assault. In actuality, the students were concerned, talked together to confirm the timeline and then used a rather innovative way to determine the timeline. The assumption fed by our implicit bias is overcome by a more reasonable and congruent story. The lesson here is to keep an open mind and avoid coming to an early conclusion that isn't supported by the data at hand.

THE PROBLEM WITH ZERO-TOLERANCE POLICIES

Simply dismissing students and restricting them from campus or the school has the potential to further anger the student, forfeits the school's ability to gather more information through an assessment and takes away the potential for education and treatment for the student. O'Toole warns schools to avoid zero-tolerance policies (2000): "In a knee-jerk reaction, communities may resort to inflexible, one-size-fits-all policies on preventing or reacting to violence" (p. 2). The school is not safer when it takes an already frustrated and potentially unstable student and sends them away with little assessment, monitoring or follow-up interventions.

Scalora et al. (2010) add from their FBI bulletin, "Do not rely on expulsion except as a last resort and unless absolutely necessary to ensure campus safety; authorities should avoid the temptation to simply expel students of concern to quickly resolve a risk. Isolated from other contingency and safety planning, this strategy sometimes can worsen matters. The final humiliation of expulsion may serve as a precipitating, or triggering, stressor in the subject's life and propel the marginalized and hostile individual toward violence" (p. 7). Instead, a BIT/CARE team approach would encourage schools to seek to gather more information to connect with the student, understand their motivation and see the assessment and intervention as a potential developmental teaching moment that would likely keep both the student and campus community safer.

Zero-tolerance approaches can also backfire in unexpected and unwanted ways. Several years ago, a major university in the South adopted a "three strikes and you're expelled from school" policy for underage drinking in the residence halls. The result was that the RAs in the hall stopped writing up incidents of underage drinking. No one wanted to be strike one or strike two, much less strike three. The school ended up missing out on documentation that a conduct office and BIT/CARE team would see as critical to documenting trends or dangerous behaviors. A similar consequence has occurred in schools who famously adopt a "single incident of cheating equals suspension" policy. The result is professors will either ignore what they see as minor incidents, or they will resolve the incidents themselves with no school-wide documentation. This allows a serial cheater to go undetected. The same consequence is analogous to much more dangerous behaviors.

MANAGING COMMUNITY IMPACT

When students engage in potentially threatening behavior, the community often reacts out of fear. When they are upset and scared, students jump to conclusions and focus on the negative outcome itself, regardless of whether or not it is likely to reoccur. Sunstein coined the term "probability neglect" in 2003 to describe this phenomenon, where the public demands legal interventions from the government or seeks clear answers for the cause. If immediate removal of a student from college is offered up by the administration to a community hungry for answers, it follows that the community then draws inaccurate conclusions that this will ultimately keep them safe.

One such example occurred on January 29, 2012, when a student at UMass Amherst distributed over 4000 letters to students living in the dormitories. The odd letter was seen as threatening by some and necessitated a law enforcement response. It is included here:

Hello,

I'm pissed off at this campus. There is no way for me to get you to understand what I'm really talking about in a page of text. There is no real way to get you to care. Someone will always be freaked out by a note getting shoved under their door, someone will always jump to conclusions, someone will always be busy, and someone will always just throw this letter away without even opening it. So please, just stop and think for one quick minute.

This is what I want to have: a group of friends that do not need to rely on common interests or activities in order to foster friendship, love, and new experiences. What I mean by this is that I don't want friends solely based on video games, having the same taste in movies, getting drunk on a Friday night, smoking pot or doing other drugs because we're too lazy to think of anything else, or talking for the sake of talking. I want to do new things, real things... and I don't want to do them alone.

So, my best friend and I are going to wait in the Blue Wall every day next week (1/30-2/3) from 6pm-7pm or so. I do not want to drink, play video games, make small talk, etc. I do not want to be a means to an end. I want to create things to do on campus, and I want to create with you. I am aware that I may seem stupid, desperate, boring, or whatever negative things you wish to think of me. But the truth is that I am stupid, desperate, and boring and want to change. Call me crazy, but I don't want to do stupid shit anymore. People can change, but most are lazy. I want to find the people who can understand this, but this school is way too big and I will never have the opportunity to meet everyone. So, I wrote you a letter to tell you that I am here.

I'm proof that at least one person is frustrated that this school is not providing an acceptable social atmosphere. So let's make it. If you want to do real things at this school, try to be an empathetic human being, and don't just want more people for your friend collection, please come to the Blue Wall or email us. If you want to talk about everyone else, not yourself, this is the place for you. I want people who I can grow with, who I can create with, who I can be human with, who I can feel real feelings with, who I can love, who are real. Time is short and I'm tired of waiting. If you have felt anything while reading this, please contact me - Not for yourself, but because you know that's what should happen. Cut the shit, human up, and make time. Even if you don't like me, there will at least be one other person there to talk to. So think about it, that's all I ask. Look for the Green Frog. Regardless of anything I've said here: If you want a friend in any form, please contact us: XXX@gmail.com. I'm afraid too.

> Remember that I love you,
> [student name]
> Please don't come if you are acquainted with me, I apologize, but just trust me.

The letter was no doubt concerning to the campus, partly due to the ominous-sounding last line. Upon a lengthy assessment and review, it was determined that the student in question did not pose a threat, and the line was explained as an attempt for him to meet new people. In the end, the student opted for a medical leave, partially due to the outrage and fear expressed by students on campus over the perceived threat. Of note, this threat occurred three weeks after the shooting in Tucson, Arizona, by another college student (Appendix B: 67), which created an atmosphere of fear and worry on campus that drove an intense reaction from students, parents, faculty and staff. Chapter 12 provides a more detailed summary on how best to respond to these public incidents involving written and social media posts by students and how to manage the concern expressed by the campus community, parents and general public.

An example in the K-12 setting occurred when a 14-year-old high-school student wrote the following poem and left it on the homeroom class local drive at school (accessible by other students in the class and the teacher):

> I want to die
> I don't care how or where
> I just need to leave this world
> This life
> I don't deserve the things I have or the things I get
> I don't deserve to be happy
> I want to feel the blood trickle down
> I want to smile as I see the world disappear from view
> I want to kill myself
> There are multiple ways I could do it
> Overdose
> Cuts
> Stabbing
> Gunshots
> Silence
> I want to fall softly to the floor

I want to be free
I want to go home
But where is home?
I want to be alone
Home is a lie
Home is a lie
Home is dead
And who says it ever existed in the first place
I don't fit in anywhere
How can I fit in here
How can I be happy
I'm so busy trying to make them feel happy
R*******
Q******
G*****
Whatever the fuck they want to be called now
I just want them to be happy
I want them to stop hurting
I want them to just leave me alone
But I want them to be happy
I want them to be happy
But how can I do that without "neglecting my feelings"
How can I do anything
How do I function
How do I even stay here
How do I stay away from the things that hurt so good but feel so bad
How
How
How
How
How
How
Someone help me
Please
Even now, they're nowhere to be seen
I don't care anymore
Why should I?
Not like they like me anyway
I don't know what it was about them
They made me feel
…things.

(Van Brunt & Solomon, 2019)

A curious classmate was looking to see what students had written that day and then brought it to the teacher. The teacher immediately asked the student not to share this with other students, took the poem off the local drive and notified the CARE team counselor. This particular campus has invested heavily in suicide-prevention training and students are very sensitive to their part in managing community impact. This did not stop the student from sharing what she read with a mutual friend of hers and the author, but it went no further than that.

The counselor notified the chair of their CARE team, the assistant principal and the student was asked to come down to the "office." This was to avoid having the student getting pulled from their next class to see the "counselor." The parents were immediately contacted, and the poem was shared. The parents provided context that the student is an artist who writes songs about serious feelings—loss of loved ones, bad relationships, suicide, etc.—but that the student is not at risk for suicide and, in fact, sees a therapist to help them understand their deep sense of empathy. A meeting with the parents, the student and the counselor was held that afternoon and the matter was resolved. A student who, at first glance, would score very high on the risk scale was given context, the context was confirmed and then the matter was reassessed and closed. The student agreed to keep their "works in progress" off the shared drive and to use other channels to share and get feedback.

There was follow-up by the team with the teacher, who was understandably very concerned. The parents and the student also asked, and were given permission, to reach out to the teacher as well. The student also asked if they could reach out to the student who initially reported finding the document to make sure they were OK. This was initially declined, but later, after speaking with that student and her parents, the two did have a meeting with the counselor present, and the reporting student was relieved (and also interested in how they get the ideas for their songs). The rumor mill at school did spread a little from the mutual friend who was not alarmed at all (knowing some of the other works of his friend), but thought it was an overreaction. The team monitored it with the cooperation of the reporting student, the author and the homeroom teacher. No other incidents arose. This level of comprehensive monitoring, prevention education and a fair amount of information-sharing helped mitigate what could have been a major campus disruption that could have been damaging to the students.

MOVING FORWARD

The next chapter takes a deeper look the spectrum of interventions available to a BIT/CARE team when working with students. From applying the conduct process to conducting a welfare check on an at-risk student, this chapter will offer practical and clear guidance on how to create interventions across a multidisciplinary team.

REFERENCES

Calhoun, F., & Weston, S. (2009). *Threat assessment and management strategies: Identifying the howlers and hunters*. Boca Raton, FL: CRC Press.

Clifton, D., Anderson, E., & Schreiner, L. (2006). *StrengthsQuest: Discover and develop your strengths in academics, career, and beyond*. New York: Gallup Press.

Early, P. & Ang, S. (2003). *Cultural intelligence: Individual interactions across cultures*. Stanford, CA: Stanford University Press.

Early, P. & Mosakowski, E. (2004). Cultural intelligence. Retrieved on March 14, 2020 from https://hbr.org/2004/10/cultural-intelligence

Federal Commission on School Safety. (2018). Final Report on the Federal Commission on School Safety. Retrieved on February 24, 2020 from https://www2.ed.gov/documents/school-safety/school-safety-report.pdf

Fitch, P., & Van Brunt, B. (2016). *Guide to leadership and management in higher education*. New York: Routledge.

Haiken, M. (2013). Suicide rate among vets and active duty military jumps—now 22 a day. Retrieved on December 26, 2019 from https://www.forbes.com/sites/melaniehaiken/2013/02/05/22-the-number-of-veterans-who-now-commit-suicide-every-day/#6073ce62e978

MSD. (2019). Marjory Stoneman Douglas High School Public Safety Commission Report. Retrieved on December 29, 2019 from www.fdle.state.fl.us/MSDHS/CommissionReport.pdf

National Threat Assessment Center (NTAC). (2019). *Protecting America's Schools: A United States secret service analysis of targeted school violence*. Washington, DC: United States Secret Service, Department of Homeland Security.

O'Matz, M. (2019). Is a threat real? Most Broward schools can't produce paperwork to document their reviews. Retrieved on December 29, 2019 from https://www.sun-sentinel.com/local/broward/fl-ne-broward-threat-assessment-audit-20190318-story.html

O'Toole, M. E. (2000). *The school shooter: A threat assessment perspective*. Quantico, VA: National Center for the Analysis of Violent Crime, Federal Bureau of Investigation.

Rath, T. (2007). *Strengths 2.0.*. New York: Gallup Press.

Rath, T., & Conchie, B. (2009). *Strengths based leadership*. New York: Gallup Press.

Scalora, M., Simons, A., & Vansly, S. (2010, February). *Campus s: Assessing and managing threats (FBI Law Enforcement Bulletin)*. Washington, DC.: Federal Bureau of Investigation

Schiemann, M. & Van Brunt, B. (2018). *Summary and analysis of 2018 NaBITA survey data*. Berwyn, PA: National Behavioral Intervention Team Association.

Van Brunt, B. & Murphy, A. (2018). *A staff guide to addressing disruptive and dangerous behavior on campus*. New York: Taylor & Francis.

Wallis, D. (2012). Coming home from war to hit the books. *New York Times*. Retrieved on December 26, 2019 from https://www.nytimes.com/2012/03/01/education/soldiers-come-home-to-hit-the-books.html

Chapter 9

BIT/CARE Team Interventions

There are a number of intervention options available to the BIT/CARE team. The previous chapter outlined some essential functional elements needed for a team to run well and be effective in its interventions. This chapter focuses on the interventions themselves. Any intervention should be developed after an initial assessment of risk and should be tailored to the unique situation at hand. Many of the lawsuits and "misses" that have occurred in K-12 and college/university settings have happened because the team has over- or underreacted to the risk. By ensuring each intervention is tied to a range of risk, the team can better ensure effective behavioral change. In this chapter, we will review the process of wellness checks, working with parents and emergency contacts, mandated assessment and treatment, applying the conduct and student discipline process, offering accommodations and working with law enforcement.

It is critical to use an objective rubric and intervention list for each case, while focusing solely on behavior. When each behavior is identified and named, a risk level is assigned based on that behavior. Interventions are then selected from the range that is commensurate with that risk level. This avoids even the appearance of discrimination that the school was choosing the intervention based on any of the protected classes—race, gender, ethnicity, national origin, religion, age, veteran status or disability. Having a solid procedure and protocol for how these behaviors are addressed, how interventions may be exacerbated or mitigated and how schools make decisions on whether to do conduct or BIT/CARE first or simultaneously provides a solid framework for protection from future scrutiny.

THE WELLNESS CHECK

The value of wellness checks cannot be overstated, especially when working with adolescents. K-12 school districts should have policies and procedures in place that trigger a wellness visit to a student's home. There are a number of reasons why a school or college may look to the police to conduct a wellness check. These may include tardiness, absenteeism, suicidal ideations, threats to others or marked changes in the student's appearance or behavior. Having a specific plan and making a careful choice on which staff should accompany police or an SRO to adequately conduct home or residence hall visits is vital for successful intervention. Additional staff may include child protective services, counseling, a school-district counselor, residence-life staff or social services. A robust, multidisciplinary team brings a wide array of perspectives, services and support to ensure the success of the interventions.

When a college student lives on campus, it becomes easier to access support staff and have better control over the environment. Like in K-12 settings, a wellness check may be requested for changes in student behaviors, suicidal thoughts or a lack of communication from the student to their family. Typically, these requests come through the Campus Police Department, Public Safety Office, the Student Affairs Office or the campus BIT/CARE team. The lower-level checks are often given to a residential-hall advisor to knock on the door and/or leave a note for the student to check-in. The majority of these are missed communications and/or the student spent the night in another location. Having the private number of your local hospitals can assist to quickly rule out that a student has been hospitalized if they are not in their room. For more serious concerns, law enforcement often accompanies student affairs staff and may involve a more detailed criminal records checks, arrest records and assessment of access to weapons. This allows the team to assess concerns such as past incarceration, recent arrests (looking for violent encounters) or contacts with law enforcement. Being prepared and completing your due diligence around checking local hospitals and background checks avoids creating an embarrassing situation for your organization.

In more dangerous scenarios, it's imperative to take a deeper dive on the immediate safety risk and gather more information prior to approaching the living space. During these checks, there are several concerns that arise related to who is part of the wellness-check staff, how to conduct this safely and the importance of developing a follow-up plan for students moving forward. Every wellness check is different and may require various resources. Any time safety is a concern, law enforcement and/or public safety should be included in the wellness check. Law enforcement and/or public safety involvement should be set at a low threshold. All the above-mentioned precautions should be adhered to, such as running the name of the student through law enforcement databases. Knowing that a student was recently detained under a mental health hold or contacted by law enforcement for illegal or violent activity may influence your decision on the approach of the wellness check, as well as provide you with a crucial piece of information.

Typically, law enforcement conducts wellness checks that involve any likelihood of risk. Law enforcement wellness checks should be in coordination with the student counseling center and staff from the residence halls. The overall goal is to keep everyone safe and support the students. Once safety is ensured, law enforcement will be more effective when they show empathy, compassion and patience. A good approach to ensuring these qualities is through providing training around mental health concerns with your law enforcement team. Campus police and law enforcement, in general, need to avoid an adversarial "us vs. them" scenario, so training officers to conduct caring and empathic wellness checks while remaining safe is essential. An officer's typical bladed stance, commanding tone and authoritative demeanor, although practical for everyday street encounters, may escalate the student in crisis. Using a more caring and empathetic approach, such as sitting down near the student, engaging in conversation about more general topics such as campus life and favorite classes and/or instructors can help build rapport before asking about mental health concerns or other sensitive issues. There are several programs that offer trainings in this area, such as the QPR Program (Question, Persuade, Refer; a national suicide-prevention training program) or Mental Health First Aid (a national program that teaches the skills needed to respond to signs of mental health disorders). All considerations must be given to officer safety, community safety and the student's safety. The challenge is balancing safety with compassion and finding a technique that works for the given student and situation. A wellness checklist can help the officer and those involved in a welfare/wellness check to ensure they don't miss gathering critical information (Table 9.1).

Additionally, law enforcement must be aware of the available interventions for students not only on campus, but off-campus as well. A robust on- and off-campus resource list should be available for law enforcement to use at any given call, especially wellness checks. It is crucial to empower law enforcement to remove obstacles for student interventions. If a student is reluctant to get off-site help because of issues like transportation or cost, this is an excellent opportunity to build rapport and assist with transport. Other areas law enforcement might be able to provide direction to students inside and outside of the educational setting might be local groups and/or activities that may connect the student, such as the backpacking club or sports activities on or near campus.

WORKING WITH PARENTS AND EMERGENCY CONTACTS

Working with parents causes a bit of separation in this section between K-12 and college/university settings. However, the central concepts of why parental involvement is important remain the same. Finding a way to bring parents or the student's emergency contact into the discussion serves two very important functions. The first is legal risk mitigation for the school, college or university. When a student is struggling, if their behavior escalates and they take their life or the lives

TABLE 9.1 Wellness Checklist

Area of Concern	Checklist
Physical Sweep	• Search of the room for people/weapons/exits • Odd smells • Look for concerning material in plain sight, i.e., journal, suicide note, drawings, photos, articles on suicide • Assessing hiding places for other people • Additional lethal means (fire, diesel, poison, chemicals, explosives)
Weapons and Firearms	• Firearm on person, in room, concealed carry permit • Access to lethal drugs or substances • Demonstrated knowledge of nearby places of height (bridges, parking garage) or danger (rushing river) • Additional lethal means (fire, diesel, poison, chemicals, explosives)
Medical Assessment	• Medical assessment needed? EMTs, Health Clinic • Are they conscious? Bleeding? Rapid heart rate? In pain? • Have they cut, burned or otherwise harmed themselves in a suicide attempt or for another reason? • Have they taken any medication or substances, or ingested other items for recreation or a suicide attempt (if so, medical transport ASAP)? • Did they have or cause a fall from height, stabbing or gunshot wound? • Assess for medical treatment requiring medical transport
Behaviors of Concern	• Assess mood (calm, anxious, worried) • Assess body language (posturing, fidgeting, clenched fists, heavy breathing, forehead sweat, pacing, target-glancing, flushed face) • Rambling speech, darting eyes, fast-paced speech • Odd thoughts, paranoia, loss of reality • Threatening speech or actions • Have they pushed, shoved, grabbed a partner or other with or without bruises or marks (such as cuts, bites and/or punches)? • Was there a weapon used to cause cuts, bruises and/or minor broken bones?

continued...

TABLE 9.1 continued...

Area of Concern	Checklist
Suicide Assessment	• Level 1: No thoughts of suicide or treatment history • Level 2: Vague thoughts of suicide with no plan and/or past treatment history of therapy or inpatient admissions • Level 3*: Currently suicidal with plan and access; limited past treatment history and/or single inpatient admissions • Level 4*: Currently suicidal with plan and access; extensive past treatment history for chronic suicide attempts *Screen for inpatient psychiatric admission
Third-Party Information	• Is the subject under a doctor's care? • Prescribed medications • Are there wants/warrants from law enforcement check? • Is there online information that should be collected? • Has there been a drastic appearance change? • Have they recently lost an important dating or intimate relationship?

of others, reaching out to involve parents or the emergency contact prior to the escalation gives them an opportunity to be part of the case management process or have significant conversations with their student. The second reason to involve is an opportunity to gather more information about the student's background, which is necessary for a more complete violence risk or suicide assessment.

Legally speaking, schools have plenty of latitude to notify parents, guardians, authorities and local resources in the event of an acute suicide risk or threat around harm to others. The Family Educational Rights and Privacy Act (FERPA), the primary student privacy law, only applies to records. Information campus administrators have about a suicidal or threatening student that is not sourced from a record is not protected by any disclosure restrictions at all. If a campus wanted to release record information, it could under FERPA, using at least three exceptions. One, it could get the written consent of a student. Two, it could contact the parents of a dependent student upon verification of dependency (Internal Revenue Service tax status). Three, it could invoke FERPA's emergency health and safety provision, which permits the release of information to anyone necessary to help address a threat.

There aren't too many gray areas here. FERPA, the Health Insurance Portability and Accountability Act (HIPAA) and every other law (including client privilege) have exceptions for health and safety emergencies. For FERPA, this is actually determined by the school. The closest thing to an exception would be if the school had a viable, good-faith belief that the parent was the cause of the suicidality or would greatly exacerbate the problem, but the school would need to show that. Residential schools also have emergency-contact forms that could/would be used. When working with the K-12 school systems, our ability to share with parents is not only allowed, but usually required, as the student is almost always a minor.

There are two groups of staff that are important to discuss when a school, university or college is moving towards sharing information with parents. The first group is campus administrators, staff and faculty; the second is those in privileged relationships with students such as doctors, counselors, psychologists and social workers. If the only person who is working with the student has privilege, for example in a clinical mental health relationship or medical treatment with a doctor or nurse, it is more difficult to share information. For clinical staff, a policy that demonstrates a similar discussion and case review of the pros and cons of notification should be located within the policy and procedure manuals of the counseling or health center. Additionally, clinical staff have a responsibility to discuss with patients who are experiencing depressive or suicidal symptoms the involvement of parents in the ongoing nature of treatment. In a university/college setting, clinical staff members who adopt the "if they are over 18, we don't talk to parents" approach to confidentiality are oversimplifying the issue and avoiding their responsibility to engage those involved in the support of students' wellbeing outside of the therapeutic hour. This is not to say all students who check "has suicidal thoughts" or "experiences fantasies about harming other people" on an intake summary immediately trigger calls to their parents. Instead, it is a call to action for clinicians to explore ways to engage parents (as well as spouses and supportive others) in their clients' treatment from the start, regardless of age.

For college and university BIT/CARE team members who are governed by FERPA rather than privilege, the sharing of information with parents should be a collective decision after a group's reflection on the best way to share the information given the best data available at the time. Legal and process problems occur when you have one department acting independently without the support or knowledge of others, such as residence-life staff making decisions in a vacuum without consulting the larger team. As with all interventions in this chapter, they are always better when considered against the backdrop of a multidisciplinary team.

In a K-12 BIT/CARE team model, the discussion becomes more related to the requirement to notify parents and how best to accomplish this requirement under the law. Generally speaking, a K-12 setting is going to have a far more difficult time explaining why the parents/guardians were not notified, as the FERPA rights actually belong to them, not the student. This seems more confusing in dual-enrollment programs (where high school students attend college classes), but it actually is not. The records kept by the college belong to the student, and the ones maintained by the high school belong to the parent. Having a well-developed, transparent policy outlined in a memorandum of understanding (MOU) between the schools that discusses when/how records are kept and when/how information is shared will resolve a lot of issues and better protect everyone involved.

MANDATED ASSESSMENT

Colleges and universities should set a clear threshold for when they require a student to complete a mandatory assessment for self-harm or harm to others. These assessments should be tied to an increase in thoughts and behavior related to self-harm and harm to others. The purpose of a violence risk assessment is to balance the risk and protective factors and determine a level of violence risk and a subsequent intervention plan. It is common for the BIT/CARE team to request that staff provide an assessment for an individual who makes a threat or poses a concern of violence through written content or on social media.

For K-12 schools, the requirement of such an assessment is often a more difficult process involving discussions with parents and law enforcement. There is a balance between the school taking protective steps for the larger community by involving off-campus law enforcement related to a potential threat and being able to work more collaboratively with parents in order to obtain permission to assess their child. The pending punitive criminal and legal action may often force the parent's hand into not providing consent for the assessment as it may be used against their child later by the courts. It is critical to ensure the parent/guardian has signed the informed consent to get the information from the assessment back to the mental health professional on the team. In some cases, this can become complicated, as they may choose to limit this sharing to protect themselves from civil or criminal liability.

In the "Angel of Darkness" case discussed in the previous chapter (Figure 8.1), there are likely significant mental illness challenges for the student that could benefit from a deeper assessment. Having a BIT/CARE team member trained to identify this writing and its reflection of a rambling, tangential thought process provides an opportunity to reach out to the student and their parents and better understand the stressors the student might be under. This would be a useful perspective for a clinical counselor or psychologist to share with the team upon the initial case review, as well as for further assessment to determine potential risk and the need for ongoing mental health support.

In addition to providing insight to the team when cases are reported, clinical staff can be useful in both assessment and treatment. *Assessment* is often one or two meetings at the request of a referral source to determine issues related to self-harm, substance use, disability accommodations or aggressive behavior.

Treatment occurs over the course of five to six meetings and is focused on changing the behavior of the student that has been assessed.

Clinical staff and non-clinical staff can assist with a threat assessment or violence risk assessment. A *threat assessment* seeks to assess the risk of violence following a threat. A *violence risk assessment* is a broader term used to assess any potential violence or danger, regardless of the presence of a vague, conditional or direct threat. Violence risk and threat assessments are not to be confused with suicide risk assessments, which are performed much more commonly by counseling center staff and present much less of a bone of contention than assessments that examine harm to others. As suicide assessments have been part of clinical graduate programs for decades, there is more training and, therefore, less discomfort when clinical staff conduct suicide assessments rather than violence risk or threat assessments.

Ideally, a violence risk assessment is conducted by a trained and experienced counselor, case manager, law enforcement officer, director of student conduct or another administrator. Counseling staff should not be the only individuals able to perform a risk assessment. However, counselors do possess helpful skills related to intake, rapport building, conducting a defensive interview and suicide assessment that may prove useful. The BIT/CARE member conducting the assessment should be trained in interviewing, rapport building, determining truthfulness and overcoming impression management. Additionally, there should be steps put in place to address cases with more complex mental health issues that may complicate the assessment.

Any BIT/CARE staff members, including clinical counseling staff, conducting a violence risk or threat assessment must be trained in these assessment techniques and have experience conducting these assessments. They should draw from existing research in violence risk and threat assessment. They should have the ability to build rapport, assess truthfulness and attempts at impression management and be skilled at developing a simple report that includes clear and research-supported recommendations. Violence risk and threat assessments are not limited to clinical staff. A well-balanced BIT should have multiple options to choose from when selecting a team member to conduct an assessment.

When approaching a mandated assessment, the BIT/CARE team should consider these questions:

1. Has the nature of the assessment been clearly outlined by the team? What is the team seeking to assess? Is this a violence risk assessment, a psychological, diagnostic-based interview or a suicide assessment?
2. What materials would be useful to have in order to complete a more detailed and accurate assessment of risk?
3. How will the information be shared back with the team? Is there a release of information that could provide a conduit for information-sharing? Is this a

voluntary or required action by the student? Is a letter required? A conversation? An email? If a written report, what areas should the report include? Where will the final results reside in terms of a database?

4. What questions are the BIT/CARE team attempting to answer? The assessment should not look to predict future behavior, but rather identify potential exacerbating factors as well as supportive and protective factors that stabilize the individual.

5. Any assessment of risk should include **both** exacerbating factors that will make the situation worse and mitigating factors that will support the situation and make it better. Good violence risk assessment is balancing the risk and protective factors.

An example of how mandated assessment could have been useful to better gauge the risk prior to an attack involves the Parkland shooting (Appendix B: 114). The attacker, like many other attackers, documented a long history of being alone and feelings of sadness and isolation throughout his life. This suicidality, marginalization, life indifference, perceived victimization and desire for fame become key risk factors to consider during an assessment (Lankford, 2013, 2018). The attacker's cell phone was recovered and there were two video clips of him discussing his attack plan (MSD Public Safety Commission, 2018). A transcription of these are provided here:

> Hello, my name is name's Nick and I'm going to be the next school shooter of 2018. My goal is at least 20 people with an AR15 and a couple tracer rounds that I think I can do it and get done. Location is Stoneman Douglas in Parkland, Florida. It's going to be a big event and when you see me on the news, you'll all know who I am. Hehehe. You're all going to die – pew, pew, pew, pew, pew. Oh yeah, can't wait.
>
> Alright, so here's the plan. I'm going to go take an Uber in the afternoon before 2:40. From there I will go to the school campus, walk up the stairs, load my bag, and get my AR and shoot people down at the main courtyard. Await and people will die.
>
> Today is the day, the day it all begins. The day of my massacre shall begin. All the kids in the school will run in fear and hide. From the wrath of my power, they will know who I am. I am nothing, I am no one. My life is nothing and meaningless. Everything I hold dear I let go beyond your half. Every day I see the world ending another day. I live alone life, live in seclusion and solitude. I hate everyone and everything. With the power of my AR you will all know who I am. I had enough of being told what to do and when to do. I had enough of telling me that I'm an idiot and a dumbass. In real life, you're all the dumbass. You're all stupid and brainwashed by the political government programs.

Cruz's Cell Phone – Notes
January 21, 2018 at 3:35 pm

"My life is a mess idk what to do anymore. Everyday I get even more agitated at everyone cause my life is unfair. Everything and everyone is happy except for me I want to kill people but I don't know how I can do it. Walk to a park, get someone to pick me up I just don't know anymore but it will happen soon."

FIGURE 9.1 Parkland Shooter's Cell Phone.

The attacker's videos and writing are provided not as an excuse for his behavior—he is solely responsible for these killings—but rather to better understand the large amount of social media and written content that existed related to his attack plan. Another example of hopelessness, marginalization and suicidal thoughts can be seen from his cell phone (MSD Public Safety Commission, 2018, p.7) and is highlighted here in Figure 9.1.

For those interested in learning more about the process of conducting a violence risk assessment, it is discussed in detail in *Harm to Others: The Assessment and Treatment of Dangerousness* (Van Brunt, 2015). This process of violence risk assessment is both an art and science, drawing on rapport-building skills, information-gathering and applying an awareness of risk and protective factors. This is not a psychological assessment, which focuses instead on a diagnostics interview, determining a threshold for involuntary commitment, medication referral and treatment planning, but rather an assessment to determine the risk of predatory or targeted violence.

MANDATED TREATMENT

Mandated treatment seeks to change existing behaviors following a violence risk assessment rather than assessing the dangerousness of the behaviors that are present. The clinician seeks to change behavior by increasing impulse control, improving frustration tolerance and teaching better anger-management skills. Used this way, mandated treatment can be a useful tool in helping students address concerning behaviors on campus and remaining within the expectations of the school code of conduct or disciplinary policy (Cohen, 2007; Snyder & Anderson, 2009). The treatment should be short-term, based on behaviors, and have a clear place in the overall services offered by a college counseling center. There are many approaches to treatment that work with defensive, unwilling or difficult clients. These include Gestalt therapy, reality therapy, transtheoretical change theory and motivational interviewing. This treatment should never be focused on addressing mental illness, but rather focused on a reduction of behaviors related to risk factors identified in the violence risk assessment and increase protective factors and social supports.

In a K-12 setting, the challenge centers around available resources and parental permission. If care is required in order for the student to continue at the school, this may be part of a larger case-management process with an off-campus provider. In this case, securing a release of information allows the school BIT/CARE or counseling staff to stay in contact with the off-campus clinical staff to better communicate and coordinate care between the school and the therapist. Some schools may have on-site clinical care that can be offered to students to address behavioral issues. The establishment of parental involvement and release of information forms among the student, therapist, parent and school BIT/CARE team should be obtained prior to any treatment.

There is some debate in the counseling field among those who see value in mandated treatment and those who see this as beyond the scope of what a college counseling center should provide or feel that it could offer a chilling effect on students seeking services. Both the 2014–2015 American College Counseling Association (ACCA) Community College Survey and the 2006–2009 Association of University and College Counseling Center Directors (AUCCCD) survey address the issue of mandated treatment. The data shows that about one-third of college counseling centers (25%–38%) offer mandated care as compared to with over half (53%–78%) offering mandated assessment (AUCCCD, 2010; ACCA, 2014). However, there are some limitations in the data, as the ACCA survey focuses on community colleges and the AUCCCD last asked the mandated-treatment question in 2008–2009. For those centers that do not wish to offer this as a service, the college or university could lean into non-clinical staff such as resident directors, non-clinical case managers and other BIT/CARE team members willing to help the student address their behaviors over time.

The National Behavioral Intervention Team Association (NaBITA) offered a white paper entitled *The Role of the Counselor on the BIT* (Van Brunt & Sokolow, 2018) that included a set of practical guidance on how to navigate mandated treatment well.

"For clinical staff considering developing a mandated therapy model, consider the following list to help maximize efficiency and avoid potential pitfalls:

- Care should be limited to behaviors, not diagnoses. It would be unreasonable to expect a student to no longer be depressed, no longer have a personality disorder, or struggle with schizophrenia. It would be reasonable to help them improve their frustration tolerance, impulse control, and appropriately access help when in crisis.
- Care should be short-term and solution-focused. It would be unreasonable to require a student to be in mandated treatment for the entire time they are

at school or even for several years. The better approach would be to require five to six sessions and then review progress as part of the case management process.

- Care can also come in the form of recommended counseling, as a conduct sanction, to identify the potential need for treatment or require an assessment and the completion of treatment recommendations.
- Students should not be required to be medication compliant. It would be more reasonable to require a medication evaluation and encourage them to follow through with recommendations, rather than creating a potential special relationship where the school or staff now have to assess or monitor medication compliance.
- Have a plan in place to notify the referral source if the student required to complete the assessment or treatment does not show up for appointments. This can be included in the initial informed consent or release of information document or through a conversation with the referring source that they should assume the student has stopped complying if the counseling center is no longer able to communicate" (p. 21).

APPLYING THE CONDUCT AND DISCIPLINE PROCESS

In the "Angel of Darkness" scenario from Chapter 8, the student conduct officer at a public school (or private in California) would be taking a risk to act on that story alone. The story is not a threat (even if Susan is the professor, she survives), it is not disruptive and it is not harassing as a stand-alone story (no matter what Professor Susan says). This is a case where pulling the BIT/CARE train out of the station first is the definitive choice.

But what if Professor Susan takes it upon herself to share this—and her "I am Susan" theory—with her colleagues and/or other students in the class? Now she will inevitably say the story has caused a disruption, but it is a disruption she created. The student did not create any disruption. In this hypothetical, Professor Susan creates the disruption the same way the officers did by arresting Mr. Cohen in the "F—K the Draft!" legal case in Chapter 5 (Cohen v. California, 403 U.S. 15, 1971). They created the only disruption, so the speech is still protected. If the student sent the story to the class and/or referenced the professor as the antagonist, that would make a significant difference. This emphasizes the importance of training the community—especially faculty—in these legal issues and the difference between conduct and BIT/CARE and about the limitations of both.

Let us say this very clearly here. The BIT/CARE team should not replace the disciplinary process. While allowing that often comes from a place of caring, it ends up doing a disservice to the school, the students and the community. While a student's cooperation with the BIT/CARE process may mitigate a sanction, it should never replace the process.

Let's say the student in Chapter 8 was sending the story to everyone, telling them the professor is evil and creating a disruptive environment in the class. The professor is upset, the class is disrupted, and the student conduct officer is notified. Given the nature of the story, the school decides to let the BIT/CARE team go first and holds off on the conduct process. The student meets with the BIT/CARE representative and explains that she lost her brother recently to a murder and is struggling with the grief. She wants to apologize the professor (and writes a letter) and agrees to see a counselor for an assessment and maybe even treatment. The professor learns of her loss and accepts the letter. She wants the matter dropped. The student is cooperating. The student conduct officer decides not to take any action at all. A year later, she relapses and does the same thing to another professor. In this case, the conduct office cannot consider the prior matter as a "prior offense," as it was never adjudicated. Any sanctions that may treat her case that way would potentially be considered biased or discriminatory. Even worse, if the school is determined to have "regarded her as having a disability," they would have potentially set the precedent of giving a pass to any disciplinary process (not outcome) as a reasonable accommodation. While these scenarios may seem to be extreme, they are easily resolved by simply putting the BIT/CARE-cooperative student through an expedited student conduct process, with sanctions that either are mitigated by her cooperation and/or mirror the activities (counseling, assessment, etc.) she is already engaged in.

The sanctioning phase is what allows schools to engage in more progressive practices that meet the need to address the behaviors. It may also allow for exacerbation of sanctions for those that do not take advantage of the BIT/CARE interventions. Also, in these days of ever-increasing internet/social media harassment and threats, a sound computer/technology use policy is even more critical. Failing to hold students accountable for their behaviors is counter to student development theory and does a disservice to the community and the student. Further, it creates an exposure point for the school moving forward. Addressing the behaviors on all fronts, even at their lowest levels, sets a clear community standard and reduces exposure.

OFFERING ACCOMMODATIONS AND IEPs

As part of a comprehensive intervention plan, the BIT/CARE team should offer a referral to accessibility services for students who may be experiencing physical or mental illness challenges that impact their ability to achieve academically. In higher-education settings, a student must self-identify to request accommodations. Federal law then requires institutions to provide otherwise-qualified students with a disability an equal opportunity to benefit from the full range of the educational experience. Under federal law, a disability is defined as a physical or mental impairment that substantially limits one or more major life activities (Americans with Disabilities Act [ADA], 1990). Examples of major life activities include caring for oneself, seeing, hearing, eating, walking, speaking, learning, reading, concentrating, thinking, communicating and working. Institutions must make reasonable accommodations to known physical or mental limitations, unless the accommodation is an undue hardship on the institution.

In K-12 settings, there are both individualized educational plans (IEPs) as well as ADA/504 disability accommodations that are available for students, and they often interact. These referral processes often have more complicated requirements and processes than their college counterparts and should be made available to students based on district policy. However, the underlying concept of offering support and accommodations to students who need it to achieve academic success and increase socialization and support are equally important in the college, university and K-12 settings. In K-12, there will also be involvement from the parents and a more detailed authorization and oversight process with required meetings and timelines.

Students coming to the attention of the BIT/CARE team related to behaviors that cause concerns to others often face unique circumstances posed by their disability and struggle to navigate systems designed to offer additional support. Here, a BIT/CARE referral and intervention plan can play a vital role in the success of students with disabilities by helping to navigate these academic and non-academic support services to align and assist with coordination (Schiemann & Molnar, 2019). Ultimately, the goal is to help prevent students from falling through the cracks by ensuring they have access to appropriate support. Students with disabilities may need mentoring and advice about navigating accommodation issues with specific faculty. Disability services providers should lead this work, but BIT/CARE members can help by making referrals and encouraging students to self-advocate.

WORKING WITH SCHOOL RESOURCE OFFICERS AND LAW ENFORCEMENT

Law enforcement should be an integral part of your campus BIT. Law enforcement is often only consulted on high-level threat cases, such as when the school feels an arrest is needed or appropriate. This limited application is a mistake and several leading law enforcement groups in the United States have directly pushed back on this idea (National Threat Assessment Center [NTAC], 2018; MSD, 2019; National Threat Assessment Center, 2019). As with other vital positions on the BIT, law enforcement should be considered as a primary role and a position that attends every meeting (Randazzo & Plummer, 2009; Van Brunt, 2012; Sokolow et al., 2014; Schiemann & Van Brunt, 2018).

Law enforcement brings a unique set of skills and resources to BIT, skills not commonly found anywhere else in the campus community. They have access to additional databases that can assist in the information-gathering stage of BIT, such as vehicle databases, firearms ownership and arrest records. Additionally, law enforcement often brings a higher level of skill when conducting interviews and obtaining witness statements. They have more flexibility and can reach beyond the traditional walls of the school setting. These "knock and talks" with students of concern or witnesses provide much needed context and additional intel on threat cases. For instance, law enforcement will have the ability to reach an on-call judge to obtain a temporary restraining order (TRO), serve a red-flag protection order confiscating firearms or take a subject into custody for a mental health hold. They have the ability to respond after traditional business hours to address students of concern or victims.

These skills and abilities are vital for schools addressing short term after-hours needs, providing a larger context to cases and assistance diffusing a crisis safely. Schools and colleges are limited to in-house conduct parameters such as "no contact" directives that, if violated, lead to discipline or removal from the school. A TRO, or protective order, can be enforced by law enforcement, and an immediate arrest can be made in most cases. Law enforcement brings an invaluable set of skills to the table and should be included in each BIT/CARE meeting that occurs.

MOVING FORWARD

The next chapter takes a deeper look at intervention and management techniques from a case-management informed process for both the K-12 and college/university settings. This chapter provides a deeper dive into the role of the case manager addressing dangerous behavior on campus. For schools that do not have a case manager, any member on the team can be trained in intervention, and this chapter outlines some important approaches to intervention.

REFERENCES

ACCA. (2014). *Community colleges: Meeting the needs of today's students in a changing and complex world.* American College Counseling Association. Retrieved on December 27, 2019 from www.collegecounseling.org/resources/Documents/ACCA-Community-College-Survey-2014-15-Final.pdf

Americans With Disabilities Act of 1990, Pub. L. No. 101-336, 104 Stat. 328 (1990).

AUCCCD. (2010). The Association for University and College Counseling Center Directors Annual Survey Reporting Period: September 1, 2008 through August 31, 2009. Retrieved on December 27, 2019 from http://files.cmcglobal.com/directors_survey_2009_nm.pdf

Cohen, V. (1971). California, 403 U.S. 15, 1971.

Cohen, V. (2007). Keeping students alive: Mandating on-campus counseling saves suicidal college students' lives and limits liability, *Fordham L. Rev*, 75, 3081–3135.

Lankford, A. (2013). *The myth of Martyrdom: What really drives suicide bombers, rampage shooters, and other self destructive killers.* New York: Palgrave Macmillan.

Lankford, A. (2018). Identifying potential mass shooters and suicide terrorists with warning signs of suicide, perceived victimization, and desires for attention or fame. *Journal of Personality Assessment*, 5, 1–12.

MSD. (2019). Marjory Stoneman Douglas High School Public Safety Commission Report. Retrieved on December 29, 2019 from www.fdle.state.fl.us/MSDHS/CommissionReport.pdf

MSD Public Safety Commission. (2018). Cruz's Cell Phone Content and Internet Searches. Retrieved on December 26, 2019 from http://www.fdle.state.fl.us/MSDHS/Meetings/November-Meeting-Documents/Nov-14-1045-am-Cruz-Cell-Phone-and-Internet-John-S.aspx

National Threat Assessment Center (NTAC). (2018). *Enhancing school safety using a threat assessment model: An operational guide for preventing targeted school violence.* Washington, DC: United States Secret Service, Department of Homeland Security.

National Threat Assessment Center (NTAC). (2019). *Protecting America's schools: A United States secret service analysis of targeted school violence.* Washington, DC: United States Secret Service, Department of Homeland Security.

Randazzo, M., & Plummer, E. (2009). *Implementing behavioral threat assessment on campus: A Virginia Tech Demonstration Project.* Blacksburg, VA: Printed by Virginia Polytechnic Institute and State University.

Schiemann, M., & Molnar, J. (2019). *A practical guide to case management in higher education.* PA, King of Prussia: The National Behavioral Intervention Team Association

Schiemann, M., & Van Brunt, B. (2018). *Summary and analysis of 2018 NaBITA survey data.* Berwyn, PA: National Behavioral Intervention Team Association.

Sokolow, B.A., Lewis, W.S., Van Brunt, B., Schuster, S., & Swinton, D. (2014). *The book on BIT* (2 ed). Berwyn, PA: The National Behavioral Intervention Team Association.

Snyder, C., & Anderson, S. (2009). An examination of mandated versus voluntary referral as a determinant of clinical outcome. *Journal of Marital and Family Therapy*, 35, 278–292.

Van Brunt, B. (2012). *Ending campus violence: New approaches to prevention.* New York: Routledge.

Van Brunt, B. (2015). *Harm to others: The assessment and treatment of dangerousness.* Alexander, VA: American Counseling Association

Van Brunt, B. & Sokolow, B. (2018). *The role of the counselor on the behavioral intervention team.* PA, King of Prussia: The National Behavioral Intervention Team Association.

Chapter 10

Case Management[1]

Threat management is an ongoing, cyclical process requiring more than a one-and-done approach. Often, threat management requires multiple appointments or meetings, the development of rapport and trust, strategic and timely interventions and routine follow-up. The field of school- and campus-based case management has evolved from this need to provide comprehensive interventions to students who pose a threat or are otherwise in need of support. Through this work, case managers aim to support their students, their school communities and the BITs with which they work. This chapter provides an overview and definition of case management, exploration of different types of case management and an in-depth discussion on the types of services case managers provide.

CASE MANAGEMENT HISTORY AND OVERVIEW

Case management has existed as a formalized field and service for decades in the community setting as a result of the deinstitutionalization movement of the 1960s and 70s (Van Brunt et al., 2012). As residential patients in behavioral-health units transitioned into the community, they needed someone to provide resources for living in their new environment. In the community setting, case managers typically serve clients with severe or persistent mental health issues by assisting them in accessing treatment, managing daily life skills, organizing finances and securing and maintaining employment. Case managers in the school or campus setting aren't limited to working with students with mental health challenges, and the type of support offered focuses on risk reduction and holistic success and wellness in direct coordination with the BIT or CARE team. School- or campus-based case managers "provide goal-oriented and strengths-based assessment, intervention, and coordination of services to students experiencing academic, personal, or

---

1. Special thanks to Makenzie Schiemann for her contributions to this chapter.

medical difficulties in order to assist them in removing barriers to success and increasing their holistic well-being" (Schiemann & Molnar, 2019, p. 2).

It is important to take a minute here and recognize that a case manager may be a dedicated, full-time staff member or it may be an existing member of the team engaging in a case-management process for a particular student (NaBITA Advisory Board, 2018). "Case management, whether as a larger philosophy for team interventions or more specifically defined as a position on the team, is about helping students overcome obstacles they encounter" (NaBITA Advisory Board, 2018, p. 8). Additionally, the U.S. Department of Education (2017) notes that case management in K-12 schools is often delivered by a school professional, in addition to their full-time job duties, in an effort to improve a student's health, educational outcomes and welfare.

Case management is therefore a critical component of the overall threat assessment and prevention work across campus, particularly with the BIT (Van Brunt et al., 2018; Schiemann & Molnar, 2019). Schiemann and Van Brunt (2018) found that having a case manager dedicated to the work of the BIT was regularly cited as a major strength of the team's overall efficacy, efficiency and functioning. The value that case-management services add to a BITs ability to identify, assess and intervene for students is widely recognized as an effective practice beyond even the self-reporting of teams with case managers (Fein et al., 2004; Jarvis & Scherer, 2015; National Association of School Psychologists [NASP], 2015; Federal Commission on School Safety, 2018). The Federal Commission on School Safety (2018) explains that it is not enough to have a reporting culture, as the reporting of threats does not mitigate the risk. In order to mitigate the risk, teams must have the capacity to appropriately respond and develop intervention and management strategies (Federal Commission on School Safety, 2018). The case-management process of conducting intakes, performing risk assessments, assisting students with accessing services, fostering behaviorial change and developing plans for academic and personal success is therefore crucial to the overall approach to threat assessment and prevention.

TYPES OF CASE MANAGERS

In the school- and campus-based setting, case managers have come to be designated as either clinical or non-clinical. Understanding the differences between clinical and non-clinical case management work is therefore important, as the designation directly impacts the scope of services provided and the level of confidentiality afforded.

Clinical case managers are individuals who are licensed *and* have been hired by the school to provide treatment (Schiemann & Molnar, 2019). The presence of a license is not in and of itself what dictates a case manager as clinical—they must have the licensure and have performing treatment or services under the licensure as part as part of their job duties. Because the treatment and services are rendered under licensure, the information and records of these services are considered privileged, or confidential, under state confidentiality laws and are stored in a privileged database (Schiemann & Molnar, 2019). Non-clinical case managers may or may not have a license, but they are "hired by the school to provide support and resource coordination, rather than mental health treatment" (Schiemann & Molnar, 2019, p 21). Because they are not rendering treatment and services under a licensure, non-clinical case management notes are considered part of the education record, stored in the BIT or similar database, and their confidentiality is governed by the Federal Educational Rights and Privacy Act (FERPA) (Schiemann & Molnar, 2019). Figure 10.1 below compares clinical and non-clinical case management.

Given the differences in the confidentiality and scope of services, clinical and non-clinical case managers tend to be located in different types of departments or units. In higher education, non-clinical case managers tend to be housed in the dean of students (46%), conduct (4.5%), academic advising (2%) or housing offices (1%) while clinical case managers are most commonly located within other units that offer confidential treatment services, such as a counseling or health center (Schiemann & Molnar, 2019). In a K-12 environment, a non-clinical case manager may report to the vice principal or principal as part of the overall student services, whereas a clinical case manager is more likely affiliated with the school mental health counselor, nurse or community mental health practitioner.

Additionally, in both higher education and K-12, the non-clinical case management services may be provided by existing school or campus staff as part of an overarching philosophical approach to delivering services and interventions (U.S. Department of Education, 2017; NaBITA Advisory Board, 2018). In this structure, the non-clinical case management duties fall to teachers, administrators, staff, etc., that have a connection to the student, are affiliated with the BIT or are otherwise well-suited given their skills or personality to provide support and interventions on a case.

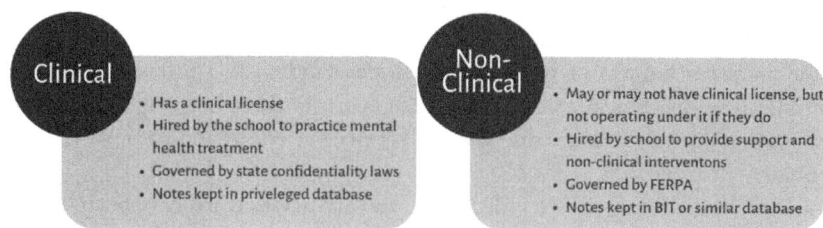

FIGURE 10.1 Clinical vs. Non-clinical Case Management. (Schiemann & Molnar, 2019, p. 22).

A PRACTICAL EXAMPLE: MIDDLE-SCHOOL BULLY THREAT

A middle-school student, Alex, creates a video on the social app TikTok that includes the text "I'm shooting up Baytown High on the 8th. Don't go that day." Alex has a history of being bullied and teased at the school because of his weight. The social media platform takes the video down after it is reported by other users. Several students fill out an online report on the schools TIPLINE reporting website. Police go to Alex's home in the early morning and exercise a search warrant. Alex is taken into custody with his computer and several hunting knives and a hunting rifle that was locked in the family's gun safe. The scene at the home is hectic, and Alex's sister Dana (who attends the high school) screams and yells, "You've ruined my life! MY WHOLE LIFE!!!!!" Alex tells police that he had no plans to do any kind of attack and it was just a really bad joke that he posted online. Once released from police custody, the school requires Alex to complete an off-campus evaluation prior to returning to classes. Parents and students start an online petition to ban Alex from returning.

Alex is a student who even prior to this incident was struggling. He was experiencing bullying and teasing at school that likely contributed to his post on the social media platform TikTok. Given the public nature of his post, and the community's reaction to it, his social status at school is likely to worsen as he returns to school. The case manager will want to attend to these issues with Alex and assess how he is handling the increase in social isolation and/or bullying behaviors. It will be important to process the bullying or teasing behaviors he is experiencing and help build appropriate skills in Alex for responding to them. For example, empowering Alex to report incidents to the school administration, engaging in self-esteem and self-confidence building and reframing negative thoughts into a more positive narrative. Additionally, it will be important to explore positive outlets to connect Alex with more positive social relationships. The case manager will want to talk with Alex about hobbies or interests he has and work to find ways to connect him with social experiences that align with his interests.

In addition to the potential for worsening social status at school, Alex's familial relationships have also been impacted by this event. The case manager should explore any tensions that now exist at home for Alex, particularly with his sister, who expressed anger at Alex for how this has impacted her. This is an opportunity for the case manager to either work with Alex on improving his communication with his family and building his skills for strengthening the relationships, or to invite the sister and family into the case management services to process what happened as a group and develop a plan for coping with the aftermath.

165

Given the existing bullying and teasing, the worsening social status at school and the tensions at home, the case manager should also asses Alex's emotional health, including an assessment of suicidality and/or non-suicidal self-injury. Alex may experience increased worthlessness, hopelessness and apathy about life as a result of the social fallout and aftermath of his post. The case manager should be prepared to ask Alex directly if he is thinking of killing or harming himself and to assess his intent, plan and access to means.

CASE-MANAGEMENT SERVICES

Clinical and non-clinical case managers often see students for similar presenting issues; however, the work they do with the students and the types of services they provide are quite different from one another. In the higher-education setting, clinical and non-clinical case managers report that emotional or mental health concerns are the most common reasons students are referred for case-management support (Schiemann & Molnar; 2019). Other common issues include suicidal ideation or attempt, death of a student, victimization/trauma, alcohol and other drug concerns, medical or health-related issues and academic concerns (Schiemann & Molnar, 2019). Similarly, case managers in the K-12 setting report that students were selected for case management based on their academic performance (55%), discipline or behavioral issues (49%), concerns from staff (47%) and attendance problems (42%) (U.S. Department of Education, 2017). While the reason for referral may be similar, remember clinical case managers are providing treatment services under a licensure and non-clinical case managers are focused on short-term interventions that provide support and reduce barriers. In this capacity, clinical case managers offer clinical assessment, diagnosis and mental health treatment, including clinical intakes and individual or group counseling (Schiemann & Molnar, 2019). Non-clinical case managers, on the other hand, "offer emotional support and coordination of resources, including psychoeducation, referral brokerage, and communication to faculty, parents and the BIT" (Schiemann & Molnar, 2019, p. 25).

Regardless of designation of clinical or non-clinical, case management is about providing wrap around interventions, support and resources to assist students in overcoming barriers to their success (Van Brunt et al., 2012; U.S. Department of Education, 2017; NaBITA Advisory Board, 2018). To operationalize this philosophy, case managers should clearly define their scope of services and develop protocols for implementing these services. Figure 10.2 below provides a sample scope of services that can guide case management work.

This scope of services provides a framework for the type of supports that case managers can use with students including one-on-one meetings, referrals to other supports, collaboration and consultation with other key stakeholders involved in the case and participation in the BIT process and interventions. A well-defined scope of services helps case managers define what work they do,

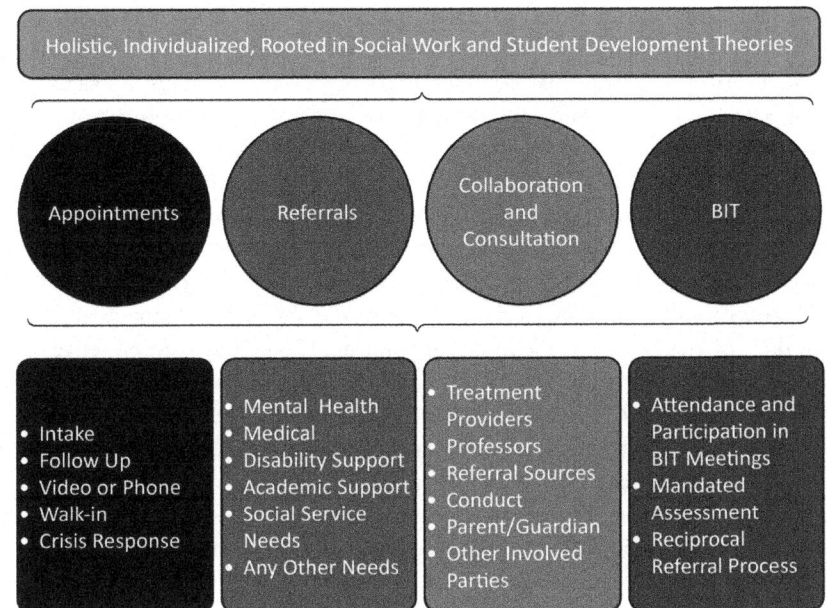

FIGURE 10.2 Sample Scope of Case Management Services. (Schiemann & Molnar, 2019, p. 53).

and what work they don't do to administration and other staff at their school as well as to the students with which they work.

APPOINTMENTS

"Paramount to case management work is the one-on-one service delivery between the case manager and the student" (Schiemann & Molnar, 2019, p. 52). One of the most effective support interventions case managers can deploy is individual meetings with the student. In these meetings, case managers can address the behaviors of concern, conduct a holistic assessment to determine additional needs and supports and partner with the student to connect them with appropriate resources. The U.S. Department of Education (2017) reports that using individual meetings to provide coaching and behavioral support was the most common type of case-management activity for high-school case managers. To implement this type of behavioral intervention and case-management service, case managers likely meet with students for an initial appointment, sometimes called an intake appointment, as well as follow-up appointments.

In the intake appointment, case managers are looking to accomplish several tasks: 1) explain case management services, 2) build rapport with the student, 3) gather holistic information regarding the student's needs across the wellness spectrum, 4) address the behavior of concern for the referral and 5) develop goals and actions for further case-management services. To aid in outlining this process and in clarifying the scope and confidentiality of case-management services, case managers should use an intake form along with a verbal explanation and overview at the beginning of the first appointment. This is particularly important for non-clinical case managers, given their broader ability to share information under FERPA, and for case managers working in K-12 environments, given their ability, and often obligation, to communicate with a parent or guardian. Additionally, the intake form and the intake appointment provide an opportunity for the case manager to explain the scope of services and what the student can expect to receive from the case manager. For the intake appointment to be the most effective, case managers should take extra care to develop rapport and gather information holistically and effectively. Borrowing from Rogers' Person-Centered Therapy, case managers can build rapport by using reflection, empathy, positive regard and authenticity (Corey, 2017). Some practical strategies for doing this include engaging in active listening, offering water, tea or snacks, having personal items in your office to build connection, using humor and self-disclosure where appropriate and finding common ground with the student.

Case management is more than a one-and-done approach. As part of the interventions for specific behaviors of concerns and the holistic approach to student support, case managers provide "regular monitoring of services and follow-up with students as needed" (U.S. Department of Education, 2017, p. 1). The frequency and duration of the follow-up appointments will vary by risk level and student needs, but the focus is to continue monitoring student progress and change in behavior over time, facilitate referrals and ensure connection to these referrals.

A PRACTICAL EXAMPLE: COLLEGE BREAK-UP THREAT

Caleb is a sophomore at Broadmore College. His on-campus girlfriend broke up with him and he went on social media and posted, "If I can't be with you, I'm going to make it my life's mission that you never find any happiness." The threat was assessed by the BIT/CARE team and found to be a low level of risk and largely transient in nature. He was given a conduct sanction, placed on probation and issued a no-contact order for his ex-girlfriend. He is required to attend weekly meetings with a case manager for the reminder of the semester to address his anger-management problems, frustration tolerance and impulse control.

Caleb's primary issues stem from his difficulty in responding to an emotionally challenging situation. In the face of frustration, anger and disappointment, Caleb responded impulsively and aggressively. The goals for working with Caleb are therefore to decrease impulsivity, build frustration tolerance and strengthen his skills for responding to difficult or frustrating events in a healthy, appropriate manner. Additionally, the case manager will want to explore Caleb's social connections and resources for support in order to increase the supports available to him.

To begin this work, the case manager will want to explore Caleb's triggers, or the common antecedents to his explosive, impulsive behavior. They will review with Caleb the most recent incident, as well as any prior incidents of impulsive behavior to explore what tends to cause, or trigger, the behavior. Is there a theme around what types of situations, emotions, statements, etc. tend to frustrate or anger him? Are there exceptions to Caleb's impulsive or aggressive behaviors? In other words, have there been times where he has experienced frustrating or upsetting situations and not responded impulsively or inappropriately? What was different about those situations?

Recognizing the triggers or warning signs will be an important first step in Caleb starting to change his behavior. Caleb will need to recognize situations ahead of time, or at least as they are occurring, that typically prompt him to respond impulsively or inappropriately. Once he can recognize these scenarios, he can begin to practice responding in a more appropriate manner. The case manager should work on building skills for Caleb to use in these scenarios by helping him learn to 1) recognize the trigger, 2) stop and take a minute to regroup his thoughts, 3) think about what is upsetting him and how he can redirect himself and 4) respond in an appropriate, healthy way. Some practical skills for stopping and thinking about his response include: deep breathing, counting to ten before responding, removing himself from the situation by asking for a few minutes to himself, running his ideas or his responses by the case manager, a trusted friend, etc. before responding and waiting or pausing at least a few hours before sending an email or text or before posting a response on social media.

To help Caleb increase his social supports and build additional factors, the case manager should consider connecting Caleb with a mental health counselor, wellness coach, or additional social activities such as clubs, organizations, recreational sports, etc. to provide a healthy social outlet. Additionally, engaging in activities like counseling and exercise will help Caleb find productive outlets for his frustration and anger.

REFERRALS

Another major function for a case manager is to serve as a referral broker. During the intake and follow-up appointments, case managers gather a holistic picture of a student's strengths and needs and develop a plan for connecting students to the appropriate referrals. Case managers serve as a conduit to other resources and provide seamless and integrated referrals to these resources. In the K-12 environment, case managers may make referrals for the student to community mental health, psychiatry or social work professionals, to disability testing services, to

169

the IEP team or to the school counselor, and they may also make referrals on behalf of the student's family such as to local food banks, housing resources, family counseling, etc. Higher-education case managers are most likely to refer to counseling services, medical or psychiatric supports, disability support services, academic resources and social services supports.

To effective serve as a referral broker, case managers should identify potential referral options at their school and within their community and then engage in intentional relationship-building with these resources prior to making the first referral. Schiemann & Molnar (2019) provide the following tips for making a strong referral:

1. **Discuss the referral with the student.** Be sure to explain how the referral might help them and what they can expect from the referral source. For K-12 students, especially elementary- and middle-school students, it is often necessary to also discuss the referral with the parents, as their involvement is critical in securing the referral.

2. **Assist the student and/or family in securing an appointment.** This may be done via phone with the student and/or family in your office, by walking them to the resource or by providing them the contact information and asking that they connect with the resource before your next follow-up appointment.

3. **Obtain a release of information if necessary.** Remember, FERPA allows non-clinical case managers to speak with staff officials at the school who have an educational need to know, but they need a release to speak to any resource outside of the institution. In K-12, case managers are able to communicate with parents without a release, and in many cases may be obligated to do so. For higher-education case managers, if a health and safety emergency exists they are able to communicate with anyone involved in resolving the emergency, including the parents, without a release. In instances where a release is required for the case manager to share information (non-staff official, parent of a college or university student in a non-emergent situation, etc.), case managers should obtain the release in advance of the referral. Additionally, when making referrals to licensed mental health or medical providers, a release is needed for the provider to communicate back to the case manager.

4. **Provide a "heads up" to the referral source.** It is often helpful to let the referral source know why you've referred the student and how you're hoping they can help. Students can struggle articulating this to the referral source themselves and by providing the information to the referral source ahead of time, you are able to maximize their ability to help.

5. **Follow up with the student.** It is important to have at least one appointment (and more if needed) with the student after you've made the referral. This allows you to confirm that the connection to the resource was successful and helpful.

COLLABORATION AND CONSULTATION

As case managers frequently make and receive referrals, they will need to communicate with these reciprocal referral sources in order to facilitate effective student support and wrap-around care. Collaboration and consultation include providing guidance to those who are concerned about a student or who have made a referral for a student, partnering with treatment providers, communicating with parents and other supports in the process and working with faculty, teachers and other school administrators to ensure continuity of care across the student's areas of interaction and impact.

A PRACTICAL EXAMPLE: HIGH-SCHOOL WHITE SUPREMIST CONFLICTS

Emmet has a history in high school of expressing white supremist thoughts. He often reposts memes on his social media accounts that include hate speech, slang and derogatory words attributed to certain minority groups. He has come to the attention of the assistant principal, school resource officer (SRO) and school counselor due to his concerning dress (wearing Nazi symbols and other white-pride slogans) and getting into fights with other students. He is called in again to discuss a post from the previous night that depicted a room of gay males being set on fire for their sins. He remains unremorseful for his behavior and says, "I live in America. That means I have free speech and I can post what I want." He is required to meet with a case manager at the school to address his fighting with other students and general angry and threatening attitudes.

Emmet clearly has a pattern of hardened beliefs and making others feel uncomfortable, diminished and threatened. What is less clear from this scenario is whether Emmet's "fighting" is physical or verbal. While it may seem like a minor detail to glean from this case, the ambiguity around the type of fighting is critical for the case manager to know. Physical aggression and fighting demonstrate an escalation in behavior that is not necessarily represented in verbal fighting and aggression alone. The case manager should clarify the specifics of the incidents that have preceded the requirement to meet so as to develop an appropriate intervention and support plan.

In the case that the fighting was limited to verbal altercations, they should begin working to build connection with Emmet. As with the other cases we've discussed, this may be difficult given that Emmet holds extremist beliefs that are likely different from the case manager's, and that Emmet remains unremorseful for his behavior and is likely reluctant to fully participate in case-management services. The case manager should look for an opportunity to share common ground with Emmet, even if it is small gains, such as similar tastes in music, hobbies, etc. Using humor, offering empathy and acknowledging that Emmet feels inconvenienced by having to meet can go a long way in building connection.

Emmet's primary issue centers around holding extremist beliefs and being on a pathway toward radicalization. The case manager will want to explore his belief system, assist Emmet in identifying the connections between his speech/behaviors and consequences and develop a plan for preventing further radicalization. Given his age and developmental stage, Emmet has likely spent most of his life basing his belief system on his parents' beliefs but is beginning to test out his own worldview and value system. In this developmental stage, the case manager should tap into Emmet's ability to think critically and to understand how his extremist views, actions and speech might not be as factual and unequivocally right as he believes. To develop this, consider working with him to identify exceptions to his belief system, times when his views turned out to be misinformed or times when his views led him into trouble.

Cases like Emmet's often circle back to the concept of free speech. The case manager should address the difference between free speech and speech free of consequence. Emmet has the right to express views, hold beliefs that are outside of the mainstream, etc., but holding these beliefs may result in consequences—either directly, if they cross out of protected speech, or indirectly, through isolation from peers who find him upsetting. The case manager should work with Emmet to help him identify instances in which his decision to exercise his free-speech rights and share his views resulted in unintended consequences. The case manager should process these examples with Emmet and work towards developing insight and acceptance of some responsibility.

Finally, to prevent further radicalization, the case manager should work with Emmet to find positive factors for Emmet and healthy social connections. What does Emmet like to do? What is going well for him? How can we strengthen relationships with peers that might have differing beliefs? The case manager should identify these positive connections and work with Emmet to develop them further by making referrals and fostering connections to clubs, organizations, etc.

BIT

Case management is most effective when it is tied to the BIT, and the work of the BIT is enhanced by its connection to a case manager. In their connection to the BIT, case managers deploy interventions, provide updates on cases, make referrals into the BIT and perform mandated assessments for the team.

In connection with the BIT, case managers often provide support and interventions to students exhibiting dangerous behavior or engaging in threatening statements (verbal or written) or actions. Violence risk and threat assessments are a critical intervention for case managers and the BIT to utilize when the dangerous or threatening statements or behaviors cross the elevated threshold on the

NaBITA Risk Rubric. Violence risk and threat assessments do not predict future violence or generate a profile for potential perpetrators of violence. Rather, violence risk and threat assessments "examine the individual to determine their risk to the greater community by asking contextual questions about the nature of the threat and risk" to determine the individual's potential dangerousness (Schiemann & Molnar, 2019, p. 144). Although similar, violence risk assessments and threat assessments occur as a result of different types of behaviors or statements. Threat assessments occur after an individual has made a vague, conditional or direct threat, whereas violence risk assessments are broader assessments used when there is concern for an individual's potential for violence, regardless of the presence of a vague, conditional or direct threat (Van Brunt, 2012, 2015).

Additionally, violence risk and threat assessments are different from psychological or mental health assessments. The outcome of a mental health or psychological assessment is a diagnosis and appropriate level of treatment, including whether the person meets criteria for hospitalization (Van Brunt & Sokolow, 2018). When attempting to understand an individual's potential for dangerousness, a mental health diagnosis and what type of treatment they need isn't that helpful, as the assumption that individuals with mental illness are a high-risk population for targeted violence lacks supportive evidence (Knoll & Annas, 2006; Van Brunt & Pescara-Kovach, 2018). Instead, the outcome of a violence risk or threat assessment is more helpful as they produce an objective understanding of an individual's specific risk and protective factors related to their potential to engage in violence. These factors are more helpful to the BIT and the case manager as they provide a framework for understanding what intervention or supports could increase the protective factors and decrease the risk factors.

Perhaps most relevant and helpful to the BIT and case manager is that violence-risk and threat assessments do not have to be performed by a licensed mental health professional given that they do not assess for a mental health diagnosis. Instead, it is recommended to train at least three individuals on the BIT to perform these assessments so that they can be completed in-house by trained, professional staff. When deciding who on the team to train, remember that these assessments should be performed by someone who can build rapport, reduce defensiveness and assess truthfulness, is knowledgeable in the literature of risk factors and is able to gather information and conduct an assessment in a seamless and effective manner (Schiemann & Molnar, 2019). Case managers often have these skills and are therefore a logical choice for conducing violence risk or threat assessments.

The need for a violence risk or threat assessment is often mandated by the BIT in writing to the student. As part of the mandated assessment process, case managers should utilize a specific scope of services and privacy form, or informed consent form if they are a clinical case manager, in order to outline the purpose, scope and length of the assessment as well as the privacy regarding how and to whom the information collected during the assessment will be shared.

A PRACTICAL EXAMPLE: COLLEGE MISOGYNIST THREAT

Asher turns in an essay to his college English class. The essay was based on an assignment prompt from the female professor, "Write what you dream about." Asher writes, "I hate women. Not all girls, but those of my generation. Those hoes and bitches who are just a bunch of sadistic individuals who only care about riding some bullshit cock carousel and getting fucked. They don't want me. They make me suffer. So, I want them to suffer. This is a genuine feeling. I want all of those blonde bitches to suffer just like Elliot Rodger did, praised be his name. I want to step on their bleeding corpses and feel the heel of my boot in their wounds, forcing out the last bit like squeezing an overripe zit." The report is shared with the BIT / CARE team and Asher is required to complete a threat assessment. Part of his judicial sanction requires him to meet with a case manager to assess and monitor his violence risk. Asher doesn't understand why he has to do this. He says, "I wrote exactly what I dream about. That bitch shouldn't ask for what she can't handle."

Perhaps the first challenge to overcome with Asher will be the fact that he does not want to be in case management and views the appointments as adversarial from the start. As is often the case with students who are required to attend case management, Asher does not see the value of the services and has difficulty seeing the rationale for his required attendance. The case manager will want to spend time up front building rapport and forming an alliance with Asher. This can be achieved by empathizing with Asher—the case manager should consider acknowledging that this process has been frustrating for him and that he doesn't want to be in case management. The case manager can find opportunities to build goodwill with him from the outset by seeing if he has fallen behind in his academics as a result and offering to help talk to his professors, checking on his housing or social relationships, etc.

Building rapport and trust quickly is important in conducting a good assessment. Asher is much more likely to be forthcoming and share information once rapport is formed. The best way to gather accurate, robust information is by conducting an assessment that flows much like a conversation and is based on respect and rapport. If Asher trusts the case manager and the case management has been transparent and empathetic, he is likely to reduce his defensiveness and provide more genuine responses. Asher's writing clearly demonstrates two significant risk factors: misogyny and objectification. In conducting the assessment, the case manager must sort out whether Asher simply dislikes women and has hardened, misogynistic beliefs about them or whether he holds these beliefs and is moving towards having, or already has, plans for an attack. The case manager should consider using a tool like the SIVRA-35 to assist in making this determination.

As part of the longer-term work with Asher, the case manager should explore some of his frustration towards women and address why writing a paper like this in class would concern others, result in consequences and require a further assessment. In his writing, Asher specifically mentions that he doesn't dislike all "girls," just those of his generation. This is a point worth exploring as it points to at least some exception to the problem—the case manager should consider asking what makes girls of his generation different, when he started feeling this way, if was there a precipitating event, if there are any girls of his generation that he does like, etc. A better understanding of the impetus behind Asher's hardened belief may help the case manager begin to shift the needle a bit on Asher's thoughts. Asher's beliefs likely align with a population known as involuntary celibates, or "incels." Within this group, individuals feel extreme rejection or unworthiness regarding romantic relationships and place the blame on women for denying them. Once trust is built with Asher, it will be important to help him recognize his own role in the dynamic of rejection and how his thoughts and behavior may be contributing to women not accepting him. Similarly, it will also be important to begin building insight into his behavior and his acceptance of responsibility for it. The case manager should discuss with Asher how his beliefs may have impacted others. Even if Asher is unable to recognize or acknowledge the emotional impact he has had and experience empathy for others, he should be able to move towards recognizing why in today's climate, given the #metoo movement, increase in school shootings and campus violence, etc., his words are threatening and concerning.

For many, perhaps particularly women, working with Asher is likely to be challenging. He holds hardened beliefs about women that most would not agree with. It will be difficult to maintain an empathetic, unbiased approach with Asher. While it is appropriate to challenge his beliefs and point out how his words and actions impact others, the case manager must do this from a place of empathy, rapport and gentle confrontation. This can be difficult when the words he uses may resonate in a personal and triggering way. As the case manager works with Asher, they should be sure to seek supervision and support for themselves.

In addition to assisting with performing violence risk and threat assessment functions, case managers have several other key roles with, and on, the BIT. While both clinical and non-clinical case managers offer important services to students, non-clinical case managers are more commonly associated with the BIT, as 29% of teams report having a non-clinical case manager as part of their core membership and only 10% report having a clinical case manager (Schiemann & Van Brunt, 2018). This prevalence of non-clinical case-manager representation on a BIT is likely due to the differences in their information-sharing capacity that we discussed above as well as their broader scope of services and ability to deploy interventions. Non-clinical case managers are able to share information openly as a member of the BIT given FERPA's permission to share information with any staff official with an educational need to know. Clinical case managers, however, must utilize an expanded informed consent or a release of information in order to share information.

Whether clinical or non-clinical, the insight and perspective of a case manager can be helpful to the team in determining the level of risk and potential interventions. To maximize the role of the case manager on the BIT, consider the following:

1. Review your caseload and determine if any students require the attention of your BIT and alert the chair. If you are a clinical case manager, obtain a release of information so that you can share information with the BIT.

2. Review the agenda and prepare case presentations with any relevant information and updates. Come to the meetings with information you gathered from your contact with the student, including any current campus resources they utilize, relevant mental health history, psychosocial dynamics and/or challenges faced by the student. Provide the BIT with your impressions and any case-management plan you may have established.

3. If the student is seeking treatment with a mental health provider, consider obtaining an ROI prior to the meeting. If the BIT would like additional insights from the treating provider, obtaining an ROI prior to the meeting allows for the BIT to obtain necessary information to determine the appropriate level of risk and response. As a case manager, you often serve as the liaison between the student, the providers and the BIT.

4. Take detailed notes on interventions the BIT would like to implement and ensure follow-through after the meeting. Be prepared to report back during the next meeting.

5. Case managers can also be a wealth of information for the BIT regarding community resources, medical system procedures and systems and insurance considerations. Providing insight into these areas can be very helpful to the BIT when making a decision about appropriate risk-rating and interventions.

A PRACTICAL EXAMPLE: COLLEGE SOCIAL MEDIA THREAT

Kirsten posts a picture on social media of her holding a handgun in a dormitory-style room. The picture goes viral quickly and students share reports with campus police and residential-life staff that Kirsten has a gun. The campus is placed in lockdown and the police take Kirsten into custody. She tells them that she was at another campus visiting a friend who showed her their new gun and that was where the picture was taken. She shares with police information of where to find her friend at the other school. Kirsten is released and is required to meet with the campus BIT/CARE team case manager to discuss the incident.

Ultimately, this case is about Kirsten making a poor decision, but not posing an actual threat, and now having to deal with the ramifications of this decision. While the case manager wants to begin by discussing the incident at hand, the decision-making process (or lack thereof) that Kirsten underwent prior to posting the photo and the impact that decision had on others, the case manager should spend the majority of the appointment on a broader assessment and support plan for Kirsten. This case is a great example of being sure to not remain overly focused on the initial reason for the referral. Talking about the referral and Kirsten's social media post is important, but likely Kirsten is experiencing distress of her own as a result of everything that has happened. The case manager should explore Kirsten's peer group and social relationships, her own emotional health and any academic challenges as a result of the incident. Working with Kirsten is likely short-term, perhaps only 2 or 3 meetings. The case manager will have to focus on quickly building rapport and buy-in to the case-management process.

Given that peers around campus and other students in the residence hall were the ones that initially reported the incident, and that the campus was placed on lockdown, there are likely to be social ramifications for Kirsten. The campus community is likely frustrated or at least having some reaction to the lockdown, and Kristen may be experiencing the brunt of this reaction. The case manager should talk with Kirsten about how this has been and explore the impact of what has happened on her friends, classmates and residence hallmates. The case manager can help Kirsten develop a plan for managing people's questions and responding to comments made about her or to her. Additionally, the case manager should assess for any mental or emotional health concerns including difficulty with mood (feelings of depression or anxiety), difficulty eating or sleeping, her own comfort level back in the residence hall, etc. If Kirsten is experiencing difficulty in these areas or expressing hopelessness regarding the situation, her social standing, etc., the case manager should be prepared to assess for any suicidal ideation or non-suicidal self-injury.

Additionally, Kirsten likely missed class and/or assignments as a result of being taken into custody and completing the police interview. Discuss with Kirsten the impact this has had on her academics and assist her in communicating with her professors. Some case managers may choose to address this topic first, as helping communicate with professors and requesting that they be flexible with Kirsten can help build rapport and demonstrate goodwill with a student who was required to come in and meet.

177

MOVING FORWARD

Case management, whether clinical or non-clinical, provides support to the assessment and offers support to assist the student to connect to resources. Another aspect to assessment and treatment of those who present threat is the management of *the contagion effect*, a phenomenon that occurs when others become motivated and inspired to follow in a student's footsteps regarding threat and dangerousness. Threats and their resulting impact do not occur in a vacuum, but rather require a detailed, planned public relations response from the school, college or university. Parents, community members and the media often engage in a panicked response driven by the concept of *probability neglect*, a disregard for reason and fact in the face of fear and terror. The final two chapters bring together the expertise of two experts in the field, Dr. Lisa Pescara-Kovach and Dr. L. Darryl Armstrong, to address these important aspects of threat management.

REFERENCES

Corey, G. (2017). *Theory and practice of counseling and psychotherapy* (10th ed). Boston, MA: Cengage Learning.

Federal Commission on School Safety. (2018). Final Report on the Federal Commission on School Safety. Retrieved on February 24, 2020 from https://www2.ed.gov/documents/school-safety/school-safety-report.pdf

Fein, R. A., Vossekuil, B., Pollack, W. S., Borun, R., Modzelski, W., & Reddy, M. (2004). *Threat assessment in schools: A guide to managing threatening situation and to creating safe school climates.* Washington, DC: United State Secret Service and United States Department of Education.

Jarvis, J., & Scherer, A. (2015). *Mass victimization: Promising avenues for prevention.* Washington, DC: Federal Bureau of Investigation.

Knoll, J. L., & Annas, G. D. (2006). Mass shooting and mental illness. In Gold, L. H. and Simon, R. I. (eds.), *Gun violence and mental illness*, 81–104. Washington, DC: American Psychiatric Association.

NaBITA Advisory Board. (2018). *NaBITA Standards for Behavioral Intervention Teams.* Berwyn, PA: National Behavioral Intervention Team Association. Retrieved from: https://cdn.nabita.org/website-media/nabita.org/wp-content/uploads/2018/09/04141609/NaBITA-Standards-FINAL-2.pdf

National Association of School Psychologists (NASP). (2015). Preventing youth suicide: Tips for parents and educators. Retrieved on March 16, 2020 from https://www.nasponline.org/resources-and-publications/resources-and-podcasts/school-climate-safety-and-crisis/mental-health-resources/preventing-youth-suicide/preventing-youth-suicide-tips-for-parents-and-educators

Schiemann, M., & Molnar, J. (2019). *A practical guide to case management in higher education.* PA, King of Prussia: The National Behavioral Intervention Team Association.

Schiemann, M., & Van Brunt, B. (2018). *Summary and analysis of 2018 NaBITA survey data.* Berwyn, PA: National Behavioral Intervention Team Association.

U.S. Department of Education. (2017). *Issue brief: Case management in high schools.* U.S. Department of Education Office of Planning, Evaluation, and Policy Development. Retrieved from: https://www2.ed.gov/about/offices/list/opepd/ppss/reports-high-school.html

Van Brunt, B. (2012). *Ending campus violence: New approaches to prevention*. New York: Routledge.

Van Brunt, B. (2015). *Harm to others: The assessment and treatment of dangerousness*. Alexander, VA: American Counseling Association.

Van Brunt, B. and Pescara-Kovach, L. (2018). Debunking the myths: Mental illness and mass shootings. *Journal of Gender and Violence*, 1–11.

Van Brunt, B., Schiemann, M., Pescara-Kovach, L., Murphy, A., & Halligan-Avery, E. (2018). Standards for behavioral intervention teams. *Journal of Behavioral Intervention Teams (JBIT)*, 6, 29–41.

Van Brunt, B., & Sokolow, B. (2018). *The role of the counselor on the behavioral intervention team*. PA, King of Prussia: The National behavioral Intervention Team Association.

Van Brunt, B., Woodley, E., Gunn, J., Raleigh, MJ., Reinach-Wolf, C., & Sokolow, B. (2012). *Case management in higher education*. Berwyn, PA: National Behavioral Intervention Team Association and the American College Counseling Association. Retrieved from: https://cdn.nabita.org/website-media/nabita.org/wp-content/uploads/2018/09/04142257/2012-NaBITA-ACCA-Whitepaper-Case-Management-in-Higher-Education.pdf

PART III

ADOPTING A CONTINUOUS MANAGEMENT APPROACH

Chapter 11

Contagion and Public Media Related to Mass Shootings[1]

Contagion doesn't solely apply to physical diseases that are spread from human to human. Thoughts, emotions and doctrines spread all too rapidly and they, like terminal illness, have led to thousands of deaths. But what makes something contagious? Just as scientists work towards treatments and cures for communicable diseases, experts are working towards preventing the spread of violent doctrines and beliefs. In both scenarios, diseases and doctrines, there is often a race against time to address them at the root.

Patients struggling with physical ailments often keep journals to describe symptoms and related emotions to their physicians. The information is then reviewed at subsequent appointments to help identify new symptoms and implement a care plan. Physicians are encouraged to tailor treatment plans to the individual patient (Alifrangis et al., 2011). In fact, in a nationwide survey (Taksler et al., 2019), there was strong overall support for doctors providing individualized preventive care recommendations for their patients. Similarly, those working on BIT/CARE teams, in law enforcement or in any related case-management role should recognize the importance of treating those who raise concerns as individuals who should be assessed and provided with an individualized plan directed towards preventing harm to others or harm to self and their inevitable contagion.

MEDIA CONTAGION AND COPYCATS

Prior to delving deep into media contagion, it is important to make a clear distinction between *media contagion* and *copycat effect*. At times, the terms are used interchangeably, but it is simply not the case that each refers to the same concept. Media contagion is similar to a communicable disease that might be lying dormant within an individual until it is triggered by repeated, sensationalized,

---

1. Special thanks to Dr. Lisa Pescara-Kovach, Ph.D. for her work on this chapter.

detailed news coverage of a violent act or suicide. The copycat effect is an act of violence that occurs due to the repeated, detailed exposure to an excess of information on suicide or violence (Johnston & Joy, 2016; Pescara-Kovach & Raleigh, 2017a). What exactly is lying dormant that sets the susceptible on a pathway to a similar act of violence? The answer is multifaceted.

With particular illnesses, there is a contagion period. For example, strep throat is contagious for up to three weeks in those who do not treat it with antibiotics. Similarly, sensationalized mass shootings are most contagious within the first 14 days (Pescara-Kovach & Raleigh, 2017a; Towers et al., 2015). As reported in Schildkraut (2019), research conducted after the Marjory Stoneman Douglas shooting (Klinger & Klinger, 2018) showed a 300% increase in threats and actual school violence within the first 30 days after the attack. The majority occurred within the first 12 days, and it's likely no coincidence that this was also the period of the most intense, sensationalized news coverage. Analogous contagion occurs subsequent to highly publicized suicides. For example, there was a 10% higher rate than expected in the months following the death of Robin Williams (Fink et al., 2018). Fink and his coauthors stated, "There was an excess of approximately 1,841 suicides in the United States in the four months after the death of Robin Williams compared to what would be expected for that time period based on forecasted models" (para. 13).

SOCIAL COGNITIVE THEORY AS AN EXPLANATION FOR COPYCAT MASS SHOOTINGS AND SUICIDES

To understand the definition of contagion as it applies to targeted violence and suicide, it is important to delve into social cognitive theory. According to Bandura (1986), we do not think in a vacuum, nor do we just take in information without our own thoughts and attributions playing a role. Bandura's perspective is that humans are actively involved in decision-making by making causal contributions to what motivates them and leads them to act. That is, we come up with our own explanations of what caused us to behave in a particular way. Our actions, thoughts, emotions and other personal experiences work together to influence what we do.

"Self-efficacy" is a term introduced by Bandura in 1977. Self-efficacy is another way of describing confidence in our own abilities. We play a role in our own behaviors, but we are also influenced by what is going on in our world. This makes contagion a result of our own thinking and emotions combined with outside influences. The greater the confidence we have in our ability to succeed in an attack or suicide attempt, the greater the likelihood of attempting such violence, especially if our emotions and experiences have been negative.

This chapter is geared towards understanding the role of media sensationalism in light of social cognitive theory. Keep in mind, internal and external influences on decision-making influence self-efficacy. It is when emotions become negative and thoughts collide with experiences such as alienation, isolation and cruelty by others that we begin to worry about a person becoming violent. Combine this with an additional external factor of sensationalized news coverage of a mass shooting, and we now have the perfect storm.

Media contagion is an example of how powerful environmental triggers are. In this case, the trigger is media sensationalism, as it often leads the individual to identify with the killers, or celebrities who died by suicide, and come to realize that they too are capable of similar acts. In other words, media sensationalism feeds feelings of self-efficacy towards an "if they can do it, so can I" mindset. This mindset has reared its head time and again, as will become evident throughout this chapter. It is likely no coincidence that incidents of mass violence and suicide triggered by media sensationalism occur in younger generations. Vettehen and Peeters (2008) speculate that emotionally arousing, sensationalized news coverage is not as upsetting to youth because they are used to hearing and seeing an array of fast-paced, arousing information via the internet. Rather than getting upset, it serves as a source of motivation. Add this to the great detail provided about these incidents and it's not surprising that some individuals seek out and find all the information they need with each act of violence, either to reproduce or outdo those before.

It is estimated that 20% to 30% of mass shootings are related to the perpetrator imitating a previous highly covered shooting. Excessive, sensationalized media coverage is not the cause of violence; rather, it is a contributor to an already at-risk individual. These future perpetrators come to learn exactly how to engage in mass or targeted violence and value the thought of retribution and fame via the killing of many. Further, they are confident they will overcome barriers as they prepare and eventually execute their plan.

WALKING THE PATHWAY TO VIOLENCE

Chapter 3 offered detailed information on risk elements for predatory violence. However, for the purpose of understanding who is susceptible to contagion, let's walk through the years that often precede an act of predatory violence that is likely due, in large part, to contagion.

Imagine for a minute that you are a young child who walks into school on the first day, hoping for a nice teacher and new friends. What you are seeking, even if you can't articulate it, is a sense of belonging. But instead of feeling a connection to others, you feel as though you don't fit in because you are repeatedly told you aren't good enough, smart enough or deserving enough for human contact. The maltreatment that occurs is repeated, hostile and intentional, and is perpetrated by classmates and, at times, teachers. When you are not being tormented, you are ignored each and every school day.

This doesn't go on for a few days or weeks, but goes on for years, and you are always on the outside looking in. To make matters worse, those mistreating you are the very students and staff members who seem to get all the breaks in life. It is you who is a "frequent flyer" to the SROs office because you get blamed for starting fights that weren't even fights—you were merely defending yourself against physical bullying.

The only people at school who give you strength are your best friend as well as your boyfriend or girlfriend, who reciprocate feelings of love. Or perhaps you feel connected to a classmate you perceive as caring about you even if it's only because of a smile flashed in class once in a while. Then one day, your loved one breaks up with you, or the classmate who offers smiles suddenly turns on you, and you realize their feelings were all in your imagination.

Now the very thought of going to school makes you anxious, and you are falling into a deeper state of depression that only seems to subside when you drink alcohol and smoke marijuana. Sometimes when you are under the influence, you talk to yourself, wondering if none of this had happened to you, would you be happy?

And what if it's the case that the bullying began when you were five years old after you watched your loving father, the greatest man you knew, die suddenly in front of you? But nobody in school has ever expressed sympathy for your loss or helped you process what happened. Instead, the bullying started because you were fascinated by death and wanted answers about what happened to your dad. Will he come back? Was it your fault? You worry about your mom and how she will support you when she has refused to leave the house since your dad passed away.

You come to realize from a young age that life isn't fair or just. Over the years, you have dark thoughts of killing yourself, but eventually decide that you are not going to go quietly. Instead, you are going to get revenge against those who represent what you have been denied, the very same type of people you feel are responsible for causing you a lifetime of pain. You decide to target those who bullied you and don't concern yourself about hurting those who get in your way.

You start wondering if it's even possible. How will you do it? Where will you do it? Then it hits you. Others have been in your shoes and they managed to carry it out, and nobody has forgotten their names. So you plan your attack. You surf the internet, studying dozens of shooters whom you come to respect because they are now forever famous for getting revenge for themselves and the other underdogs. You think, if they could do it, I can do it. You learn this with a click of your keyboard. Details were immediately revealed regarding the weapons used, the way the bombs were made, how they entered the buildings, what they wore and how many they killed or injured.

You realize that you will be famous and you will belong to a group that you hold in high regard: those you deem fighters against injustice. Like them, you want to rid this world of those you feel are unworthy of life. You get pleasure from planning, using your grandfather's AR-15 assault weapon and your newly purchased handgun to shoot at paper "human" targets and following instructions you learned from news coverage of a recent shooter. As you walk out the door of your house carrying your weapons, extra ammunition and explosives, you tell your best friend that today is the best day of your life and you will be popular forever.

WHAT WAS ON THE PATH?

The fictional depiction of "your" life was written to parallel the findings of the recently released U.S. Secret Service report (National Threat Assessment Center [NATC], 2019). The scenario depicted above has played out repeatedly in our nation, as is evident in their findings. The Secret Service examined 41 targeted shootings that took place from 2008 to 2017 in an effort to protect America's youth and our nation as a whole. The report's (2019, executive summary) major findings are summarized as follows:

- there is no profile of a student attacker, nor is there a profile for the type of school that has been targeted;
- attackers usually had multiple motives, the most common involving a grievance with classmates;
- most attackers used firearms, and firearms were most often acquired from the home;
- most attackers had experienced psychological, behavioral or developmental symptoms;
- half of the attackers had interests in violent topics;
- all attackers experienced social stressors involving their relationships with peers and/or romantic partners;
- nearly every attacker experienced negative home-life factors;
- most attackers were victims of bullying, which was often observed by others;
- most attackers had a history of school disciplinary actions, and many had prior contact with law enforcement; and
- all attackers exhibited concerning behaviors. Most elicited concern from others, and most communicated their intent to attack.

The report elaborated upon the aforementioned findings to shed light on the factors that played a role in leading towards the targeted attacks. Previous chapters applied the report to predatory violence and the need for a behavioral intervention or CARE team comprised of individuals from multiple disciplines, in addition to appropriate training, policies and tools such as those offered through the National Behavioral Intervention Team Association (NaBITA).

THE IMPACT OF MEDIA SENSATIONALISM ON THOSE AT RISK OF PREDATORY VIOLENCE

In addition to the aforementioned findings in the Secret Service report, media coverage is yet another factor of concern as it works as a catalyst, triggering the already-struggling individual. Environmental factors, as well as internal factors, contribute to thoughts of violence. For example, with the excessive media coverage, the impact of the Columbine attack (Appendix B: 20) is so powerful that it has proliferated in a generation that was yet to be born the year the shooting transpired. Columbine lives in the minds of those who feel they relate to and identify with the perpetrators. According to Follman and Andrews (2015) and Pescara-Kovach and Raleigh (2017a), Columbine was the exemplar across 74 plots and 30 states, but with the caveat that this generation of shooters wants to take the lives of more people than were taken in Columbine.

But what is media sensationalism? Udeze and Uzuegbunam (2013) shared an interesting fact that raises concern when applied to targeted shootings. They state, "Sensationalism is seen as a type of editorial bias in mass media in which events and topics in news stories are over-hyped to increase viewership or readership figures" (pp. 70–71).

We are often drawn to the unusual and the violent. Think back to Maslow's hierarchy of needs as it applies to motivation. Maslow stressed the need for humans to have their deficiency needs met prior to being able to reach higher levels of personal growth needs. In fact, not only are physiological survival needs like air, water, shelter, food and sleep needed to survive, humans also require a sense of safety. As such, security, safety and a sense of order are also central to our personal growth and stability. It seems logical that humans are drawn to information that without which their health and safety could be at risk and ultimately our species could cease to exist. As stated in Vettehen and Peeters (2008), "…sensationalism has also been connected to human evolution. The basic argument is that over the course of biological and cultural evolution, the human brain has become adapted to the task of noting information that may increase chances of survival and reproduction, in particular information about real or potentially threatening situations" (p. 320).

HEADLINE GRABBING AND MASS SHOOTINGS

Through the years, the media seems to have turned sensationalism of mass shootings into a science. It begins with an attention-grabbing statement at the beginning of the televised news, then the desk reporter begins to describe the incident in graphic detail, speculating on why it happened and how many injuries and fatalities have occurred before "going live" to an on-site reporter. The on-site reporter then interviews traumatized eyewitnesses, classmates or coworkers on the air, asking what happened and what exactly they saw. Coverage goes on for days and weeks, to the extent that it is reminiscent of the sharing of a detailed recipe for how to commit a mass shooting. Likewise, print news sources draw in the reader by using emotionally salient terms like "massacre," "slaughter" and other graphic descriptors within the headline. Table 11.1 highlights some examples of headlines that appeared in print newspapers the day following each respective incident.

The accurate term for these practices is *headline-grabbing*. Sisask and Varnik (2012) and Pescara-Kovach and Raleigh (2017b) stress that headline-grabbing is a concern due to its link to media contagion. McManama O'Brien et al. (2017) describe headline-grabbing as sensational wording geared towards receiving attention and publicity. In the media market, there is fierce competition for not only the quickest coverage, but also the most detailed and graphic. Within the table, it is likely some key terms jumped out at you. It's hard to stomach reading *massacre, bloodbath, horrific, monsters, mourning, bloodied, murdered, deadliest, slaughter* and *terror* when one reads headlines that describe violent acts young children and young

TABLE 11.1 Examples of Headline Grabbing (Mass Shooting)

Columbine	High School Massacre: Columbine Bloodbath Leaves Up To 25 Dead *Denver Post*	Horrific: Giggling Gunmen Invade High School – Killing up to 25 *Daily News*	The Monsters Next Door: What Made Them Do It? *Time Magazine*
Virginia Tech	Massacre and Mourning: 33 Die in Worst Mass Shooting in U.S. History *San Jose Mercury News*	Bloodied Campus Asks: Where Were the Warnings? *Chicago Tribune*	Bloodbath: 33 Die in Nation's Worst Shooting *The Detroit News*
Sandy Hook	20 Children Murdered: Unthinkable *Tampa Bay Times*	Massacre of Innocents: 20 Children, 7 Adults Killed/2nd Deadliest Shooting in U.S. *Republican American*	Slaughter: Gunman Kills 26, Including 20 Kids at Connecticut Schools *Standard Speaker*
Parkland	Terror, Again, in School *The Boston Globe*	A Horrific, Horrific Day *Pensacola News Journal*	We Know What Will Happen Next *The Boston Globe*

adults were subjected to. It seems as though media sources forget that witnesses, survivors and loved ones are also hearing and reading the news.

We have a reason to be concerned. As stated in Pescara-Kovach and Raleigh (2017b), Gould (2001) found a higher-than-normal likelihood of a public mass shooting within about two weeks of an incident that received sensationalized publicity. Towers et al. (2015) discovered that within 13 days of four school shootings, there is a fifth. Though the two-week timeframe is common, Sandy Hook and Columbine remain powerful influences on those who identify with the shooters.

We can be certain media contagion is an issue and that shooters identify, and sometimes worship, those who came before them. Court documents and written and spoken manifestos make the connection those at risk feel to one another clear. Clues are easy to identify in thwarted plots as well. Take Elizabeth Lecron (Appendix B: 137) from Toledo, Ohio. Lecron and her male accomplice were plotting to commit a mass shooting in an upscale bar. Thankfully, a phone call to authorities about Lecron and her boyfriend's suspicious behavior was taken seriously, as a search of her residence revealed firearms, ammunition and materials to build explosives. Lecron was influenced by Columbine. She had even traveled to Littleton, Colorado, to walk the grounds of Columbine. But she's not the first and will not be the last to emulate the Columbine shooters. The Sandy Hook shooter (Appendix B: 75) had collected dozens of articles on Columbine, as did an 18-year-old from Vermont who was reported to law enforcement by a concerned friend. Upon a search of his home, they found books about Columbine and a journal which contained his plans to commit a shooting at his former high school (Appendix B: 116). These plots were thwarted, but others were carried out. Contagion is deadly more often than not.

MEDIA CONTAGION AND THE COPYCAT EFFECT WITH SUICIDE

As if sensationalism of such shootings isn't enough, media contagion is an issue of concern in suicides as well. In 1974, Phillips described the increase in suicide that occurs after a media-sensationalized suicide. This phenomenon is known as the "Werther Effect" (Pescara-Kovach & Raleigh, 2017b; Phillips, 1974(Philips 1974)). Sisask and Varnik (2012) echoed the sentiments in their research from 2012 and many have demonstrated its existence since that time.

Think back to a time you heard of a suicide on the news. Aside from deaths occurring within religious cults (e.g., Branch Davidians), suicide does not get as much attention as targeted shootings. But it is likely you remember at least one suicide that hit you hard, often that of a celebrity such as Robin Williams, Chris Cornell, Chester Bennington or Kate Spade. These tragedies were sensationalized and discussed in detail with the same headline-grabbing tactics used in news of mass shootings.

Again, humans are drawn to this type of news. It heightens the emotional state and brings to our attention a topic that remains taboo among the mainstream.

The 24/7 news cycle is only as successful as the top story on a given day and, given what they know about sensationalism being a draw, they continue to spend considerable time reporting on celebrity suicides. News channels do not even acknowledge those suicides that are difficult to sensationalize. As stated in Pescara-Kovach and Raleigh (2017a), as with coverage of public mass shootings, only the most graphic and disturbing cases are "worthy" of attention in the media.

HEADLINE GRABBING AND SUICIDES

Headline-grabbing poses a risk in relation to suicide as well as mass and targeted shootings. The media doesn't set out with the goal of triggering copycat suicides or shootings, but this outcome is unfortunately an unintended result. Research conducted in 2012 (Sisask and Varnis) found that those at the greatest risk of being impacted by media contagion are near the same age as the individual who died by suicide. In addition, suicides that are the most contagious are those in which the deceased died at their own hands by extreme means. Table 11.2 is a

TABLE 11.2 Examples of Headline Grabbing (Suicide)

Robin Williams	Robin Williams Slit His Wrist Before Killing Himself *The Economic Times*	Hanged: Robin Tied Belt Around His Neck *Daily News*	Slashed Wrist with a Pen Knife *Daily News*
Chris Cornell	Chris Cornell Hanged Himself, Medical Examiner Says *CNN*	Update: Police Say Chris Cornell Had Band Around His Neck *Associated Press*	Chis Cornell's Bleak Final Facebook Post *Sunshine Coast Daily*
Chester Bennington	'He's Dead, He's Been Hanging;' Chester Bennington's Housekeeper Discovered Singer's Body: 911 Call *Toronto Sun*	Chester Bennington Dead: Linkin Park Singer Died on Chris Cornell's Birthday: Here's Why the Date is so Important *The Independent*	Chester Bennington's Housekeeper Heard Wailing As Driver Called 911 to Report Suicide *Daily News*
Kate Spade	Kate Spade Killed Herself 'After Her Husband Demanded a Divorce and Moved Out' as Her Sister Says She Suffered from Manic Depression for Years and Was Obsessed with Robin Williams' Suicide *Dailymail.co.uk*	'Not Your Fault' Kate Spade Dead at 55 – Designer's Heartbreaking Suicide Note to Daughter, 13, Before She Was Found Hanged in New York Apartment *The Sun*	Kate Spade Killed Herself with Scarf *Pop Culture*

sample of headlines that followed the suicide death of a celebrity where there was a related spike in copycat suicides.

GUIDELINES TO MINIMIZE THE LIKELIHOOD OF A COPYCAT SUICIDE

Given the knowledge we have regarding contagion, it is necessary to work towards preventing its likelihood to guide someone towards suicide. As parents and caregivers, it is important to understand contagion and what types of information lead to contagion. A little-known fact is that media guidelines were established over twenty years ago. Specifically, the media worked towards minimizing the sensationalizing of celebrity suicides. It is likely this occurred due to the available research on the Werther effect. What is truly disappointing is, in the last decade, media sensationalizing of suicide seems to have reared its head once again. It is likely no coincidence that suicide rates among youth have also increased significantly in parallel with the increase in sensationalism.

Not only is news coverage putting the vulnerable at risk, so too are television series and films. The series that immediately comes to mind as an example of potentially dangerous programming is Netflix's *13 Reasons Why*. McManama et al. (2017) conducted research on binge-watching and discovered that young people are the most susceptible to being influenced by highly emotional programming. As stated by Sisask and Varnik (2012),

> "Although the media is only one feature of the social environment in which suicidal behaviors can be learned and the effect is probably smaller than that of other psychosocial risk factors for suicide, it is a significant agent in social construction of reality, especially for vulnerable persons" (p. 124).

13 Reasons Why details the pre-suicide experiences of Hannah, who lived through various types of bullying, sexual assault, physical assault, negative comments about her appearance, isolation, alienation and a lack of support by the school counselor. Let's face it, Hannah is relatable to vulnerable youth who are living through similar experiences. Our world isn't sunshine and roses at that age. Bullying is common and many feel alienated and isolated. Sexual assaults and dating violence are plaguing the young, as is the vulnerability brought about by chasing "likes" on social media.

In the first season, rather than arriving at a safe, positive ending, Hannah ends her life in a graphic depiction of suicide. The series could have proven to be a positive recipe for surviving the turmoil of adolescence and young adulthood. Instead, it served us a recipe for suicide as a means to end suffering.

However, a graphic suicide is how it ended *before* the National Association of School Psychologists (NASP) and other organizations banded together against the series' introductory season and especially the ending. Subsequently, the network responded by deleting the graphic scene, but Hannah still died by suicide. Prior to the scene deletion, Hannah dies as a result of cutting her radial artery and veins deeply in a sawing motion. The scene was disturbing even to those who are not at risk of suicide. The creators of the series also responded to criticism by showing the contact information for the National Suicide Hotline after each episode. In addition, experts provide information on suicide with each episode. The concern is, at the age this is viewed, young people are in a time in which their peers are the "experts" and the adults are seen as preaching and out of touch with what they're going through. Thus, while the information is provided, it's likely not being received. And now there isn't just one season of *13 Reasons Why*; there are four.

The creators try to make the case that the series is a great learning tool to teach about the negative impact of the aforementioned life experiences. However, unless it is viewed with a trusted adult and the issues are discussed with a focus on how suicide is not the answer, we cannot be sure of the lesson young people are taking away. NASP reacted to season one with opposition, but the series remained, so NASP released guidelines for educators and families (NASP, 2017; Appendix C).

For Parents: From a practical perspective, parents should be aware of popular media geared towards young people. Series like *13 Reasons Why* should be avoided or if viewed, parents and caregivers should watch them with their children or adolescents. Related to this, it's a good idea to avoid open access to all types of media. One can easily find suicide tutorials on YouTube, for example. Like *13 Reasons Why*, these are likely to serve as a trigger to an already-struggling individual. Just as those at risk of violence should not be allowed to view sensationalized violence and play-by-play explanations of how a shooting was perpetrated, so too should those at risk of suicide not be permitted open access to YouTube and its detailed suicide depictions.

As you're reading this, you might be thinking this is impossible given Generation Z's attachment to their electronic devices and social media apps. If we keep our youth busy and connected to in-person relationships, they are less likely to seek the same from an online source. Watch television shows and movies together as a family. Fear of missing out (FOMO) will diminish if healthy relationships are formed and activities are planned away from social media. Part of this starts with the adults. Children learn through observation. We model and they repeat the behaviors. We too have to put our phones down and engage. It's also very important that all parents and caregivers are aware of warning signs and risk and protective factors.

According to the National Association of School Psychologists (NASP) in *Preventing Youth Suicide: Tips for Parents and Educators* (NASP, 2015), there are typically warning signs in advance of a suicide attempt. They are:

- a change in appearance, thoughts, feelings and/or behavior;
- a suicide plan;
- sleeping too much or not able to sleep at all;
- significant weight loss or gain;
- online posts or handwritten notes about wanting to die or disappear;
- giving away items they previously enjoyed;
- expressing feelings of hopelessness (e.g., "things will never get better," or "what's the point of living?");
- previous suicide attempts;
- indirect statements (e.g., "I wish I was never born," or "The world would be better without me"); and/or
- direct statements (e.g., "I want to kill myself," or "I want to die").

In addition to warning signs, there are risk factors that make someone susceptible to suicide. Risk factors include, but are not limited to, a family history of suicide, the suicide of a close friend or classmate, family discord, alienation, isolation and lacking a connection with peers or family.

The good news is there are steps parents and caregivers can take to work towards preventing suicide. First and foremost, hope is a key to prevention. That is, young people can feel as though what they are feeling is going to last forever. It might be bullying, being abandoned by friends or a breakup that is triggering their thoughts. Remind them that life gets better and that whatever they are going through will pass. Stay with them. Stay calm. Do not leave them unsupervised or in the presence of lethal means. And talk. Talk about suicide.

Talking about suicide does not cause suicide. In fact, discussing their pain and being reassured that there is hope, help and someone to rely on is a relief. As a reminder, this isn't personal. Parents and caregivers often get their feelings hurt or they feel like they're bad caregivers if their child or teen is suicidal, so they avoid the conversation. However, as you've read above, there are warning signs and risk factors we can detect. And for every risk factor, there is a protective factor. Open communication, destigmatizing suicide, removing media triggers and getting professional help will go a long way. However, if a loved one is at imminent risk of attempting suicide, take them to the emergency room where they can be immediately evaluated and put on their way to a care plan.

For School and Campus Personnel: The school and campus environment is a powerful context that can act as either a risk or protective factor. The key is student connectedness and a climate that openly discusses mental health and suicide. All school and campus personnel involved in the lives of students should be aware of the risk factors and warning signs. In addition, it is important to foster an environment where students feel good about themselves, accepted and able to work on coping skills. NASP (2015) provided the following statement on their website:

"The entire school staff should work to create an environment where students feel safe sharing such information. School psychologists and other crisis response team personnel, including the school counselor and school administrator, are trained to intervene when a student is identified at risk for suicide. These individuals conduct suicide risk assessment, warn/inform parents, provide recommendations and referrals to community services, and often provide follow up counseling and support at school"

(para. 6).

Teachers and professors must be in tune to current social media and viewing trends. By extension, prior to assigning a chapter, book or film to students, educators should do their research. Far too many required the *13 Reasons Why* book or series without realizing the potential for media contagion.

For Media: Even before the release of *13 Reasons Why*, the CDC, in conjunction with suicide prevention and intervention experts, worked to educate the media on how to discuss suicide. The result was a key document, *Reporting on Suicide* (n.d.), geared toward preventing suicide contagion. Their recommendations to media are to avoid sensationalizing both non-celebrity and celebrity suicides. Media outlets should not provide method details, photos or videos, and never share details of a suicide note or post. Further advice to media is to never report suicide as a crime or interview a first responder in regard to a suicide. In addition, media sources are discouraged from using the terms "failed attempt," "committed suicide," "successful" or "unsuccessful" in relation to a suicide-attempt outcome. These terms are sensationalistic and must be avoided if we are to work towards diminishing tragic deaths by suicide.

As for detailed media reporting in relation to mass shootings, general guidelines (*save.org*) can be summarized as: (1) lessen reporting on perpetrators; (2) never show victim and perpetrator photos together; (3) limit photos of the shooter; (4) do not stigmatize mental illness; (5) do not sensationalize or glorify a shooting; (6) be sensitive when interviewing survivors and their families; (7) show how the community is coming together to get through the difficult period; and (8) do not place blame on those targeted (if there are specific targets) or their school or community.

Schildkaut (2019) supports applying the same World Health Organization (WHO) guidelines on reporting suicides to reporting mass shootings. This is an excellent approach, especially because many shooters are also suicidal. WHO recommends not prominently placing a suicide news story on a page, news report or website. The same should apply to mass shootings, given what we know about contagion. WHO also stresses the avoidance of the word "suicide" within a headline and avoidance of details on method. Similarly, "massacre," "bloodshed" and other salient terms should not be used in reference to mass shootings.

195

As discussed, Columbine stands out as the exemplar to this day. Somehow it transcends the previously mentioned two-week, high-risk time period. That is, the shooters have a following among "Columbiners," who know every detail about the shooting. Most mass shooters since 1999 reference Columbine in their spoken or written posts or manifestos. Columbine was the top news story of 1999 with months of reports, graphic details, interviews and 911 calls eventually released to the public. This information remains available and is sought after by at-risk youth who identify with the shooters and see them as martyrs or heroes. But what if there wasn't such extensive reporting on every aspect of the Columbine shootings? The information simply wouldn't be widely available and the infamous day that will forever be replicated by those who carry out their plans would be a distant memory for all but those involved.

Media contagion exists. It's undeniable. However, all of us play a role in minimizing the likelihood of suicides and school or campus shootings. Whether you're a parent who knows to talk openly about suicide and spend time watching programming with your child, or you work as a teacher or school or campus administrator and know that it's so important that students feel connected, you play a role in prevention. We all do. We know the power of the media in contributing to suicides, but imagine if outlets were educated on how to report and what to report. Maybe then they could lessen the likelihood of suicides and shootings. We're not there yet. The best we can do is learn what to do right by studying what went wrong. It is so important that schools and campuses have BIT or CARE teams in place because, until we live in a perfect world, we have to ensure we're at least trying to catch at-risk youth before they fall.

MOVING FORWARD

The next chapter addresses the issue of how a school or college should share information with the media. There is a temptation to shut down and avoid connecting with the media during a crisis and, in many ways, this can be the worst approach. The "Feed the Bears" motto serves school officials well when it comes to giving the media something to focus on during a crisis. If you don't feed the bears, they will go through the garbage looking for something to eat.

REFERENCES

Alifrangis, C., Koizia, L., Rozario, A., Rodney, S., Harrington, M., Somerville, C., Peplow, T. & Waxman, J. (2011). The experience of cancer patients. *QJM: An International Journal of Medicine*, 104(12), 1075–1081.

Bandura, A. (1986) *Social foundations of thought and action: A social cognitive theory*. Englewood Cliffs, NJ: Prentice Hall.

Fink, D.S., Santaella-Tenorio, J. & Keyes, K.M. (2018). Increase in suicides the months after the death of Robin Williams in the US. *PLoS ONE*, 13(2): e0191405. https://doi.org/10.1371/journal.pone.0191405.

Follman, M. & Andrews, B. (2015). How Columbine spawned dozens of copycats. Mother Jones. Retrieved on February 15, 2020 from www.motherjones.com/politics/2015/10/columbine-effect-mass-shootings-copy-cat-data/

Gould, M. S. (2001). Suicide and the media. *Annals of the New York Academy of Sciences*, 932(1):200–224.

Johnston, J. & Joy, A. (2016). Mass shootings and the media contagion effect. *Symposium presented at the Annual Conference of the American Psychological Association.* Retrieved on March 28, 2020 from www.apa.org/news/press/releases/2016/08/media-contagion.aspx

Klinger, A. & Klingr, A. (2018). Violent threats and incidents at school. Retrieved on March 28, 2020 from http://eschoolsafety.org/violence

McManama O'Brien, K.H., Knight, J.R., & Harris, S.K. (2017). A call for social responsibility and suicide risk screening, prevention, and early intervention following the release of the Netflix series 13 Reasons Why. *Journal of the American Medical Association Internal Medicine*, 177, 1418–1419.

National Association of School Psychologists (NASP) (2015). Preventing youth suicide: Tips for parents and educators. Retrieved on March 16, 2020 from https://www.nasponline.org/resources-and-publications/resources-and-podcasts/school-climate-safety-and-crisis/mental-health-resources/preventing-youth-suicide/preventing-youth-suicide-tips-for-parents-and-educators

National Association of School Psychologists. (2017). *13 Reasons Why Netflix series: Considerations for educators* [handout]. Bethesda, MD: Author.

National Threat Assessment Center (NTAC). (2019). Protecting America's schools: A United States Secret Service analysis of targeted school violence. United States Secret Service, Department of Homeland Security.

Pescara-Kovach, L. & Raleigh, M.J. (2017a). The contagion effect as it relates to public mass shootings and suicides. *Journal of Behavioral Intervention Teams* (5), 35–45.

Pescara-Kovach, L., Raleigh, M.J. (2017b). The contagion effect as it relates to public mass shootings and suicides. *Journal of Behavioral Intervention Teams*, 5, 35–45.

Philips, D. (1974). The influence of suggestion on suicide: Substantive and theoretical implications of the Werther effect. *American Sociological Review* (39), 3, 340–354.

Sisask, M. & Varnik, A. (2012). Media roles in suicide prevention: A systematic review. *International Journal of Environmental Re- search and Public Health*, 9, 123–138. Retrieved from www.ncbi.nim.nih.gov/pmc/articles/pmc3315075/.

Schildkraut, J. (2019). A call to the media to change reporting practices for the coverage of mass shootings, *Washington University Journal of Law & Policy*, 60, 273–292.

Taksler, B., Mercer, M., Fagerlin, A., Rothberg, M. (2019). Assessing patient interest in individualized preventive care recommendations. *MDM Policy and Practice* 4(1).

Towers, S., Gomez-Leviano, A., Khan, M., Mubavi, A. & Castillo-Chavez, C. (2015). Contagion in Mass Killings and School Shootings. *PLoS ONE* 10(7): e0117259. DOI:10.1371/journal.pone.0117259.

Udeze, S.E. & Uzuegbunam, C.E. (2013). Sensationalism in the media: The right to sell or the right to tell. *Journal of Communication and Media Research*, 5, 69-78.

Vettehen, P.H. & Peeters, A. (2008). Explaining effects of sensationalism on liking of television news stories: The role of emotional arousal. *Communication Research*, 35, 319–338.

Chapter 12

Optics and the Media
"Feeding the Bears"[1]

Consider the last time you experienced a crisis, either in your personal or business life. Organizations under attack during a crisis "feel" just as we do as humans; there is a simultaneous and overwhelming sense of shock, outrage, fear and confusion. "How could this happen to us?" "Will we survive?" "What do we do?" "Who can we trust?" "Do we have friends out there that can help?" "Why didn't we prepare for such a situation?" "Will this ever end?"

Welcome to the world of crisis management.

Managing a crisis is the enterprise of telling the ugly truths about an incident. It is the polar opposite of what most of us do daily through our school or university work. The objective of such management is to make a bad situation less so. If conventional public relations have been disparaged as telling pretty lies, then crisis management should be praised as telling ugly truths (Dezenhall and Weber, 2007).

Crisis management is all about storytelling, and any good story begins by recognizing the warnings set out before us. When Chief Brody in the movie *Jaws* said that Quint's crew would need a bigger boat, he was doing more than observing; he was assessing strategically both the practical tools that would be required to catch the great white shark and determining the resolve of the shark-hunting team (Dezenhall and Weber, 2007). To manage a crisis, the organization and leadership must have the tools and resolve to survive to fight another day.

The speed at which a situation can become a crisis is literally within seconds. As mentioned in Chapter 2 and Chapter 11, the advent of social media changed the entire landscape of working with the public and the media in the past two decades. No matter what else happens, schools and universities need to know the story is going to be told by the press, and now is the time for leadership to prepare. They need to be prepared to tell the story.

---

1. Special thanks to Dr. L. Darryl Armstrong, Ph.D., for his work on this chapter.

AN OUNCE OF PREVENTION

The secret to preventing some crises is a practical issue/threat-management program. Employees in such a culture are "situationally aware" and trained and authorized to move issues forward to management. The leadership listens and takes action on issues in their earliest stages. Conflict does not materialize, or if it does, management is ready to deal with it.

"Issues" are adverse events, incidents, problems or situations; they do not typically interrupt overall business operations. A student transported to the hospital for a suicide attempt is a problem. However, it does not usually threaten the long-term bottom-line or negatively impact the reputation of the school or college. An issue may affect people, the environment and business operations; it may jeopardize your brand or reputation for the short-term. If dealt with quickly and efficiently, most issues will not rise to the level of crises.

There are several levels of issues that require different responses. The issue may be "latent," previously identified and tracked as part of an issue-management program, such as growing concerns about a lack of speaker diversity at a national medical conference (Hughes, S., 2020).

On the other hand, the issue may be "smoldering" when it has been partially addressed, perhaps even by legislation yet not resolved, as is the case with sexual harassment and the #MeToo movement issue (McDonald, 2018). Latent and smoldering issues can often be mitigated by dealing with them when discovered, preventing them from maturing into crises.

Schools, colleges and universities could also imagine a more "eruptive" issue. An eruptive issue can be as mundane as a sewer leak into a nearby creek, or as scandalous as the chief of campus security getting arrested in a prostitution sting, or as traumatic as a Facebook post that contains a hit-list of students to be killed. No matter what the problem is, your response must be timely and will influence the public's perception (the optics) of you, the organization and your leaders' ability to handle the situation.

Your organization may not be directly involved or responsible for the initial problem; however, the staff is responsible for the media response. If you do not adequately address an issue and communicate your actions, the issue can become a crisis that can damage your organization's reputation. To maintain your brand and reputation, you must communicate with your various audiences. Properly communicating promptly with the media, the public, your employees and other stakeholders during a crisis is critical. Only then will you recover and survive to fight another day.

Take the incident at Lake Worth High School on October 7, 2019 (Appendix B: 147). A student in the school posted a threat on Snapchat, tagging the school in the location. The post is provided in Figure 12.1. A concerned student shared the threat through the StudentProtect app, a tool implemented by the Palm Beach County Schools. The case was handled by the Palm Beach Sheriff's office, and the

FIGURE 12.1 Lake Worth Highschool Snapchat threat.

student who had made the threat was taken into custody. The incident strongly impacted the school, with hundreds of phone calls and media requests and an armed police presence at the school for several days.

The time to prepare for these kinds of incidents is not the morning they are unfolding but months ahead of time with forethought and multidisciplinary planning.

FOUR KEYS TO PREPAREDNESS

Richard Stephenson, CEO of YUDU Ltd., shares his thoughts on how to deal with a crisis in the public (Twitter) sphere. "In the forty years, I have been running businesses big and small; there has never been a time when we have less time to think before we act. Preparation is the only medicine" (BCI, 2018, p. 1).

In a crisis, the chief executive officer must be the chief crisis officer, or if not the CEO, the business-unit chief who has the authority to make fundamental decisions and not be paralyzed by analysis or insecurity. It is important to remember that, although the staff they work with may be large, effective crisis-management leadership teams should remain small. While they collect input, advice and counsel from various internal and external sources, these teams are not esteem-building sessions. The smaller the team, the more efficient it can be.

There are four areas where we need to ensure we are better prepared for future crises and emergencies.

1. **Have a crisis communications guidance document.** An organization must have a Communications Governance (CG) document that is easy to understand and use and that everyone who may be engaged in responding has agreed to use. Most importantly, this document must be approved and agreed

to by the leadership. It must have the "sign-off" of those in command and agreement to use it for guidance during all crises and emergencies.

The CG document, as the name implies, spells out the authorities and who can approve messages. It clearly states who is responsible for drafting the emergency notifications (many of these can be done in advance) and the follow-on tactical or strategic communications, who can edit these statements and who must approve them.

2. **Have a written crisis/emergency plan agreed to by leadership.** In corporate, university and non-governmental communications, having a crisis plan is an absolute must for the organization hoping to survive. Having leadership buy-in and practicing that plan is even more important. This plan must be simple, easy to understand and use. Develop the program with a cultural mindset that recognizes the importance of timely responses for both crises and emergencies. An emergency plan is critical to saving lives and property. Exercise and train to the plan, knowing that all plans require leadership resiliency.

Your emergency plan should aim to respond and reduce the impact of any immediate risks or threats that your business has identified. The plan should take into account as many scenarios and threats as possible for the organization, even though you recognize and accept that it will not be all-inclusive.

3. **Have pre-written and approved templates for messaging.** These are critical to have on hand and to be able to update quickly for a timely response. The time to write a media holding statement is not in the chaos of a crisis. We will discuss how to prepare these and provide examples below. These statements must be readily available to use so there is no delay in being timely with initial responses. Guidance on how to prepare key messaging is in Appendix E.

4. **Use all available communication tools to share with the public and the media.** While many companies have a communications or public-relations department or a social media lead, many organizations consider social media to be an afterthought. A study by Weber Shandwick (2020) found that only 54% of lawyers surveyed have received instruction on how social media impacts their companies, leaving nearly half of law firms unprepared for managing an incident that goes public.

If you do not have social media platforms up and running and/or are not using them on a regular and consistent basis, now is the time to get that underway. Also, if you have not developed working relationships with your external partners, including the media, law enforcement, first responders, contractors, media and suppliers, start doing so now in a planned and systematic outreach. Forge alliances with your industry experts, nonprofit organizations, reporters and others before a communications crisis occurs so that they can help when trouble arises (Jackson, 2012).

201

"Organizations must ... become more conscious of the risks they face, understand their duty of care to employees, implement robust risk management procedures, explore insurance solutions, and embed a culture of crisis resilience throughout the company. Ignorance is not an option. Firms need to learn how to anticipate, prevent, respond, and recover."

Paul Bassett, the Managing Director of Crisis Management at Arthur J. Gallagher

LEADERSHIP AND CRISIS MANAGEMENT

Crisis management requires leaders who can make decisions with minimal amounts of information and a cultural mindset that is resilient and adaptable. To survive and minimize any long-term consequences, leaders must have confidence in their communications and crisis-management professionals, and "leaders must lead."

Some leaders fail or delay accepting responsibility during a crisis. Even when they understand the consequences of the need to respond promptly, they create unique problems for themselves. Such management wants to blame others downstream for their failure to plan appropriately, coordinate, contract and collaborate with their crisis-management team, emergency responders and other officials. When confronted by the media or stakeholders, they often imply that "all will be okay, this too shall pass." They may be backed by legal and PR counsel that don't want to contradict leadership or encourage the supposed safety of "no comment." They are in perpetual denial that such a thing could happen to them and their enterprise.

In a business crisis, being "unavailable for comment" won't make the story or the damage that it inflicts go away; it will just encourage opponents to fill in the blanks and motivate reporters to dig deeper (Jackson, 2012). Leaders often "silo" their decision-making, and instead of collaborating with their communicators and other members of their crisis team to respond quickly, they insulate themselves from the crisis. When all else fails in handling the crisis and recovering swiftly, they litigate or proceed to "lawyer up" to regain their reputation and try to restore their brand.

These leaders fail to understand that social media has overtaken the traditional news media and that many stakeholders now rely on LinkedIn, YouTube, Twitter, Instagram, Snapchat, Facebook and other social platforms for their news. Before the advent of social media, these leaders had the luxury of time to gather the facts and formulate a response. Lawyers could tweak and pontificate for hours before a reply was issued, usually by a public-relations person who served as a "talking head." This approach is no longer an option. "The natural storytellers who might be inclined to twist [and spin] the narrative should be locked away along with the grey suits. The spokesperson should have command of the facts, and not drift into speculation but deliver what is known with gravitas and compassion for those impacted," says Richard Stephenson (BCI, 2018, p. 1).

Leaders with such an orientation do not understand the damage such a philosophy and approach can do to an organization's reputation and ability to recover. Social media is a communications tool just like the traditional media platforms of newspapers, radio and television, and anything you post on the platforms can and most likely will be shared instantly and infinitely. When untruthful information, misinformation or rumors appear on social media, they will be shared as truth indefinitely.

A plan of action that details appropriate response, correction of misinformation and dealing with rumors is essential because things can go bad quickly. Your answers must be authentic, truthful, sincere and issued with an appropriate tone. While the wrong thing going viral can spell disaster for a company ill-prepared to deal with it, social media can also be a powerful tool for connecting with audiences on a more personal level and getting across vital information that can help you weather the storm (BCI, 2018).

Imagine the social media post that occurred on April 7, 2019, at Bonita Vista High in Chula Vista, California (Appendix B: 139). A student posted the following (Figure 12.2). These are the kinds of challenges facing schools today that demand a coordinated response. A leader must find the exact chord to roll out a plan of action which is truthful, genuine and addresses the fear experienced by students, teachers, parents and the community.

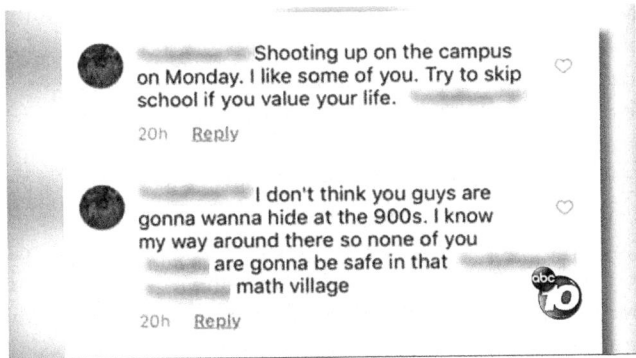

FIGURE 12.2 Bonita Vista High Threat.

"A commander, who does not either take the initiative, in planning or attack, lies in his continual search for something. Indeed anything in which to react. It is his greatest weakness. He is vulnerable to the ploys of his opponent."
The Cambridge Illustrated History of Warfare

CRISIS- AND COMMUNICATIONS-MANAGEMENT PROCESSES

When developing your crisis-management program, establish confidence, integrity and trust between all the parties. You can accomplish this through a collaborative process where the various partners are at the leadership's table. This approach keeps all parties informed and educated about issues and provides guidance and counsel. Communicators and crisis managers are team players, along with human resources, general counsel, security and business and operations managers. When issues arise, the communicator understands the situations the management faces and is better informed to help navigate through the crisis because they are part of the leadership team and the past decision-making.

It is useful to remember that people want to hear from a sincere spokesperson who understands their frustrations, fears and feelings. In March 2019, a chemical fire broke out at the Intercontinental Terminals Company. The fire burned for 10 days, spreading noxious fumes for miles around the Houston-area petrochemical storage company, before CEO Brent Netland released a brief video "apologizing" for the chemical fire (Associated Press, 2019). Harris County Commissioner Adrian Garcia called Netland and other senior ITC executives "cowardly" for not being more visible and transparent in the aftermath of the days-long fire (Associated Press, 2019).

It is, of course, essential to coordinate with your legal counsel and to manage the legal aspects of a crisis. Yet equally important is communicating in simple, understandable, compassionate and empathetic language that relates to the concern and doing so promptly. To communicate effectively with impacted stakeholders, you must acknowledge where they are in their thinking and feeling about the situation.

Leslie Lillard says, "There's been a lot of executive training that has occurred in the last few years around the use of 'empathy statements.' You see them used in so many press conferences now that they've become almost trite: a mere check-off on a list of things that 'should be said'" (Lillard, 2020).

However, real, meaningful empathy statements go far beyond "Our thoughts and prayers are with you," or "I understand your frustration." These spokespeople acknowledge the pain experienced and admit wrongdoing (when and if appropriate), sincerely apologize when appropriate and demonstrate through their behaviors the commitment to resolve the situation. Empathy statements show diligence to prevent it from happening in the future by "doing the right thing."

Examples of meaningful and sincere empathy statements include:

- "We don't have all the answers right now. What I do know is that many people are hurting. We want to be part of the solution to that."
- "I know there are no words I say that will alleviate the pain. Understand, though, I am committed to working find a way to make things right with everyone impacted."

- "This is such a tragic event. We grieve that our company may have had any part in causing it in any way. To those that have been affected, first I want to say, I'm deeply sorry. I want to hear your concerns and need your help to find a path to recovery." (When there is a fault by the company.)

"A true leader has the confidence to stand alone, the courage to make tough decisions, and the compassion to listen to the needs of others. He does not set out to be a leader, but becomes one by the equality of his actions and the integrity of his intent."
Douglas MacArthur

RESPONDING TO EMERGENCIES

Emergencies present a direct threat to the health and safety of both your employees and the public. They demand immediate attention to preserve the public's health and safety. An emergency can cause extensive loss or damage to people, property and the environment. Emergencies include events such as tornadoes, hurricanes, wildfires, floods, protests, active shooters and civil disruptions.

Emergency planning, communications, training and exercising are an integral part of any enterprise, regardless of its size. Failure to plan spells disaster and reputational damage. During crisis and emergency events, the public's greatest fear is that your organization has not adequately prepared itself to handle the situation efficiently and effectively. The ability to communicate quickly and with confidence as soon as possible establishes the foundation of the public's perception and helps you control the narrative.

We live in a 24-hour news cycle, and crises and emergencies drive news coverage. In the news business and on social media, "if it bleeds, it leads." When a crisis erupts, the organization and its leaders can and will become the headline of the moment. Being prepared, trained and exercised for crises will help you have and convey the confidence needed. How you respond to a crisis can reduce and even allay public fears and makes the difference in the time it takes you to recover. It is critically important to understand that a 24-hour news cycle will repeat endlessly what the situation is and how you are responding to it. If you do not control the narrative from the outset, you will invariably be on the defensive.

In today's world, exercise and training should use the most recent and advanced training and technology. The days of tabletop training exercises that fail to provide the realism of social media engagement are over. Leadership that does not seek out the latest in training does a disservice to itself and its employees and, of course, the stakeholders. An example of this process is provided in Appendix D. When you fail to respond appropriately to a crisis or an emergency, you will create negative optics and damage your brand, reputation, trustworthiness and credibility.

205

There are numerous 2018 crisis examples gathered by PRDaily.com and Ragan.com (Working, 2018). They include such fiascoes as the state of Hawaii's mistaken siren alert that North Korea had launched missiles, Roseanne Barr's single late-night racist tweet, a Burger King with rats, the H&M charges of racism in its advertising and J.P. Morgan's debacle at the Biological Innovation Organization Boston convention with topless dancers promoting its brand on their painted bodies. Each of these examples shows how quickly an organization, person, business or an institution can lose its brand, reputation, trust and credibility the audiences have in them.

CRISIS COMMUNICATION

The ultimate goal of crisis communications is timeliness. Our communication goal should be that during any situation, we want to get the right information to the right people at the right time so they can make the right decisions and issue the right communications (Lortz, 2017).

Many organizations compound and even prolong a crisis. They do not diagnose the problem, start the fix and promptly communicate what it is they are doing. They become paralyzed and fearful of what to do and say. Delays in response to a crisis in today's world of social media are not acceptable to your stakeholders, and not prudent.

An example of this comes from Rutgers University, where basketball coach Mike Rice was fired after a videotape of him was aired showing Rice shoving, grabbing, yelling homophobic and misogynistic slurs and throwing balls at his players (Nall, 2013). The school was aware of abuse allegations months before the video surfaced, and Nall makes the point that leaving this for unaddressed for four months was like an open wound, quadrupling the negative impact on the university's reputation.

Whether you uncover a cybersecurity breach, learn of a government investigation, discover sexual harassment or see a threatening YouTube video posted by a student, the enemy remains the same—time. According to a survey by Deloitte (2014), almost 90% of executives say that damage to their reputation is the most critical risk they face.

Your stakeholders need to know and understand that you and your team are prepared to handle any event. During an emergency, they want to know what is going on as soon as possible. After the crisis, they will look at what you did to keep the situation from worsening and how will you prevent such incidents in the future.

Failure to be resilient and adaptive and to communicate effectively and comprehensively at any stage of a crisis affects the organization's brand, reputation and the public's perception and impacts the recovery process.

"The speed of communication is so critical in a crisis or a building crisis. For example, our college was put on probation during an accreditation process.

This can be devastating to a college. The local and national media was alerted, and we began getting calls. I immediately alerted our faculty, staff, and students, and explaining to them that it was because of the university not giving us enough freedom to control our own programs, academic integrity. This was a year-long crisis brewing. But we had teams of folks helping to manage the message and assessing the problem and solutions. Most of all, we managed the news going out to the media; I did interviews often with them and sent them information to assure them we had an excellent institution. We, again, had a focused approach, open, positive, and informative on the crisis at hand, no hidden veils of secrecy."

Dr. Jim Kerley, a retired college president with 25 years of service.

THE TRUTH SETS US FREE

It is critical to crisis management to tell the truth. People intrinsically understand when they are not getting all the facts, and they get frustrated and turn their anger towards the people who try and "spin" them, and they can and do become disgusted when the truth is not told.

- Former U.S. Congressman Anthony Weiner was disgraced and ruined by sending lewd text messages to a variety of women, but mostly because he lied to cover it up.
- Former Ohio State University football coach Jim Tressel, a great leader and role model for his players, resigned because he lied about transgressions.
- Former baseball player Roger Clemens—arguably one of the greatest pitchers ever—went on trial in July, not for using steroids, but for allegedly lying to Congress about it (on July 14, a judge declared a mistrial.)
- Former President Bill Clinton was disgraced and humiliated when he pointed with a crooked finger at the American public and lied, "I did not have sexual relations with that woman."

How different would these outcomes have been if these people had told the truth, regardless of the consequences?

"When it comes to communicating about a crisis in the world of social media, speed, and frequency are key. No longer will the public accept the slow and unresponsive onsite investigations. All responding agencies must provide timely, factual, and frequent information as the event unfolds. Facts need to be validated, and rumors dispelled as quickly as possible. At the same time, give care to crafting the message. Responses can take a life of their own. *Never lie*, even if the information is known but can't be revealed at the time. Be honest with the public. Always assume every comment and action will go viral, even if it doesn't because there is an infinite supply of digital ink at someone's disposal."

Taylor Hayes, former publisher of the Kentucky New Era in Hopkinsville, Kentucky

DON'T BE QUIET

There is a mistaken impression that panic is the greatest threat to an organization during a crisis. Actually, the most severe threat to any organization is to do nothing and hope it goes away, or to fall victim to the canard of we have not "PR-ed" them enough or else they would like us.

It makes no difference the level of the crisis facing you; our society is seen by most of the public as scandal-ridden, and the crisis-obsessed media and the public expect a few specific things from the crisis-stricken organization and its leadership. They want to see someone out front explaining themselves and the company. In today's world, silence equals guilt, as does the legalistic and disdainful "no comment."

We recognize there are situations when out of necessity, you must issue a written statement as you seek to get yourselves together and secure verifiable information. It is best to stay below the radar in such situations. However, when people's lives are significantly affected, or there are real health and safety risks involved, you must share with people what you know.

Stepping out first and accurately characterizing the situation (while avoiding liability risks) positions you and your leadership as credible and reliable players in whatever happens next in the crisis. Understanding the expectations and the needs of the public, media and stakeholders can help with this (Table 12.1).

TABLE 12.1 What the Public, Media, and Stakeholders Expect

Prompt alerts and communications

Respect for their feelings and concerns

Timely and consistent information release and updates

Two-way communications

People talking in language and on a level that the listener can understand, and who can empathize with their feelings and understand their fears

Understandable answers to their questions

Organizational accountability

Explanation of what happened and why

Objective investigations into the problem that determines the "root cause," and how the problem was handled and how it will be corrected and prevented in the future

Leaders that "walk their talk"

You need to learn from your mistakes

LEARN TO LISTEN

Listen with care. Observe and monitor what is trending on social media. Step outside your role and into their world. What would you want to know? How would you feel? Only then should you set about meeting the informational needs. Useful messaging addresses both the thinking and feeling needs of the receiver of the information.

In a crisis and emergency, it is not about winning; it is about developing and sustaining two-way communications and engaging with the working relationships we have built over time. It is about collaborating to find real solutions to real problems to ease the pain and resolve the situation. Ten steps to listening well are included in Appendix G.

MEDIA HOLDING STATEMENTS

Bears are always hungry and looking for their next meal. Think of social and traditional media as bears. These bears are always looking for their next story. If you don't feed them, they are going to go digging through your trash. They are going to interview frustrated students, cold-call faculty and staff to let them vent and talk to the community and parents.

Crises invariably seem to happen at odd and late hours; whatever the hours, we must feed the social and traditional media "bears." Therefore, *media holding statements* are valuable. They are the appetizer on the bear's menu.

A holding statement consists of a few brief sentences you issue via social and traditional media venues within the first 15-30 minutes after the crisis occurs. The media and the public recognize you might not have all the facts and information to provide a full statement, but they expect timely information from you confirming that you know something has happened.

Holding statements buy you some time to get your investigation and fact-gathering underway, but they are not a panacea for more than an hour or so. This first statement merely explains to the audience that you know an incident has occurred. Statements from this point forward should answer as best as is known what happened, who was involved, when it happened and if known, why it happened.

Approved media holding statements are critical to handling any crisis, and if you do not have them at the ready, you are playing defense from the outset. They should be prepared in advance and be available at a moment's notice when an incident arises. The ability to respond quickly using holding statements can get the organization back in control of the narrative. Remember, the goal is to control that narrative. Therefore, write your generic holding statements now. Get them approved by all required parties. Load them to a readily accessible site on computers that the crisis-communications manager and the team can easily access.

An initial statement can be concise: "We are aware of the incident that occurred this afternoon at the campus. Currently, we are gathering further details and will issue an update within the next hour."

The task seems relatively simple. However, this straightforward statement took an organization two-hours to draft and then secure approval from their executive leadership team following an accident and the ultimate death of an employee. Three hours later, and long after social media released the information, the statement was issued.

Other examples of applicable initial holding statements can be:

- "We are in contact with the victim's family and doing everything we can to support them."
- "We are investigating the incident and have a team on the way to the scene."
- "Our campus security is cooperating with the authorities."
- "All of us are devastated. We have had an excellent safety record, and this is the first accident of this kind to occur at one of our facilities in the last decade."

Social media demands posting such an initial statement quickly. However, such statements only buy some time. The "follow-on statement," which is the soup or salad of the bear's menu, must begin to provide verifiable information. This statement explains in more detail what you know happened. If possible, it reveals who was involved and when it happened. If known, it tells why it happened, but be careful to never speculate, and be aware that the media will attempt to get you to speculate.

Here are some examples of possible follow-on messages to use in various venues such as your website, additional tweets, verbal messages to employees, etc.

- "As a result of an incident/s at the (name of facility), employees have been asked to evacuate the building/premises."
- "Currently, efforts are focused on ensuring the health and safety of all individuals on and adjacent to the premises."
- "Emergency plans are activated, and actions to address the potential incident are being carried out jointly with police and first responders."
- "When we have confirmed further details, we will be providing that information to the media and the public."
- "The media briefing will be at (time and location.)"
- "We also will be providing updated information on our website: (insert website address) as well as notifications via Facebook and Twitter. #ABCEvent"
- "We ask all campus employees and individuals in the general area to assist in the response by following the direction of campus security and local law enforcement officials."

Recognize that even the follow-on statement is, at best, a second holding statement.

Earlier, we mentioned the importance and value of a CG document. Now is the time to refer to the checklist of the leadership in the plan to confirm, for example, who will approve statements that are more detailed when you write and edit them. All the necessary information you need to contact them immediately should already be available, including cell and landline telephone and pager numbers and email addresses.

Everything you have done in advance to strengthen the understanding of the need for speed during a crisis will now return dividends.

> "In 45-years of dealing with crises, only one time have I ever had a crisis start and end during office hours, and that was a kidnapping unrelated yet affecting my organization. However, experience has shown me that you must prepare in advance. Prepare for the very worst that can happen. Train, exercise, secure leadership buy-in to handle situations. Be resilient. Only then can you survive and recover more quickly, irrespective of when the event occurs."
>
> - L. Darryl Armstrong, Ph.D., Behavioral Psychologist

BUILDING TRUST, INTEGRITY AND CREDIBILITY WITH STAKEHOLDERS AND THE MEDIA

The general public, your stakeholders and the media will determine if you are trustworthy as a crisis communicator and source for their stories.

• **Reporters need to know if you are competent.** To be seen as relevant, you must be knowledgeable and have a level of technical expertise to explain what is happening during a crisis. However, you do not want an analytical, technical person who has few social and interpersonal skills explaining what happened to the media. At least, not at first, although you may use them later as a subject-matter expert.

You do not want the president of your enterprise explaining why a sewer system design led to an explosion and release of harmful gasses. Leave that to a person that understands such systems. Nor do you want an executive apologizing for an incident who cannot show sincerity, compassion, empathy and real concern.

Your communicator during a crisis must be able to explain what happened in relatable and understandable language that behaviorally shows concern, empathy and compassion. Provide explanations in language my 80-year-old grandmother with a sixth-grade education can understand. Communicators must have a robust set of rapport-building and interpersonal skills to deliver such messages. They must be comfortable in front of a camera. They must be able to relate to how others feel in the situation.

- **You must be seen and heard as objective and fair in your analysis and communications.** The strategy is not to "to win." Instead, you are speaking to explain, educate and inform, answer tough questions and reassure the stakeholders that you have the situation under control. When a communicator approaches a crisis with anything less than transparency, openness and total honesty, no one will be capable of believing them to be objective and fair. You are not "out to win;" your job is to explain, inform and educate the audiences. The best communicators are the best teachers.

  When you demonstrate consistency in your messaging and by your behaviors and show goodwill in your sharing of information, you are behaviorally showing concern and care for others in the short- and long-term.

  There is no dishonor in admitting you do not know an answer when dealing with reporters. When you tell the media and the public, "I don't know," you are human. You must commit to getting the answer quickly, though. Then, when you get the response, you must then share it with all your audiences. This behavior enhances your trust and credibility because you kept your word.

- **You will lose credibility when you do not keep your promises, do not meet deadlines you set and do not deliver on your commitments.** If you tell the media you will hold a briefing at a specific time and for whatever reason you cannot meet the promise, you should still show up and explain why you are not yet ready to brief them.

- **How do you know you are losing credibility?** Watch for changes in the way reporters treat you. When reporters start going around you to other sources inside your organization and share information anonymously, your credibility is minimal.

Appendix I provides some additional advice on how to work more effectively with reporters.

DURING AND AFTER A CRISIS

If the crisis or emergency continues or matures, you will be conducting media briefings, interviews and possibly press conferences, which are the main entrée of the bear's meal. In press conferences and briefings, you share the verifiable and most up-to-date facts and data you have acquired. Examples of how to prepare, conduct and manage the aftermath of the interview are provided in Appendix H.

When posting statements, if you are using Twitter, use your organization's verified handle and choose a hashtag carefully, such as #EventABCCampus. Use social media information in emails and news releases. Use this information to direct the media to your Twitter and Facebook accounts and website for further background information and updates.

Realistically, you do not want anyone and everyone in a crisis to be talking to the media or the stakeholders. You want only trained and practiced spokespeople doing that job. There are occasions when your president or chief executive will need to address the media and the public. Using executives as spokespeople depends on the severe nature of the event.

Now is the time to ensure that your organization has a clearly outlined media policy. Be sure to have written and leadership-agreed-to protocols about who can speak for your institution. The guidance should tell your employees who are not spokespeople how to direct a media inquiry to your officially designated spokespeople.

You also need a well-defined social media policy tailored to your organizational needs. We recommend consulting with social media consultants and institutions relevant to your business who have been successful in deploying social media.

The dessert on the bear's menu is the media interactions in the days and weeks following the crisis. You know more about what happened. Perhaps you now understand why the event occurred. Maybe you can update the media on the condition of the people involved in the situation. Even days and weeks after the event, you can and should expect "aftershocks."

Aftershocks are inquiries and questions from reporters doing more in-depth and investigative reporting after the incident has been resolved. Think of such programs as *60 Minutes* and *20/20* as examples of media coverage that goes more in-depth. The questions asked by these reporters will be very pointed and seek information you said would be available after the incident investigation. At this time, reporters will want to know how well the organization is recovering, what went wrong, how those that were affected are recovering, why the crisis occurred and, importantly, what is being done to prevent such an event in the future.

You will have time after the crisis winds down to breathe, organize data, validate information, understand the lessons learned and prepare for the more in-depth interviews as the media engages you in aftershock questions. Use this time wisely to prepare yourself. Even organizations that handled the crisis well can and do stumble at this stage. Be mindful that on each anniversary of a significant crisis event, you can expect the media to contact you for a "reaction" or "your memories or thoughts" about the event.

MOVING FORWARD

Our final word of advice: get started now. When you plan, train and exercise for the worst possible events that can happen to you and your organization, you are prepared as well as you can be. Right now is the time to prepare yourselves to feed the bears. Bears do not forgive you when they miss a meal, and you never know when they will come calling.

In the end, perhaps the best-laid plans will require us to "improvise, adapt and overcome." However, maybe now we can do so with much more confidence.

REFERENCES

Associated Press. (2019). CEO of Texas Petrochemical Tank Facility Apologizes for Fire. Retrieved on March 28, 2020 from https://www.insurancejournal.com/news/southcentral/2019/03/29/522322.html

BCI (2018). Handling social media in a crisis: Dos and don'ts. Retrieved on February 17, 2020 from https://www.thebci.org/news/handling-social-media-in-a-crisis-dos-and-don-ts.html

Deloitte. (2014). Global survey on reputation risk. Retrieved on February 17, 2020 from https://www2.deloitte.com/content/dam/Deloitte/pl/Documents/Reports/pl_Reputation_Risk_survey_EN.pdf

Dezenhall, E., & Weber, J. (2007). *Damage control: Why everything we know about crisis management is wrong.* New York: Portfolio.

Hughes, S. (2020). Lack of women speakers spurs conference to make changes. Retrieved on February 17, 2020 from https://www.medscape.com/viewarticle/923907?src=rss

Jackson, J. (2012). 10 Communications lessons That you can learn from Harry Potter. Retrieved on February 17, 2020 from http://prsay.prsa.org/2011/08/29/10-things-that-you-can-learn-from-harry-potter/

Lillard, L. (2020) Senior Associates, Nusura Personal Interview.

Lortz, M. (2017). Crisis communications messaging best practices. Retrieved on February 17, 2020 from https://www.everbridge.com/blog/crisis-communications-best-practices/

McDonald, L. (2018). McDonald's workers in 10 cities across the U.S. to stage walkout on Tuesday calling for reform on the company's sexual harassment policy. Retrieved on February 17, 2020 from https://www.dailymail.co.uk/news/article-6161163/McDonalds-workers-strike-week-companys-sexual-harassment-policy.html

Nall, M. (2013). Rutgers PR crisis stems from months of woeful inaction. Retried on February from http://prsay.prsa.org/2013/04/08/rutgers-pr-crisis-stems-from-months-of-woeful-inaction/

Weber Shandwick (2020). Social media's role in crisis management: A call for greater legal vigilance. Retrieved on February 17, 2020 from http://webershandwick.co.uk/wp-content/uploads/2015/11/SocialMedia-Crisis-Nov4_ML.pdf

Working, R. (2018). Top 10 PR blunders of the year—so far. Retrieved on February 17, 2020 from https://www.ragan.com/top-10-pr-blunders-of-the-year-so-far/

Appendix A

Tabletop Exercises

ANTELOPE KILLER (ELEMENTARY SCHOOL)

Narrative: An elementary school encounters a problem within its community. Someone is writing notes and leaving them in the cafeteria, bathrooms and hallways. The notes included language like, "You will all die soon," "Death is here for Antelope Elementary" and "No one is safe. You will all die." Each includes a drawing of a circle with an extended plus sign through it. This causes panic and hysteria among many of the students; others joke about it and call them the AK (Antelope Killer). Some even joke about giving them suggestions on which teachers to take out first.

A student in fourth grade, Shane, is discovered leaving one of the notes. He admits to doing this and says he was just kidding and then kind of liked the attention. He is somewhat remorseful for what he did but doesn't understand why it's a such a big deal. He had been watching a documentary on the History Channel about the Zodiac Killer, and that's what gave him the idea for the symbols on the notes.

DISCUSSION QUESTIONS:

Foundational Level

1. How would you characterize these threatening notes: transient or substantive?
2. What initial risk level would you rate this case at (see Appendix J)?
3. Identify the stakeholders in this case (who it impacts). Hint, there are at least 10 groups.

Intermediate Level

4. What kind of assessment and questions would be useful to use with Shane to confirm the initial level of risk? Who would be best to ask these questions? Describe the dangers of using a mental health assessment only.

5. What referrals or sanctions would be used in this case? At what stage would parents become involved?
6. Why kind of insight would you expect from members of a BIT/CARE team? Think about psychological assessment, criminal, law enforcement, special education, case management, counseling and ADA/504.

Advanced Level

7. What are some ways the school could address the students making light of the threats?
8. How could the school address the public-relations challenges of this case (reference Chapter 12)? What are some ways to do this within the school?
9. What kind of case-management, therapeutic or mentoring support would Shane benefit from moving forward (reference Chapter 10)? List some areas to focus on to reduce future concerning behaviors as well as supporting Shane.

ANTELOPE KILLER: VRAW² SCORING

Scoring Key: 0 = Not Present; 1 = Unsure or moving toward a full 2; 2 = Present. Scores of 5 or more in each subsection indicate full endorsement for the factor.

FACTOR A: FIXATION AND FOCUS

Sub-Factor	Score	Notes
A.1: Naming of Target	1	Vague mentions of "all" and "Antelope Elementary"
A.2: Repetition of the Target	2	Repeated through multiple notes found at the school
A.3: Objectification of Target	0	No negative adjectives or descriptors
A.4: Emphasis of Target	0	No emphasis on particular groups or targets
A.5: Graphic Language	0	No graphic language related to deaths
Overall Score:	3	Factor Endorsed: No

FACTOR B: HIERARCHICAL THEMATIC CONTENT

Sub-Factor	Score	Notes
B.1: Disempowering Language	0	No mention of "less than" language
B.2: Glorified Avenger	0	No mention of motive or seeing target as "less than"
B.3: Reality Crossover	2	Actual notes found at school
B.4: Militaristic Language	0	No mention of tactical or militaristic language
B.5: Paranoid Content	0	None present
Overall Score:	2	**Factor Endorsed:** No

FACTOR C: ACTION AND TIME IMPERATIVE

Sub-Factor	Score	Notes
C.1: Location of the Attack	2	Antelope Elementary
C.2: Time of the Attack	1	Vaguely mentioned as "soon"
C.3: Weapons and Materials	0	Not mentioned
C.4: Overcoming Obstacles	0	Not mentioned
C.5: Conditional Ultimatum	0	Not mentioned
Overall Score:	3	**Factor Endorsed:** No

FACTOR D: PRE-ATTACK PLANNING

Sub-Factor	Score	Notes
D.1: Discussion and Acquisition of Weapons	0	Not mentioned
D.2: Evidence of Researching or Stalking the Target	2	Likely aware of the school and individuals
D.3: Details Concerning Target	0	None provided
D.4: Fantasy Rehearsal for Attack	1	Some elements of fantasy through creating fear and relishing in the coming panic
D.5: Costuming Description	0	Not mentioned
Overall Score:	3	**Factor Endorsed:** No

FACTOR E: INJUSTICE COLLECTING

Sub-Factor	Score	Notes
E.1: Perseverating on Past Wrongs	0	Not mentioned
E.2: Unrequited Romantic Entanglements	0	Not mentioned
E.3: Desperation, Hopelessness and Suicide Ideation/Attempt	0	Not present in notes
E.4: Amplification/Narrowing	2	Use of the Zodiac symbol
E.5: Threats to Create Justice	0	Not mentioned
Overall Score:	2	Factor Endorsed: No

Endorsed:

Not Endorsed:

- Factor A: Fixation and Focus (3)
- Factor B: Hierarchical Thematic Content (2)
- Factor C: Action and Time Imperative (3)
- Factor D: Pre-Attack Planning (3)
- Factor E: Injustice Collecting (2)

ANTELOPE KILLER: LOOKING GLASS SCORING

		Element	Rationale	Score
		Escalation Elements		
Author	1.	Suicidal Content	Not present in the example given	0
	2.	Isolation and Hopelessness	Not present in the example given	0
	3.	Fame/ Meaning-Seeking	A larger part of the transient nature of these threats combined with the Zodiac fear	2
	4.	Injustice/ Grievance-Collecting	Not present in the example given	0

continued...

		Element	Rationale	Score
Tone	5.	Hardened, Black/ White Thinking	Can be inferred from the threats and desire to kill others expressed in the note	1
	6.	Overall Graphic and Violent Descriptions	No graphic or violent content beyond a general statement of killing others	0
Content	7.	Target Detail	Mentioning of the school location, no narrowing beyond this.	2
	8.	Weapon Detail	No mentions of what weapons would be used in the attack	0
	9.	Threat Plan Detail	No detail given beyond a comment about it happening "soon"	0
	10.	Previous Attack Detail	No mention of previous attacks	0
		Escalating Total		**5**
		Mitigating Elements		
Author	1.	Trolling	This is likely a trolling case where a student is posting transient threats for a reaction	2
	2.	Developmental Delay	The student in question is young and does not appreciate the level of disruption	2
	3.	Tangential, Rambling or Incoherent	Not present in this case	0
	4.	International, Native Language	Not present in this case	0
	5.	Creative Author	Not present in this case	0
Content	6.	Writing for Class	Not for a class assignment	0
	7.	Therapeutic Journal	Not for a therapeutic process	0
	8.	Rhetoric or Opinion	Not an attempt to change opinions	0
	9.	Retaliatory Expression	Does not seem to be focused on a response to any frustration	0
	10.	Affective/Reactive	Is not an immediate reaction to an event	0
		Mitigating Total		**4**

The overall Looking Glass score is calculated by subtracting the Mitigating Elements (4) from the Escalating Elements (5), for an overall score of 1. This puts the case in the moderate category.

Score	Risk	General Summary	Suggested Interventions
-20 to -5	MILD		
-4 to 2	MODERATE	Elements of concern present in the written content or post. Consider further threat assessment and information-gathering to better assess the risk. It would be unlikely that suspension or separation would occur at that stage.	• Consider the voluntary use of violence-risk or threat assessment • Hold individualized meeting with student and parent/guardian to identify a safety plan • Discuss how to reduce triggers, increase protective factors and review/adjusted plan regularly • Use bullying protocols (if needed) • Refer for student discipline and/or behavior-management process; address emerging behaviors under an academic disruption/ discipline policy • Engage in skill-building for social and emotional learning, conflict management, interpersonal conflict resolution, problem-solving
3 to 9	ELEVATED		
10 to 20	CRITICAL		

THIS I BELIEVE (HIGH SCHOOL)

Narrative: A creative writing professor in high school follows the "This I Believe" approach (https://thisibelieve.org) and makes the following assignment to his class: write a brief, personal essay about a core belief and discuss how it was formed.

A student in class, Jack, turns in the following for the assignment:

I believe in the chaos of the Joker. I have been faking a smile for my entire existence. I am Jack's sardonic smile. I am the Joker.

I have always been alone. I've tried to make friends, but they have vandalized my heart. They have raped my soul. Women are the WHORES or the Madonna; in either case, not interested in a freak like me. Trust me, I've tried; the black pill went down easy, Mr. Rodger. Thank you, dear prophet. Be a God, and slaughter them like the sheep they are.

I am in the corner now with a gun pressed to my temple, waiting for my special day. But I am no scared animal; you sadistic pieces of SHIT. You give me stained toilet paper to clean my wounds. You have annihilated me. Destroyed my creations. So, I rise from those ashes, with my Joker's smile, to wipe you from the earth.

I will be part of something phenomenal. I will take the spotlight, smash your iPhones; I will smash you all, you jars of clay, and watch your guts spill out on the parched earth. Cognac. Your million-dollar homes. Your BMWs and Mercedes. You roll around like PIGS in your fat surpluses. I will be the clarifying fire. I am the space cowboy. I am a ghost in the machine. I am Shinji Aoba.

The things you used to own. You know what? Now they own you. The sun rises to humiliate, not bring light. I Am Jack's Smirking Revenge. You will see what comes. There will be deer grazing on the overgrown highways.

The Joker brings truth. When I was younger, I was kicked to the ground. My sign was taken and broken on the black pavement. But now, I am going to take out the clones. I am waiting for my special day. That day of retribution. The purity of the fire.

I could have left. I could have fled. Don't doubt my pain. Don't doubt my lack of purpose. Everyone assuming you are a freak for not acting like everyone else. I have run before, but I'm not running anymore. Look at my face. Your guns and filters and morals will not stop me. A metal detector does not stop the fire.

What? You don't see it? Mentally, I have carved it in. I assure you; it is there.

You will see. I am the Joker. I stand above you with my face white and lips blood-red. Knife in one hand, match in the other. I am excited for what is to come. One flip of the coin, Mr. Dent, Mr. Caleb Sharpe, and our path is determined.

I am the heat of the crucible. The time for penance has passed. None will escape the blaze.

When initially confronted by the BIT/CARE around the concerning writing sample, Jack responded with a shrug. He said, "I was asked to write how I feel. This is how I feel." Jack has a history of being edgy with his writing and interactions with teachers. He enjoys pushing limits and challenging the status quo.

DISCUSSION QUESTIONS:

Foundational Level

1. The story has concerning themes that touch in popular movies such as *Joker* and *Fight Club*, and past attacks such as Virginia Tech (Appendix B: 44), Isla Vista (Appendix B: 87),and Freeman High (Appendix B: 108). What concerns do you have when reading it? What escalates your concerns? What helps mitigate them?
2. What initial risk level would you rate this case at (see Appendix J)?
3. Identify the stakeholders in this case (who it impacts).

Intermediate Level

4. What kind of assessment (if any) would be useful to use with Jake to confirm the initial level of risk? Who would be best to complete the assessment(s)? Describe the dangers of using a mental health assessment only.
5. Would this be considered a violation of the student discipline or code of conduct at your school? Would this cross the threshold of a criminal action? Discuss the dangers of under and overreacting to this content.
6. What kind of insight would you expect from members of a BIT/CARE team? Think about psychological assessment, criminal, law enforcement, special education, case management, counseling and ADA/504.

Advanced Level

7. What are some ways to address the concerns of other students, parents or the community who learn of the story? How would the school's response differ if this occurred in an online post?
8. What kind of education and advertising does your school or school system use to ensure the teacher would share this concern forward with the BIT/ CARE team?
9. What kind of case-management, therapeutic or mentoring support would Jake benefit from moving forward (reference Chapter 10)? Identify are some individuals who could work with him to encourage his writing, but reduce his writing escalating a potential attack fantasy.

THIS I BELIEVE: VRAW² SCORING

Scoring Key: 0 = Not Present; 1 = Unsure or moving toward a full 2; 2 = Present. Scores of 5 or more in each subsection indicate full endorsement for the factor.

FACTOR A: FIXATION AND FOCUS

Sub-Factor	Score	Notes
A.1: Naming of Target	2	Implied the rich, those with privilege: "Your million-dollar homes, your BMW's and Mercedes. You roll around like PIGS in your fat surpluses..."
A.2: Repetition of the Target	2	Repeated as a theme throughout
A.3: Objectification of Target	2	"You roll around like PIGS in your fat surpluses..."
A.4: Emphasis of Target	2	"PIGS" and "SHIT" in all caps; references to "I am..." from *Fight Club* movie
A.5: Graphic Language	2	"...raped my soul...," "...stained toilet paper to clean my wounds...," "...watch your guts spill out..."
Overall Score:	10	Factor Endorsed: Yes

FACTOR B: HIERARCHICAL THEMATIC CONTENT

Sub-Factor	Score	Notes
B.1: Disempowering Language	2	"...sadistic pieces of SHIT...," "You roll around like PIGS in your fat surpluses..."
B.2: Glorified Avenger	2	Author sees protagonist as rising from pain and punishing others: "I am the heat of the crucible...," "I will be the clarifying fire..."
B.3: Reality Crossover	2	Reference to past attacker in a studio in Kyoto and amine The Space Cowboy: "I am a ghost in the machine. I am Shinji Aoba...;" reference to Freeman High attack, "One flip of the coin, Mr. Dent, Mr. Caleb Sharpe..."
B.4: Militaristic Language	1	Several mentions of fire: "A metal detector does not stop the fire...," "I am the heat of the crucible..."
B.5: Paranoid Content	1	Odd phrases: "I am the space cowboy. I am a ghost in the machine...," "Thank you, dear prophet...," "The sun rises to humiliate, not bring light..."
Overall Score:	8	Factor Endorsed: Yes

FACTOR C: ACTION AND TIME IMPERATIVE

Sub-Factor	Score	Notes
C.1: Location of the Attack	0	Not mentioned in narrative
C.2: Time of the Attack	0	Not mentioned in narrative
C.3: Weapons and Materials	2	Frequent mentions of fire: "…a gun pressed to my temple…;" references to past Kyoto fire attack
C.4: Overcoming Obstacles	2	"Your guns and filters and morals will not stop me. A metal detector does not stop the fire…"
C.5: Conditional Ultimatum	0	No way out of the pending threat: "The time for penance has passed. None will escape the blaze…"
Overall Score:	4	Factor Endorsed: No

FACTOR D: PRE-ATTACK PLANNING

Sub-Factor	Score	Notes
D.1: Acquiring Weapons	0	None mentioned
D.2: Researching the Target	0	None mentioned
D.3: Details Concerning Target:	1	Some references to the rich and privileged
D.4: Fantasy Rehearsal	2	There is a relishing quality throughout the story around righting past wrongs: "I am excited for what is to come…," "Be a God, and slaughter them like the sheep they are…"
D.5: Costuming Description	2	"…with my face white and lips blood-red…"
Overall Score:	5	Factor Endorsed: Yes

FACTOR E: INJUSTICE COLLECTING

Sub-Factor	Score	Notes
E.1: Perseverating on Past Wrongs	2	"You have annihilated me. Destroyed my creations...," "I am the heat of the crucible. The time for penance has passed..."
E.2: Unrequited Romantic Entanglements	2	"I have always been alone...," "Women are the WHORES or the Madonna; in either case, not interested in a freak like me..."
E.3: Desperation, Hopelessness and Suicide Ideation/Attempt	2	"I have always been alone...," "I am in the corner now with a gun pressed to my temple..."
E.4: Amplification/ Narrowing	1	Use of CAPS, repetitive us of *Fight Club* "I am..."
E.5: Threats to Create Justice	2	"One flip of the coin, Mr. Dent, Mr. Caleb Sharpe, and our path is determined...," "I will smash you all, you jars of clay, and watch your guts spill out on the parched earth...," "...to wipe you from the earth..."
Overall Score:	9	Factor Endorsed: Yes

Endorsed:

- Factor A: Fixation and Focus (10)
- Factor B: Hierarchical Thematic Content (8)
- Factor D: Pre-Attack Planning (5)
- Factor E: Injustice Collecting (8)

Not Endorsed:
- Factor C: Action and Time Imperative (4)

THIS I BELIEVE: LOOKING GLASS SCORING

		Element	Rationale	Score
		Escalation Elements		
Author	1.	Suicidal Content	"I am in the corner now with a gun pressed to my temple…"	1
	2.	Isolation and Hopelessness	"I have always been alone…," "You have annihilated me. Destroyed my creations…," "None will escape the blaze…"	2
	3.	Fame/ Meaning-Seeking	"You will see. I am the Joker…," "I will be part of something phenomenal. I will take the spotlight…," "I am waiting for my special day…"	2
	4.	Injustice/ Grievance-Collecting	"I was kicked to the ground. My sign was taken and broken on the black pavement…," "I am the heat of the crucible. The time for penance has passed…"	2
Tone	5.	Hardened, Black/ White Thinking	Right/wrong coin flip: "One flip of the coin, Mr. Dent, Mr. Caleb Sharpe…," "The things you used to own. You know what? Now they own you…"	1
	6.	Overall Graphic and Violent Descriptions	"I will smash you all, you jars of clay, and watch your guts spill out on the parched earth…," "You give me stained toilet paper to clean my wounds…," "Be a God, and slaughter them like the sheep they are…"	2
Content	7.	Target Detail	The rich and privileged: "Your million-dollar homes, your BMWs and Mercedes. You roll around like PIGS in your fat surpluses…"	1
	8.	Weapon Detail	Several references to the use of fire, "A metal detector does not stop the fire…"	1
	9.	Threat Plan Detail	Several references to the use of fire, "I will be the clarifying fire…," "None will escape the blaze…"	1
	10.	Previous Attack Detail	"I am Shinji Aoba…," "the black pill went down easy, Mr. Rodger…," "One flip of the coin, Mr. Dent, Mr. Caleb Sharpe,…"	2
		Escalating Total		15

continued…

		Element	Rationale	Score
		Mitigating Elements		
Author	1.	Trolling	Jack has a large history of pushing limits. While this seems to be related to his feelings, he shows responsibility around the essay.	2
	2.	Developmental Delay	While young, this does not seem to be part of this writing assignment or case.	0
	3.	Tangential, Rambling or Incoherent	The story, while disturbing, has an internal logic and references to past attacks	0
	4.	International, Native Language	Not present in this case	0
	5.	Creative Author	This seems to be a critical element in this case.	2
Content	6.	Writing for Class	This was an assignment for class. While the content was graphic and harsh, it does fit writing the parameters of the assignment.	2
	7.	Therapeutic Journal	Not for a therapeutic process	0
	8.	Rhetoric or Opinion	Not an attempt to change opinions	0
	9.	Retaliatory Expression	There are some elements in the writing that seem to relate to Jack's life and experience. This piece fits with a retaliation for past mistreatment.	2
	10.	Affective/Reactive	This seems to be more of a thoughtful and chosen writing approach, rather than something immediate and reactive.	0
		Mitigating Total		8

Final Looking Glass score is calculated by subtracting the Mitigating Elements (8) from the Escalating Elements (15), for an overall score of 7. This puts the case in the elevated category.

Score	Risk	General Summary	Suggested Interventions
-20 to -5	MILD		
-4 to 2	MODERATE		
3 to 9	ELEVATED	A higher level of concern that should trigger a required, in-person violence- or threat-assessment process. It is more likely that a suspension or separation would occur pending a mandated evaluation.	• Evaluate the need to assess immediate safety through welfare/safety check with in-house counseling staff, SRO or police • Meet with student and parent/guardian to assess and plan • Coordinate a mandated assessment with BIT/CARE staff trained in violence and/or threat assessment. • Referral to support services such as counseling, ADA/504, IEP • Coordinate transitions at beginning and end of in-school or out-of-school suspensions with school discipline • Coordinate with school resource officer, local law enforcement, etc. to discuss plan for safety, community, response, etc.
10 to 20	CRITICAL		

GET RID OF THE DAMN NIG*AS! (COLLEGE)

TRIGGER WARNING: *This case study involves extremely racist language toward the African-American community. Sadly, this kind of hatred and bigotry is common in the assessment of written threat, thus its inclusion. The authors share their apologies.*

Narrative: A community college has been receiving a series of concerning and racist emails from a current student. The student, Karl, is a 28-year-old Caucasian male majoring in business administration with a 3.2 GPA. He works part-time doing security at the local mall. It is reported he is often isolated and alone, disconnected from others and has difficulty making friends. Last month, he was admitted to the hospital for suicide attempt. He has little family support and there have been reports that he has lost his off-campus apartment and is living out of his car. A sample of the emails are included in the following text. Several Bible verses were shared graphically by the student to the conduct officer, college president and the African Student Success Program (ASSP) leadership. An example is provided here in Figure A.1.

[Email to faculty leader of ASSP]
Those student in ASSP—the fucking nig**rs who rape the pasty bitches who are now corrupt. HIVAIDS HIVRACISTHIV HIV NIG**RS HIV BURN TO THE GROUND AND SALT THE FIELDS. YOU ARE A CURSE HIV RACIST HIVHIVIV—go cut the genitals of your females you fuzzy apes. NIGNOG

[Email to college president and board of trustees]
YOU are racist. GET them NIG**RS DEAD and OFF CAMPUS. The college is a trap to keep me still. To weaken me to take me life again.

[Email to conduct officer]
You have no seat of power. You are evil and wicked. Your laws are not Gods laws. You should have not let [Leader of ASSP] try to fuck you with his floppy dick. My hard dick would have been much better for your pasty ass. You'll shout my name to the campus, bitch.

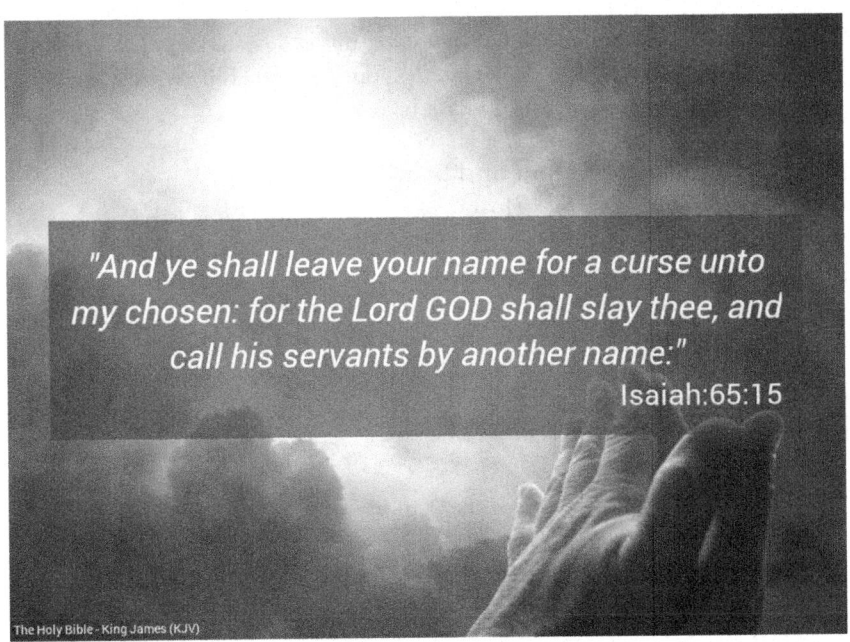

FIGURE A.1

[Email to college president]

Next time nig**r [leader of ASSP] walks into an office talking about killing someone just grab him and hold him down and slit his throat. Those brave enough and saw off his head and drag it around campus.

[Email to college president and board of trustees]

Staff Name 1; Staff Name 2; Staff Name 3

Need to die. Take them out and lynch them. They are guilty of their sins!

[Email to conduct officer]

You brought these troubles in and handled things the way you did and now it has escalated. And it wotnbe forgotten. Maybe read up on how Mr. Tarrant handled Jews and Nig**rs. Maybe I'll get me some attention like my good old boy Dylaan.

[Email to faculty leader of ASSP]

You and your nig**rs ruined my woman. But no matter, I am married to her. I should have never given you remission for your sins. Just like Cleopatra took the bite from the ASSP. There will be a reckoning. There will be justice-→ Deuteronomy 32:35

[Email to college president]

I have left the state and have no food and no money. I drove past the freeways and felt my anger at how you are killing the state, this evil [state name]. All my problems are now multiple. More bullets in the gun to my head. Now we are here and you will all will suffer your sins. I won't be overlooked.

[Email to college president and board of trustees]

Clean up your fucking campus, [name of college president]!

[Email to faculty leader of ASSP]

Stop crying victim and say its owed and due to you NIG**R ASS!!! Your boot is on my neck ready to snap it like a noose snaps a hanging corpse (Figure A.1).

Discussion questions:
Foundational Level

1. How would you characterize these threatening notes: transient or substantive (review Chapter 5)?
2. What initial risk level would you rate this case at (see Appendix J)? Discuss both the risk (Chapter 3) and protective factors (Chapter 4).
3. These threats and racist comments are obviously charged and are going to be very upsetting to members of the community. What are some initial ways your BIT/

CARE team can manage potential bias/reactive responses and remain focused on the true nature of the threat without responding to the racism and bigotry associated with it (which will be handled through student conduct separately)?

Intermediate Level

7. What kind of assessment and questions would be useful to use with Karl to confirm the initial level of risk? Who would be best to ask these questions? What are some of the challenges in talking with Karl that the interviewer would have to overcome?
8. Why would blocking Karl's ability to email faculty and staff be a cause for concern? What are some other options beyond blocking his email?
9. Discuss what departments on campus would be involved in a multidisciplinary assessment in this case.

Advanced Level

10. What are some ways the college would need to address the reasonable fear and anger of the targeted staff and African-American student groups? How does the college navigate FERPA when having these discussions?
11. How would the school approach a warning to the individuals who were threatened? To the larger community? Would a Clery Act warning be appropriate? Discuss the pros and cons of a notification of this behavior to Karl's off-campus security job. Should the school notify his supervisor?
12. Given the progressive nature of the discipline process, at what point would the college look at expelling Karl? What are some ways to mitigate the risk related to that decision (keeping him on campus, suspending or expelling)?

Get Rid of the Damn Nig**rs: VRAW^2 Scoring

Scoring Key: 0 = Not Present; 1 = Unsure or moving toward a full 2; 2 = Present. Scores of 5 or more in each subsection indicate full endorsement for the factor.

FACTOR A: FIXATION AND FOCUS

Sub-Factor	Score	Notes
A.1: Naming of Target	2	Three staff members listed in email followed with "need to die;" "those ASSP students shouldn't have raped and murdered...;" "this evil [state name]...;" "Next time nig**r [leader of ASSP] walks into an office talking about killing someone just grab him and hold him down and slit his throat. Those brave enough and saw off his head and drag it around campus...;" "Maybe read up on how Mr. Tarrant handled Jews and Nig**rs..."
A.2: Repetition of the Target	2	Repeated threats to the school president and leadership in ASSP program; "...get the nig**rs dead and off campus..."

continued...

Sub-Factor	Score	Notes
A.3: Objectification of Target	2	Frequent calling of others "nig**r;" "the college is a trap to keep me still…;" "Clean up your fucking campus, [name of college president]…;" "pasty bitches"
A.4: Emphasis of Target	2	Use of all caps, use of AIDS HIV RACIST
A.5: Graphic Language	2	Throughout the emails, "just grab him and hold him down and slit his throat. Those brave enough and saw off his head and drag it around campus…;" "go cut the genitals of your females you fuzzy apes. NIGNOG"
Overall Score:	10	Factor Endorsed: Yes

FACTOR B: HIERARCHICAL THEMATIC CONTENT

Sub-Factor	Score	Notes
B.1: Disempowering Language	2	Frequent "nig**r;" "pasty bitches;" "floppy dick"
B.2: Glorified Avenger	2	"Now we are here, and you will all suffer for your sin…;" "You brought these troubles in and handled things the way you did and now it has escalated. And it wotnbe forgotten. Maybe read up on how Mr. Tarrant handled Jews and Nig**rs. Maybe I'll get me some attention like my good old boy Dylaan…;" "There will be a reckoning. There will be justice-→ Deuteronomy 32:35…"
B.3: Reality Crossover	2	Actual emails with names of students, faculty and staff mentioned; "this evil [state name]…;" "Maybe read up on how Mr. Tarrant handled Jews and Nig**rs…" (Christchurch attack reference); Maybe I'll get me some attention like my good old boy Dylaan…;" (Charleston church attack)
B.4: Militaristic Language	1	Brief mention of Christchurch and Charleston attacks
B.5: Paranoid Content	2	"You brought these troubles in and handled things the way you did and now it has escalated. And it wotnbe forgotten…;" "You and your nig**rs ruined my woman…" (referring to a past female student); "I am married to her…" (he is not); "You have no seat of power…"
Overall Score:	9	Factor Endorsed: Yes

FACTOR C: ACTION AND TIME IMPERATIVE

Sub-Factor	Score	Notes
C.1: Location of the Attack	0	Not mentioned directly
C.2: Time of the Attack	0	Not mentioned directly
C.3: Weapons and Materials	0	Not mentioned directly
C.4: Overcoming Obstacles	0	No mentioning of overcoming obstacles
C.5: Conditional Ultimatum	2	Frequent mentions of removing black students to campus or order to avoid punishment
Overall Score:	2	**Factor Endorsed:** No

FACTOR D: PRE-ATTACK PLANNING

Sub-Factor	Score	Notes
D.1: Discussion and Acquisition of Weapons	0	No direct weapons mentioned
D.2: Evidence of Researching or Stalking the Target	1	There is connection to targets, but no mention of stalking; the harassing emails seem to indicate a personal knowledge, "You are evil and wicked. Your laws are not Gods laws..."
D.3: Details Concerning Target:	0	No personal details about targets
D.4: Fantasy Rehearsal for Attack	1	Some fantasy-based language and desire to make things right; "You should have not let [Leader of ASSP] try to fuck you with his floppy dick. My hard dick would have been much better for your pasty ass...;" Bible verse picture shared Isaiah 65:15, "... for the lord GOD shall slay thee...;" "You are evil and wicked. Your laws are not Gods laws..."
D.5: Costuming Description	0	No costuming
Overall Score:	2	**Factor Endorsed:** No

FACTOR E: INJUSTICE COLLECTING

Sub-Factor	Score	Notes
E.1: Perseverating on Past Wrongs	2	Frequently mentioned in emails; "Stop crying victim and say its owed and due to you NIG**R ASS!!! Your boot is on my neck ready to snap it like a noose snaps a hanging corpse..."
E.2: Unrequited Romantic Entanglements	1	No direct comments about the women he is interested in rejected him, but a consistent feeling that others [nig**rs] are keeping him from his relationships; "You and your nig**rs ruined my woman... "
E.3: Desperation, Hopelessness, and Suicide Ideation/Attempt	2	Past suicide attempt last month; "To weaken me to take me life again...;" "Your boot is on my neck ready to snap it like a noose snaps a hanging corpse..."
E.4: Amplification/ Narrowing	2	Narrowing on targets throughout, specific names mentioned frequently, emails directly to conduct officer and potential sexual threats; "You should have not let [Leader of ASSP] try to fuck you with his floppy dick. My hard dick would have been much better for your pasty ass...;" "You and your nig**rs ruined my woman... "
E.5: Threats to Create Justice	2	Frequent and throughout emails with references to god punishing; "I should have never given you remission for your sins...;" "get the nig**rs dead and off campus...;" "Just like Cleopatra took the bite from the ASSP. There will be a reckoning. There will be justice-→ Deuteronomy 32:35..."
Overall Score:	9	Factor Endorsed: Yes

Endorsed:
- Factor A: Fixation and Focus (10)
- Factor B: Hierarchical Thematic Content (9)
- Factor E: Injustice Collecting (9)

Not Endorsed:
- Factor C: Action and Time Imperative (2)
- Factor D: Pre-Attack Planning (2)

GET RID OF THE DAMN NIG**RS: LOOKING GLASS SCORING

		Element	Rationale	Score
		Escalation Elements		
Author	1.	Suicidal Content	Suicide attempt last month; "To weaken me to take me life again...;" "Your boot is on my neck ready to snap it like a noose snaps a hanging corpse...;" "All my problems are now multiple. More bullets in the gun to my head..."	2
	2.	Isolation and Hopelessness	Repetitive theme and mentioned directly during phone discussion with BIT/CARE staff when reviewing the case; "Your boot is on my neck ready to snap it like a noose snaps a hanging corpse..."	2
	3.	Fame / Meaning-Seeking	"Maybe I'll get me some attention like my good old boy Dylaan... " (referencing Charleston attack); "You'll shout my name to the campus, bitch...;" "Now we are here and you will all will suffer your sins. I won't be overlooked..."	2
	4.	Injustice/ Grievance-Collecting	Consistently mentioned through fear nig**rs are impregnating his "pasty" bitches; upset at lack of attention to his needs; "Stop crying victim and say its owed and due to you NIG**R ASS!!! Your boot is on my neck ready to snap it... "	2
Tone	5.	Hardened, Black/ White Thinking	Inflexible opinions expressed about racial inequity and lack of attention from the school; "You and your nig**rs ruined my woman" (referring to a past female student); "Maybe read up on how Mr. Tarrant handled Jews and Nig**rs;" "YOU ARE A CURSE HIV RACIST HIVHIVIV"	2

continued...

		Element	Rationale	Score
	6.	Overall Graphic and Violent Descriptions	"...just grab him and hold him down and slit his throat. Those brave enough and saw off his head and drag it around campus...;" "Your boot is on my neck ready to snap it...;" "...go cut the genitals of your females you fuzzy apes..."	2
Content	7.	Target Detail	Three staff members listed in email followed with "need to die;" "those ASSP students shouldn't have raped and murdered...;" "evil [state named]..."; "Next time nig**r [leader of ASSP] walks into an office talking about killing someone just grab him and hold him down and slit his throat. Those brave enough and saw off his head and drag it around campus...;" "Need to die. Take them out and lynch them. They are guilty of their sins!..."	2
	8.	Weapon Detail	No mentions of what weapons would be used in the attack	0
	9.	Threat Plan Detail	No detail given about the threat	0
	10.	Previous Attack Detail	"Maybe I'll get me some attention like my good old boy Dylaan..." (referencing Charleston attack); Just like Cleopatra took the bite from the ASSP. There will be a reckoning. There will be justice--→ Deuteronomy 32:35..."; Maybe read up on how Mr. Tarrant handled Jews and Nig**rs..." (Christchurch attack reference)	2
			Escalating Total	16
		Mitigating Elements		
Author	1.	Trolling	There is some evidence of trolling with the repetitive, single-sentence emails back and forth with staff members	1
	2.	Developmental Delay	Does not seem present in this case	0

continued...

		Element	Rationale	Score
	3.	Tangential, Rambling or Incoherent	There is a stark shift in email tone between examples 1-3 and 4-9; Rambling, disconnected thoughts expressed; "I am married to her..." (he is not); "you have no seat of power...;" "You and your nig**rs ruined my woman..."	2
	4.	International, Native Language	Not present in this case	0
	5.	Creative Author	Not present in this case	0
Content	6.	Writing for Class	Not for a class assignment	0
	7.	Therapeutic Journal	Not for a therapeutic process	0
	8.	Rhetoric or Opinion	Some evidence of politized, white-supremist viewpoints, but advocating violence negates scoring here	0
	9.	Retaliatory Expression	Less a reaction to gain face, more emotional in reactions; some threats are related to past wrongs perceived or experienced; "Now we are here, and you will all suffer for your sin..."	1
	10.	Affective/Reactive	Consistent history of vague, disorganized and transient threats, that while concerning, lack a substantive quality; "You should have not let [Leader of ASSP] try to fuck you with his floppy dick. My hard dick would have been much better for your pasty ass...;" "Next time nig**r [leader of ASSP] walks into an office talking about killing someone just grab him and hold him down and slit his throat. Those brave enough and saw off his head and drag it around campus..."	2
			Mitigating Total	6

Final Looking Glass score is calculated by subtracting the Mitigating Elements (6) from the Escalating Elements (16), for an overall score of 10. This puts the case in the critical category.

Score	Risk	General Summary	Suggested Interventions
-20 to -5	MILD		
-4 to 2	MODERATE		
3 to 9	ELEVATED		
10 to 20	CRITICAL	Highest level of concern, indicating many of the elements in the writing sample match previous attackers' writings. Likely removal of student from campus, coordination with police around arrest and mental health professionals around involuntary admission.	• Immediate wellness check/ initiate evaluation for involuntary hold/initiate suicide protocols • Required contact with parent/ emergency contact • Evaluate need for emergency notification to school community or to specific, impacted parties • Initiate mandated assessment once immediate safety has been established • Determine and share process of assessment and action-planning with parent/guardian • Coordinate with necessary parties (school resource officer, local law enforcement, FUSION center, discipline, legal and/or threat consult, etc.) to create plan for safety, response, interventions, suspension, etc. • Connect with off-campus resources as appropriate such as case manager, child protective services, juvenile justice • Provide guidance, support, and safety planning to impacted parties, such as teachers and other students

Appendix B

Case Review of Attacks and Social Media Threats

1. 08/01/66: University of Texas Tower Shooting, Austin, Texas
2. 12/30/74: Olean High School Shooting, Olean, New York
3. 05/28/75: Brampton Centennial Shooting, Brampton, Ontario, Canada
4. 05/20/88: Hubbard Woods Elementary School Shooting, Winnetka, Illinois
5. 09/14/89: Standard Gravure Shooting, Louisville, Kentucky
6. 09/18/89: Jackson County High School, McKee, Kentucky
7. 12/06/89: École Polytechnique Massacre, Montreal, Quebec, Canada
8. 11/01/91: University of Iowa Shooting, Iowa City, Iowa
9. 08/24/92: University Shooting, Montreal, Quebec, Canada
10. 01/18/93: East Carter High School Shooting, Grayson, Kentucky
11. 03/25/94: Etowah High School Shooting, Woodstock, Georgia
12. 04/19/95: Oklahoma City Bombing, Oklahoma City, Oklahoma
13. 02/02/96: Frontier Middle School Shooting, Moses Lake, Washington
14. 03/13/96: Dunblane Massacre, Dunblane, Scotland
15. 02/19/97: Bethel Regional Shooting, Bethel, Alaska
16. 10/01/97: Pearl High School Shooting, Pearl, Mississippi
17. 12/01/97: Heath High School Shooting, West Paducah, Kentucky
18. 04/24/98: Parker Middle School Dance Shooting, Edinboro, Pennsylvania
19. 05/20–21/98: Thurston High School Shooting, Springfield, Oregon
20. 04/20/99: Columbine Shooting, Littleton, Colorado
21. 07/27–29/99: Atlanta Day Trading Shootings, Atlanta, Georgia
22. 01/30/01: De Anza College Thwarted Attack, Cupertino, California
23. 03/05/01: Santana High School Shooting, Santee, California
24. 10/28/02: Arizona Nursing College Shooting, Tucson, Arizona
25. 05/09/03: Case Western Reserve University Shooting, Cleveland, Ohio
26. 09/24/03: Rocori High School Shooting, Cold Spring, Minnesota
27. 10/03: H.B. Thompson Middle School Horror Movie, Syosset, New York
28. 02/09/04: Columbia High School Shooting, East Greenbush, New York

29. 03/16/04: Malcolm High School Thwarted Attack, Malcolm, Nebraska
30. 02/04: St. Paul Harding High School Threat, St. Paul, Minnesota
31. 10/14/04: Humbolt High School Poetry, St. Paul, Minnesota
32. 03/21/05: Red Lake Reservation High School Shooting, Red Lake, Minnesota
33. 11/08/05: Campbell County High School Shooting, Jacksboro, Tennessee
34. 01/30/06: Goleta Postal Service Shootings, Goleta, California
35. 04/23/06: Puyallup Threat, Puyallup, Washington
36. 08/30/06: Orange High School Patricide Attack, Hillsborough, North Carolina
37. 09/02/06: Shepherd University Shootings, Shepherdstown, West Virginia
38. 09/13/06: Dawson College Shooting, Montreal, Quebec, Canada
39. 09/14/06: Bay East High School Threat, Green Bay, Wisconsin
40. 09/27/06: Platte Canyon School Hostage Crisis, Bailey, Colorado
41. 09/29/06: Weston High School Shooting, Cazenovia, Wisconsin
42. 10/02/06: Amish Schoolhouse Shooting, Nickel Mines, Pennsylvania
43. 11/20/06: Emsdetten School Shooting, North Rhine, Germany
44. 04/16/07: Virginia Tech Shooting, Blacksburg, Virginia
45. 04/23/07: Cary-Grove High School Essay, Cary, Illinois
46. 10/10/07: Plymouth Whitemarsh Thwarting, Plymouth Meeting, Pennsylvania
47. 11/07/07: Jokela School Shooting, Jokela, Tuusula, Finland
48. 12/07: University of Arkansas Threat, Fayetteville, Arkansas
49. 02/14/08: Northern Illinois Shooting, DeKalb, Illinois
50. 06/04/08: Penn High School Thwarted Attack, South Bend, Indiana
51. 09/23/08: Kauhajoki School Shooting, Kauhajoki, Western Finland, Finland
52. 03/17/09: Attleborough Academy Threat, Norfolk, England
53. 04/03/09: American Civic Association Immigration Center, Binghamton, New York
54. 04/10/09: Henry Ford Community College Shooting, Dearborn, Michigan
55. 05/18/09: Larose Cut Off Middle School Attack, Larose, Louisiana
56. 08/04/09: LA Fitness/Collier Shooting, Collier, Pennsylvania
57. 11/05/09: Fort Hood Shooting, Killeen, Texas
58. 11/17/09: Beauvais Thwarted Attack, Beauvais, France
59. 12/09: Mortuary Trocar Threat, Minneapolis, Minnesota
60. 02/12/10: University of Alabama Shooting, Huntsville, Alabama
61. 02/18/10: Austin IRS Plane Attack, Austin, Texas
62. 02/23/10: Deer Creek Middle School Shooting, Littleton, Colorado
63. 10/26/10: Combat Vet Essay, Baltimore, Maryland
64. 12/10/10: Elonis v. U.S., Bethlehem, Pennsylvania
65. 12/14/10: School Board Shooting, Panama City, Florida
66. 01/05/11: Millard High School Shooting, Omaha, Nebraska
67. 01/08/11: Tucson Shooting, Tucson, Arizona
68. 04/07/11: Rio de Janeiro Shooting, Rio de Janeiro, Brazil
69. 04/29/11: University of Central Arkansas, Conway, Arkansas

70. 07/22/11: Norway Attacks, Oslo and Utoya Island, Norway
71. 08/17/11: Freedom High Thwarted Attack, Tampa, Florida
72. 01/29/12: UMass, Tyler Molander Letter, Amherst, Massachusetts
73. 02/27/12: Chardon High School Shooting, Chardon, Ohio
74. 07/20/12: Aurora Theater Shooting, Aurora, Colorado
75. 12/14/12: Sandy Hook Shooting, Newtown, Connecticut
76. 01/10/13: Taft Union High School Shooting, Kern, California
77. 05/27/13: West Albany Bomb Plot, Albany, Oregon
78. 06/27/13: League of Legends Threat, San Antonio, Texas
79. 07/03/13: University of Washington Thwarted Attack, Seattle, Washington
80. 10/21/13: Sparks Middle School Shooting, Sparks, Nevada
81. 12/13/13: Arapahoe High School Shooting, Centennial, Colorado
82. 01/28/14: Verona Area High School Threat, Verona, Wisconsin
83. 03/14: Loughborough Attempted Attack, Leicestershire, England
84. 03/04/14: Columbine Obsession, Danbury High School, Danbury, Connecticut
85. 04/09/14: Franklin Regional High School Stabbing, Murrysville, Pennsylvania
86. 04/29/14: Waseca High School Shooting Plot, Waseca, Minnesota
87. 05/23/14: Isla Vista Killings, Isla Vista, California
88. 05/31/14: Slender Man Attack, Waukesha, Wisconsin
89. 05/31/14: FSU Strozier Library Shooting, Tallahassee, Florida
90. 06/05/14: Seattle Pacific University Shooting, Seattle, Washington
91. 06/08/14: Las Vegas Walmart Shootings, Las Vegas, Nevada
92. 10/24/14: Marysville Pilchuck High School Shooting, Marysville, Washington
93. 11/03/14: Newcastle College Plot, Newcastle Upon Tyne, United Kingdom
94. 06/17/15: Charleston Church Shooting, Charleston, South Carolina
95. 08/26/15: Live TV Shooting, Roanoke, Virginia
96. 10/01/15: Umpqua Community College, Roseburg, Oregon
97. 10/02/15: 4chan Threat, Philadelphia, Pennsylvania
98. 11/17/15: Kean University Twitter Threats, Union, New Jersey
99. 01/04/16: Columbia South Carolina Bomb Threats, Columbia, South Carolina
100. 02/12/16: Independence High School Murder Suicide, Glendale, Arizona
101. 02/29/16: Madison Junior-Senior High School, Middletown, Ohio
102. 09/22/16: Fargo South High Threat, Fargo, North Dakota
103. 01/01/17: West Liberty-Salem High School Attack, Salem, Ohio
104. 03/13/17: Greenwood County Facebook Threat, Greenwood County, South Carolina
105. 03/15/17: Ware Shoals Threat, Greenwood County, South Carolina
106. 05/26/17: Portland Train Attack, Portland, Oregon
107. 06/08/17: Weis Market Attack, Eaton Township, Pennsylvania
108. 09/13/17: Freeman High School Shooting, Rockford, Washington
109. 10/01/17: Las Vegas Music Festival Shooting, Las Vegas, Nevada
110. 10/03/17: San Antonio Strip Threat, San Antonio, Texas

111. 11/05/17: Sutherland Texas Shooting, Sutherland Springs, Texas
112. 12/07/17: Aztec High School, Aztec, New Mexico
113. 01/23/18: Marshall County High School Shooting, Benton, Kentucky
114. 02/14/18: Stoneman Douglas High School Shooting, Parkland, Florida
115. 02/14/18: ACES Alternative High School Plot, Everett, Washington
116. 02/15/18: Fair Haven School Shooting Threat, Fair Haven, Vermont
117. 02/15/18: Broome High Snapchat Threat, Spartanburg, South Carolina
118. 02/15/18: Belton-Honea Path Threat, Honea Path, South Carolina
119. 02/16/18: Abbeville High Bomb Threat, Abbeville, South Carolina
120. 02/18/18: Jessamine County Snapchat Threat, Nicholasville, Kentucky
121. 02/18/18: Broome High Copycat Threat, St. Petersburg, Florida
122. 02/19/18: Conway Jr High Threat, Conway, Arkansas
123. 02/19/18: Mountain Pine School District Threat, Mountain Pine, Arkansas
124. 02/19/18: Calhoun Falls Charter School Bomb Threat, Calhoun Falls, South Carolina
125. 02/19–20/18: Westview Middle School Bomb Threat, Goose Creek, South Carolina
126. 03/2–21/18: Austin Serial Bombings, Austin, Texas
127. 03/27/18: Upper Darby Threat, Drexel Hill, Pennsylvania
128. 04/20/18: Forest High School, Ocala, Florida
129. 05/18/18: Santa Fe High School, Santa Fe, Texas
130. 05/25/18: Noblesville West Middle School, Noblesville, Indiana
131. 05/30/18: Spanish River Snapchat Threat, Boca Raton, Florida
132. 06/04/18: Buchanan High School Threat, Clovis, California
133. 10/18: Shelby County High Threat, Lawrenceburg, Kentucky
134. 10/24/18: Bartow Florida Satanic Killer Thwarted Attack, Bartow, Florida
135. 10/27/18: Pittsburgh Synagogue Shooting, Pittsburgh, Pennsylvania
136. 10/22/18–11/01/18: United States Attempted Mail Bombing, Aventura, Florida
137. 12/08/18: Toledo Plot, Toledo, Ohio
138. 03/15/19: Christchurch Shootings, Christchurch, New Zealand
139. 04/07/19: Bonita Vista High Threat, Chula Vista, California
140. 04/26/19: Christchurch Revenge Plot, Los Angeles area, California
141. 04/30/19: UNCC Shooting, Charlotte, North Carolina
142. 05/20/19: Wiregrass Ranch High Threat, Wesley Chapel, Florida
143. 08/03/19: El Paso Walmart Shooting, El Paso, Texas
144. 08/05/19: Texas Grandma Thwarted Threat, Lubbock, Texas
145. 08/06/19: Florida Walmart Threat, Winter Park, Florida
146. 08/10/19: Texas Walmart Threat, Harlingen, Texas
147. 08/12/19: School Rezoning Threat, Lake Worth Beach, Florida
148. 08/12/19: Charles Town Threat, Charles Town, Virginia
149. 08/14/19: Albert Lea Threat, Albert Lea, Minnesota

150. 08/14/19: iFunny Threat, Boardman, Ohio
151. 08/15/19: Oakwood High Snapchat, Oakwood, Ohio
152. 08/15/19: Norwalk CT Thwarted Attack, Norwalk, Connecticut
153. 08/16/19: Edison High School Snapchat Threat, Fresno, California
154. 08/16/19: Volusia County Threat, Volusia County, Florida
155. 08/16/19: Claremore Facebook Threat, Claremore, Oklahoma
156. 08/18/19: Daytona Beach Text Threat, Daytona Beach, Florida
157. 08/19/19: Perry County Threat, Hazard, Kentucky
158. 08/19/19: Maui Tweet, Kahului, Hawaii
159. 08/19/19: Rapid City Threat, Rapid City, South Dakota
160. 08/20/19: UHD Snapchat Threat, Houston, Texas
161. 08/21/19: Marriott Threat, Long Beach, California
162. 08/21/19: Chicago Women's Reproductive Health Clinic Threat, Chicago, Illinois
163. 08/22/19: Nova High School Threat, Davie, Florida
164. 08/22/19: St. Mary Magdalen Threat, Altamonte Springs, Florida
165. 08/22/19: Burns Middle School Snapchat Threat, Brandon, Florida
166. 08/28/19: Gulf Coast High Snapchat Threat, Naples, Florida
167. 08/28/19: High Point University Threat, High Point, North Carolina
168. 08/29/19: St. Paul Threat, St. Paul, Minnesota
169. 09/08/19: Desert Hot Springs High School Threat, Desert Hot Springs, California
170. 09/13/19: Christopher Columbus High School Threat, Miami, Florida
171. 09/13/19: Gloucester Plot, Gloucester, England
172. 09/15/19: McAlester High Threat, McAlester, Oklahoma
173. 09/17/19: College Place High Threat, Walla Walla, Washington
174. 09/19/19: Riverside Middle School Snapchat, Watertown, Wisconsin
175. 09/24/19: Great Oak High School Threat, Temecula, California
176. 10/07/19: Lake Worth High School Snapchat Threat, Lake Worth Beach, Florida
177. 10/20/19: Albany High School, Albany, New York
178. 10/24/19: Cedar Ridge High School, Hillsborough, North Carolina
179. 10/27/19: Elmhurst College, Elmhurst, Illinois
180. 11/19: Valley Forge Kindergartener, Valley Forge, Pennsylvania
181. 11/01/19: Concord High Threat, Concord, New Hampshire
182. 11/01/19: Pizza Inn Shooting Threat, McAlester, Oklahoma
183. 11/05/19: West Hills College Threat, Lemoore, California
184. 11/06/19: Albion Middle School Threat, Orleans County, New York
185. 11/14/19: Saugus High School Shooting, Santa Clarita, California
186. 11/18/19: Ramona High School Threat, Riverside, California
187. 11/21/19: St. Mary's College, Moraga, California
188. 11/23/19: Ánimo Mae Jemison Charter Middle School, Los Angeles, California

189. 11/26/19: Tokay High Bathroom Wall, Lodi, California
190. 12/01/19: Cypress Bay High School Threat, Weston, Florida
191. 12/03/19: Estancia High Threats, Orange County, California
192. 12/06/19: Naval Air Base Shooting, Pensacola, Florida
193. 12/06/19: Falcon Cove Middle School Threat, Weston, Florida
194. 12/09/19: DeSoto Bathroom Threat, DeSoto, Texas
195. 12/11/19: Lakeland High School Threat, Suffolk, Virginia
196. 12/12/19: Henry M. Gunn Senior High School, Palo Alto, California
197. 12/16/19: Volusia County Threat, Volusia County, Florida
198. 01/03/20: Gulf Coast High Yolo Threat, Naples, Florida
199. 01/05/20: Napoleon Community Schools, Napoleon, Michigan
200. 01/19/20: Warrensburg High School, Warrensburg, New York
201. 01/22/20: Tallahassee Airport Graffiti, Tallahassee, Florida
202. 01/28/20: Waterloo Community School Bomb Threat, Waterloo, Iowa
203. 01/19/20: Huntsville High School, Huntsville, Alabama
204. 02/10/20: North Dorchester High School Threat, Dorchester County, Maryland
205. 02/12/20: School for Creative and Performing Arts Threat, Cincinnati, Ohio
206. 02/14/20: Mainland High School Threat, Daytona Beach, Florida

13 Reasons Why Netflix Series

Considerations for Educators

Schools have an important role in preventing youth suicide and being aware of potential risk factors in students' lives is vital to this responsibility. The trending Netflix series *13 Reasons Why,* based on a young-adult novel of the same name, is raising such concerns. The series revolves around 17-year-old Hannah Baker, who takes her own life and leaves behind audio recordings for 13 people who she says in some way were part of why she killed herself. Each tape recounts painful events in which one or more of the 13 individuals played a role.

Producers for the show say they hope the series can help those who may be struggling with thoughts of suicide. However, the series, which many teenagers are binge-watching without adult guidance and support, is raising concerns from suicide-prevention experts about the potential risks posed by the sensationalized treatment of youth suicide. The series graphically depicts a suicide death and addresses in wrenching detail a number of difficult topics, such a bullying, rape, drunk driving and slut-shaming. The series also highlights the consequences of teenagers witnessing assaults and bullying (i.e., bystanders) and not taking action to address the situation (e.g., not speaking out against the incident, not telling an adult about the incident).

CAUTIONS

We do not recommend that vulnerable youth, especially those who have any degree of suicidal ideation, watch this series. Its powerful storytelling may lead impressionable viewers to romanticize the choices made by the characters and/ or develop revenge fantasies. They may easily identify with the experiences portrayed and recognize both the intentional and unintentional effects on the central character. Unfortunately, adult characters in the show, including the second school counselor who inadequately addresses Hannah's pleas for help, do not inspire a sense of trust or ability to help. Hannah's parents are also unaware of the events that lead to her suicide death.

While many youths are resilient and capable of differentiating between a TV drama and real life, engaging in thoughtful conversations with them about the show is vital. Doing so presents an opportunity to help them process the issues addressed, consider the consequences of certain choices and reinforce the message that suicide is not a solution to problems and that help is available. **This is particularly important for adolescents who are isolated, struggling or vulnerable to suggestive images and storylines.** Research shows that exposure to another person's suicide, or to graphic or sensationalized accounts of death, can be one of the many risk factors that youth struggling with mental health conditions cite as a reason they contemplate or attempt suicide.

What the series does accurately convey is that there is no single cause of suicide. Indeed, there are likely as many different pathways to suicide as there are suicide deaths. However, the series does not emphasize that common among most suicide deaths is the presence of treatable mental illnesses. Suicide is **not** the simple consequence of stressors or coping challenges, but rather, it is most typically a combined result of treatable mental illnesses and overwhelming or intolerable stressors.

School psychologists and other school-employed mental health professionals can assist stakeholders (e.g., school administrators, parents and teachers) to engage in supportive conversations with students as well as provide resources and offer expertise in preventing harmful behaviors.

Guidance for Educators

1. While we do not recommend that all students view this series, it can be appreciated as an opportunity to better understand young people's experiences, thoughts and feelings. Children and youth who view this series will need supportive adults to process it. Take this opportunity to both prevent the risk of harm and identify ongoing social and behavioral problems in the school community that may need to be addressed.
2. Help students articulate their perceptions when viewing controversial content, such as *13 ReasonsWhy*. The difficult issues portrayed do occur in schools and communities, and it is important for adults to listen, take adolescents' concerns seriously and be willing to offer to help.
3. Reinforce that school-employed mental health professionals are available to help. Emphasize that the behavior of the second counselor in the series is understood by virtually all school-employed mental health professionals as inappropriate. It is important that all school-employed mental health professionals receive training in suicide risk assessment.
4. Make sure parents, teachers and students are aware of suicide-risk warning signs. **Always take warning signs seriously, and never promise to**

keep them secret. Establish a confidential reporting mechanism for students. Common signs include:

- Suicide threats, both direct ("I am going to kill myself," "I need life to stop") and indirect ("I need it to stop," "I wish I could fall asleep and never wake up"). Threats can be verbal or written, and they are often found in online postings.
- Giving away prized possessions.
- Preoccupation with death in conversation, writing, drawing and social media.
- Changes in behavior, appearance/hygiene, thoughts and/or feelings. This can include someone who is typically sad who suddenly becomes extremely happy.
- Emotional distress.

5. Students who feel suicidal are not likely to seek help directly; however, parents, school personnel and peers can recognize the warning signs and take immediate action to keep the youth safe. When a student gives signs that they may be considering suicide, take the following actions:
   - Remain calm, be nonjudgmental and listen. Strive to understand the intolerable emotional pain that has resulted in suicidal thoughts.
   - Avoid statements that might be perceived as minimizing the student's emotional pain (e.g., "You need to move on," or "You should get over it").
   - Ask the student **directly** if they are thinking about suicide (i.e., "Are you thinking of suicide?").
   - Focus on your concern for their wellbeing and avoid being accusatory.
   - Reassure the student that there is help and they will not feel like this forever.
   - Provide constant supervision. **Do not leave the student alone.**
   - Without putting yourself in danger, remove means for self-harm, including any weapons the person might find.
   - **Get help.** Never agree to keep a student's suicidal thoughts a secret. Instead, school staff should take the student to a school-employed mental health professional. Parents should seek help from school or community mental health resources. Students should tell an appropriate caregiving adult, such as a school psychologist, administrator, parent or teacher.

6. School or district officials should determine how to handle memorials after a student has died. Promote memorials that benefit others (e.g., donations for a suicide prevention program) and activities that foster a sense of hope and encourage positive action. The memorial should not glorify, highlight or accentuate the individual's death. It may lead to imitative behaviors or a suicide contagion (Brock et al., 2016).

7. Reinforcing resiliency factors can lessen the potential of risk factors that lead to suicidal ideation and behaviors. Once a child or adolescent is considered

at-risk, schools, families and friends should work to build these factors in and around the youth:

- Family support and cohesion, including good communication.
- Peer support and close social networks.
- School and community connectedness.
- Cultural or religious beliefs that discourage suicide and promote healthy living.
- Adaptive coping and problem-solving skills, including conflict resolution.
- General life satisfaction, good self-esteem and a sense of purpose.
- Easy access to effective medical and mental health resources.

8. Strive to ensure that **all** student spaces on campus are monitored and that the school environment is truly safe, supportive and free of bullying.
9. If additional guidance is needed, ask for support from your building- or district-level crisis team. The team may be able to assist with addressing unique situations affecting your building.

See Preventing Suicide: Guidelines for Administrators and Crisis Teams for additional guidance.

Suicide Awareness Voices of Education (SAVE) and the JED Foundation have created talking points for conversations with youth specific to the *13 Reasons Why* series, available online.

GUIDANCE FOR FAMILIES

1. Ask your child if they have heard or seen the series *13 Reasons Why*. While we don't recommend that they be encouraged to view the series, do tell them you want to watch it with them or to catch up, and discuss their thoughts.
2. If they exhibit any of the warning signs above, don't be afraid to ask if they have thought about suicide or if someone is hurting them. Raising the issue of suicide does not increase the risk or plant the idea. On the contrary, it creates the opportunity to offer help.
3. Ask your child if they think any of their friends or classmates exhibit warning signs. Talk with them about how to seek help for their friend or classmate. Guide them on how to respond when they see or hear any of the warning signs.
4. Listen to your children's comments without judgment. Doing so requires that you fully concentrate, understand, respond and then remember what is being said. Put your own agenda aside.
5. Get help from a school-employed or community-based mental health professional if you are concerned for your child's safety or the safety of one of their peers.

See Preventing Youth Suicide Brief Facts (also available in Spanish) and Preventing Youth Suicide: Tips or Parents and Educators for additional information.

SAFE MESSAGING FOR STUDENTS

1. **Suicide is never a solution. It is an irreversible choice regarding a temporary problem. There is help. If you are struggling with thoughts of suicide or know someone who is, talk to a trusted adult, call 1-800-273-TALK (8255) or text "START" to 741741.**
2. Don't be afraid to talk to your friends about how they feel and let them know you care about them.
3. Be an "upstander" and take actions to reduce bullying and increase positive connections among others. Report concerns.
4. Never promise to keep secret behaviors that represent a danger towards another person.
5. **Suicide is preventable.** People considering suicide typically say something or do something that is a warning sign. Always take warning signs seriously and know the warning signs.
    *   Suicide threats, both direct ("I am going to kill myself") and indirect ("I wish I could fall asleep and never wake up"). Can be verbal, written or posted online.
    *   Suicide notes and planning, including online postings.
    *   Preoccupation with death in conversation, writing, drawing and social media.
    *   Changes in behavior, appearance/hygiene, thoughts and/or feelings.
    *   Emotional distress.
6. Separate myths and facts.
    *   **MYTH:** Talking about suicide will make someone choose death by suicide who has never thought about it before. **FACT:** There is no evidence to suggest that talking about suicide plants the idea. Talking with your friend about how they feel and letting them know that you care about them is important. This is the first step in getting your friend help.
    *   **MYTH:** People who struggle with depression or other mental illness are just weak. **FACT:** Depression and other mental illnesses are serious health conditions and are treatable.
    *   **MYTH:** People who talk about suicide won't really do it. **FACT:** People, particularly young people who are thinking about suicide, typically demonstrate warning signs. Always take these warning signs seriously.
7. **Never leave the person alone; seek out a trusted adult immediately.** School-employed mental health professionals like your school psychologist are trusted sources of help.

8. Work with other students and the adults in the school if you want to develop a memorial for someone who has died by suicide. Although decorating a student's locker, creating a memorial social media page or other similar activities are quick ways to remember the student who has died, they may influence others to imitate or have thoughts of wanting to die as well. It is recommended that schools develop memorial activities that encourage hope and promote positive outcomes for others (e.g., suicide-prevention programs).

Read these helpful points from SAVE.org and the JED Foundation to further understand how *13 Reasons Why* dramatizes situations and the realities of suicide. See Save a Friend: Tips for Teens to Prevent Suicide for additional information.

ADDITIONAL RESOURCES

- National Suicide Prevention Hotline, 1-800-273-TALK (8255) or text "START" to 741741
- Center for Disease Control Suicide Datasheet
- SAMHSA Prevention Suicide: A Toolkit for High Schools
- Suicide Prevention Resource Center, After a Suicide: Toolkit for Schools
- Memorials: Special Considerations for Memorializing an Incident

WEBSITES

- National Association of School Psychologists, www.nasponline.org
- American Association of Suicidology, www.suicidology.org
- Suicide Awareness Voices of Education, www.save.org
- American Foundation for Suicide Prevention, https://afsp.org/
- www.stopbullying.gov
- Rape, Abuse & Incest National Network, www.rainn.org

REFERENCES

Brock, S. E., Nickerson, A. B., Louvar Reeves, M. A., Conolly, C., Jimerson, S., Pesce, R, & Lazarro, B. (2016). *School crisis prevention and intervention: The PREPaRE model* (2nd ed.). Bethesda, MD: National Association of School Psychologists.

Contributors: Christina Conolly, Kathy Cowan, Peter Faustino, Ben Fernandez, Stephen Brock, Melissa Reeves, Rich Lieberman.

Document may be adapted or excerpted with proper acknowledgement. Please cite as:
National Association of School Psychologists. (2017). *13 Reasons Why Netflix series: Considerations for educators* [handout]. Bethesda, MD: Author.

Appendix D[1]

Realism Provided by Nusura's SimulationDeck Technology[2]

All organizations these days are subject to crisis- and emergency-management disasters. Those that take the time to plan for their worst-case scenarios and prepare in advance will survive and even thrive. Those that believe it "can't happen to us" will not.

Perhaps equally important, whether they are nonprofit organizations, local, state or federal agencies, large or medium-sized businesses or universities and colleges, those folks that don't understand the impact that social media can have on crisis and emergency management are destined to suffer even more severe consequences than they may realize.

Imagination is the real sign of intelligence, some say. When it comes to technology and crisis and emergency management, which is evolving daily at speeds often beyond our comprehension, there can be no argument that imagination often makes the difference between the mundane and the next level of creativity.

Recently we teamed with a relatively new company based in Denver, Colorado: Nusura, Inc. "Nusura" is a Swahili term meaning "one who survives." This company is one of the newest innovative companies on deck offering a way for organizations to test their social media and public outreach skills through the use of a training tool they call SimulationDeck.

SimulationDeck is a secure web portal that replicates online communications tools, including social media sites as Facebook, Twitter and YouTube, as well as organizational websites and blogs.

As many of my readers know, for years my firm has offered strategic crisis planning and issue management alongside emergency-operations planning, training and webinars. When we were asked by a client to consider how best to bring them into the real world of social media, we sought out and found Nusura, Inc.

---

1. Written by L. Darryl Armstrong, Ph.D.
2. https://ldarrylarmstrong.wordpress.com/2017/10/19/realism-provided-by-nusuras-simulation-deck -technology/

The teaming partnership has resulted in a significant contract with a federal agency. We believe our combined resources, talents, experience and a similar set of values on how to handle clients and business in general brought us to the front of the bidder pack.

Nusura's president is Jim Chestnutt, an experienced public-information officer formerly with the Federal Emergency Management Agency (FEMA). Chestnutt and his team of former FEMA employees set out to train people on how to get information out to their stakeholders in a timely, accurate and coordinated fashion during emergencies.

We saw benefit and value to the application of their technology for not just life-threatening situations; we also saw the benefit to planning for the always-prevalent developing crisis around such internal issues as reorganizations, downsizing, sexual harassment charges, ethics charges and legal entanglements that any organization can face.

Chestnutt and I both found that in after-action reports from actual and exercise events—be it an internal crisis or an external emergency—the public-information function in major exercises was not being tested in a realistic way, which is what sent me out to find a way to correct the issue for my clients.

Chestnutt says that the pressure created by mock media and those tasked with testing the public-information element in simulated exercises didn't compare to the reality of handling even a small emergency.

Nusura, Inc. has former public-information officers and field agents from all levels of government who have experienced all sorts of internal and external crises and emergencies. SimulationDeck is the creative offspring of this group of talented professionals to mimic what happens online and in the media during an actual crisis or emergency.

The simulation web portal has nine websites, which emulate social media sites: SimulationBook includes Facebook's core features; Bleater simulates Twitter; the blogging platform is called Frogger; their YouTube lookalike is Ewe Tube; there is a site for agency or organizational news; incident information; the Exercise Times Daily, a web-based newspaper that features live reader comments; SimDeck News, a web-based TV station; and KEXN Radio.

SimulationDeck doesn't require special software, so it can work on any platform or internet-connected device. Chestnutt notes that one person working the SimulationDeck could act as 10 people. This person can file a newspaper article, then post on the agency's website and then act as the Governor's press secretary and announce a surprise press conference.

Chestnutt told emergencymgmt.com that "Things happen instantly, and any simulation player can generate an enormous amount of injects, as fast as they can type and enter it."

The tool was recently used during the Vibrant Response 13, a U.S. Army North national-level field training exercise that included 9,000 service members and civilians from the military, as well as state and federal agencies.

Dan Manuszewski, chief of public affairs for the U.S. Army North, told the editor at www.emergencymgmt.com that it's increasingly important to practice all forms of communication, and that includes social media as it becomes increasingly popular.

We note that many of our college and university clients, who have been reluctant to engage in social media as a communication tool, are becoming aware of its importance when they see that their students and staff are more quickly informed through Twitter and Facebook smartphone communications than the organization's systems. We see significant opportunity to bring these folks and many other organizations and agencies into the real social media and mass-media world through such applications as SimulationDeck.

Like it or not, social media is becoming a major communication platform, especially for current generations. Those organizations that fail to train their employees in the proper use of social media are doing a disservice to the employees and their stakeholders.

Manuszewski says that we need to make sure we understand the entire information environment—from the traditional media to the media that people are using now, like social media.

Chestnutt says that the company is listening carefully to feedback from its users and continually making improvements.

Appendix E

How to Prepare Key Messages

September 11, 2001. The event brought the need for crisis planning and a resilient crisis mindset to the forefront of all leaders' minds. It also made crisis communicators stop and think about the most efficient and practical approach to developing and communicating key messages.

The following five guidelines provide an overview of the process for developing key messages.

Identify your audiences: Audiences (stakeholders) may include employees, customers, partners, victims, victims' loved ones, individuals who are directly affected, neighboring communities not directly affected, elected officials, the media, people with access and functional needs, industry, businesses, etc.

Identify the shared, overarching concerns of the audience: Attempt to identify what the audience needs and wants to know. Refer to the questions in the messaging triangle to determine what the audience wants to know. Other questions may include the following:

What is the most critical information to share?

Example: hazard or safety information, service restoration, the status of a facility in an affected community, etc.

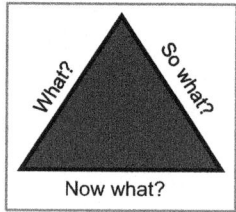

What will be the most pressing issues?

Power outages, loss of community members, active shooters, etc.

What will be the most pressing questions?

What do I do, where do I go, what is the campus doing to mitigate the problem, etc.?

Develop three key messages that address the concerns of the audience: These three messages are what goes in the first set of boxes. Messages

254

should be brief, concise and written at the sixth-grade reading level. Messages should parallel your crisis-communication objectives. Where possible and appropriate, messages will reinforce: the commitment to health, safety and welfare; commitment to openness and transparency; and collaboration with external partners.

List supporting facts for each key message: These facts should support and elaborate on the message.

Finalize and distribute the messaging: Messaging should be approved by the crisis-communication manager and shared with the crisis-communication team to help guide the development of information products (e.g., news releases, talking points, tough questions with 30-second sound-bite answers, etc.).

A United Airlines Cautionary Tale

Melissa Agnes is the author of *Crisis Ready: Building an Invincible Brand in an Uncertain World*, and is a leading authority on crisis preparedness, reputation management and brand protection. Her explanation of the United Airlines' mishandling of a crisis is pivotal in understanding what not to do (https://melissaagnes.com/)

(BCI, 2018).

Dr. Dao, a paying United Airlines customer, expected the flight from Chicago to Louisville to be uneventful. He was mistaken. Randomly picked by the airline so that a crewmember could get to Louisville for a crew change, he suffered humiliation and injury when he was dragged from his seat on that infamous April flight in 2017. Thanks to YouTube and China's microblogging site Weibo, within 48 hours on April 10, 2017, more than 100 million people in the United States and 210 million people in China saw the United Airlines passenger violently removed from the flight. It took the CEO almost 24 hours to respond. United Airlines stock lost $1.4 billion in value the following day, according to *Fortune* magazine's Lucinda Shen.

United's CEO, Oscar Munoz, who ironically had been named "Communicator of the Year in 2017" by *PRWeek*, responded the next day on April 11th in a manner that was thought to be "tone-deaf and insensitive" by thousands on social media. As more video footage revealed the extent of the passenger's injuries, including bleeding from a cut on his head and the loss of teeth, the Federal Department of Transportation stepped in to investigate.

The incident got the attention of Congress. Twenty-one senators wrote to Munoz expressing their "deep concern." Congress began to look at legislation to prevent airlines from involuntarily bumping paying passengers from overbooked flights. The outrage continued to grow after Munoz sent an email to his employees defending his staff's actions and calling the passenger "disruptive and belligerent." The anger spread globally with customers and potential customers questioning the policies of the airline's overbooking practices and threatening boycotts. The boycotts never materialized.

Eleven days later, April 21st, United Airlines announced that Munoz would remain CEO but would not take broader control of the company as previously announced and planned. He had been chosen to assume the role of chairman of the board at the 2018 annual stockholders' meeting. Munoz announced he would step down as CEO of United Airlines in May 2020.

Mr. Munoz stumbled, no doubt; however, he also did eventually recover. He apologized personally to Dr. Dao. The airline privately settled, and the terms are not public. The settlement was sufficient enough that Dr. Dao's lawyer spoke highly on what the airlines paid.

Mr. Munoz went on ABC's *Good Morning America* and said he felt "ashamed" when he saw the video. He apologized and vowed that it would never happen again on a United flight. In May, he took his mea culpa to Congress. Lawmakers proclaimed with much flair the complaints of their constituents to him (Stewart, 2017).

However, Mr. Munoz gets it. He emphatically stated, "Ultimately, our actions will speak louder than words." During a crisis, the public and the media measure and assess words and actions. Leadership must understand that they must "walk their talk."

"That was the right thing to do," said Steve Barrett, editor of *PRWeek* magazine. "They should have done it immediately. United made it a much bigger story than it ever would have been."

PRWeek was thrust into the somewhat awkward position of criticizing Mr. Munoz's handling of the affair less than a month after it had honored him as the 2017 Communicator of the Year. The award is the public relations equivalent of an Oscar. The honor was for his rehabilitation of the airline's tattered image and for reaching labor agreements that had eluded United management for years. The magazine did not retract the honor, but after the Dao incident, Mr. Barrett said, "The episode and subsequent response will be quoted in textbooks as an example of how not to respond in a crisis" (Stewart, 2017).

Yes, Mr. Barrett, it is.

Still, United "has suffered considerable reputational damage," Mr. Barrett said. "No one is going to forget that video anytime soon" (Stewart, 2017).

REFERENCES

BCI (2018). Handling social media in a crisis: Dos and don'ts. Retrieved on February 17, 2020 from https://www.thebci.org/news/handling-social-media-in-a-crisis-dos-and-don-ts.html

Stewart, J. (2017). The boycott that wasn't: How United weathered a media firestorm. Retrieved on February 17, 2020 from https://www.nytimes.com/2017/07/27/business/how-united-weathered-a-firestorm.html

The Lost Art of Listening
10 Steps to Develop Your Skills[1]

There are 10 steps to use to develop your listening skills, which are critically important in the processes of achieving collaborative, informed consent in the process of building your plans to handle a crisis.

1. **Don't assume you've heard the story before.** The Earl of Chesterfield Phillip Stanhope once said, "Many a man would rather you heard his story than granted his request." And who knows, you may pick up on something you missed before. Every problem deserves a thorough hearing. People want to be respected, and the highest respect we can show them is to listen to what they have to say.

2. **Don't second-guess the speaker.** Nothing is more irritating than to begin talking and then have the listener jump into the middle of one of your sentences, saying, "I know what you're talking about." The speaker gets the impression you are in a hurry and you want to ease them out of the office or get them off the telephone. Even though you may be trying to empathize with them, you need to hear all of the information before commenting. And, more importantly, they need to be able to tell you all the information.

3. **Suspend your judgment** until you've heard the situation through to the end.

4. **Take notes.** Frequently, someone who has a problem will tell you more than you need to know about a situation. You must listen for the key facts and taking notes can help you zero in on the real issues.

5. **Be careful about showing your negative nonverbal signals as you listen.**

6. Much of how we feel is transmitted through facial expressions or how we hold our bodies during the conversation. **Be as relaxed as you can be and keep your facial expressions and body movements**

---

1. https://ldarrylarmstrong.wordpress.com/2016/11/08/the-lost-art-of-listening-10-steps-to-develop-your-skills/

noncommittal. When you sit with arms crossed and leaning back in your chair, let's face it, you are communicating with your body language. The body language of both the speaker and the listener plays a pivotal role in communication. Learn the roles for specific situations and you'll increase your effectiveness.

7. **Be patient.** It helps a person to vent (remember, this is a therapy for them) and gives you time to think.

    The other day at the airport, I was sitting and reading a business article and enjoying my coffee. A stranger sat down beside me. I acknowledged him nonverbally, and then he started talking and talking and talking. He spoke for almost 10 minutes about a bad experience he had that morning at breakfast and the terrible service he had received. I listened intently. I learned that his name is George and that he is the CEO of a major company in Atlanta. He gave me his card, and I shared mine. Finally, as his business companion approached, he said, "You know you would make a good therapist. Thanks for listening." I told him I have a great deal of practice. You see, an excellent facilitator is a better listener. And one day, he may need an excellent facilitator. You never know.

    As my grandfather always said, "God gave us two ears and one mouth." The next time your client or even a stranger needs to talk, take the time to listen.

8. **Don't feel obligated to reply to every statement.** Keep listening and only respond to the essential points. Remember, you can't fix everything.

9. **Listen to understand** rather than spending the time mentally preparing your next remark.

10. **Be sure to ask inviting and open-ended questions** that can result in more informative answers. Then, recap what you heard and clarify any points you didn't understand.

    Listening is truly an art and one that is learned and improved upon with experience.

    Socrates said, "Wisest is he that knows he does not know" in 399 BC. It was true then, and it is true now. We learn from those who have a story to share. We should not feel awkward listening to folks at all levels.

    We first must learn—and listening is the first step—before we can teach. And even then, there is more to learn.

Checklists—Preparing for the Interview

What to Do Before, During and After the Interview[1]

The day will come when you need to do an interview with the media. Now is the time to prepare yourself for this actuality. Start by going to YouTube, a valuable resource where you can see examples of various media interviews. Learn by watching examples of the good, the bad and the ugly. The following checklists provide you tips, techniques and things to do or not to do when it comes to working with reporters:

RESEARCH AND PREPARATION

- Learn what you can about the reporter (conduct online research and gather intelligence from your colleagues).
- Respond quickly and expertly.
- Respond to all questions.
- Clarify and repeat the reporter's question before replying.
- Prepare for your interview with facts and develop three key messages.
- Be accurate and complete in the information provided.
- Never, ever, ever lie!
- Use examples, stories and analogies.
- Don't say something that you don't want to appear on the news or as a headline.
- Don't lose your temper or get flustered.
- Don't expect, or even ask to see, an advance copy.
- Don't be surprised by misquotes, unfortunate contexts or lack of fair and balanced reporting.

---

1. https://www.atsdr.cdc.gov/risk/riskprimer/media.html

WHERE IT CAN GO WRONG: THE TRAPS—INTERVIEW TACTICS

- The often-repeated question.
- The negatively phrased question.
- Multiple questions packaged as one.
- Silence—does not have to be filled by you, the interviewee.
- Hostility towards you.

FIXING THE PROBLEM—INTERVIEW TACTICS

- Change the subject by using conversation bridges.
- Bridge to another topic by saying something like, "I think your readers might also like to know…"
- Buy thinking time: Repeat a part of or the entire question when being interviewed for an article.

EXCEPTIONS—INTERVIEW TACTICS

- When asked a negative question, never repeat the negative.
- Don't repeat the question on camera.
- Count a few beats before answering.
- Try the simple technique of waiting 3 seconds before answering.
- Correct any misinformation.
- If the reporter quotes the wrong statistic or fact, you have the right to correct them politely.

BEFORE YOUR INTERVIEW—TIPS

- Ask who will be conducting the interview.
- Ask which subjects they want to cover.
- Develop at least the 10 toughest questions you and your team can brainstorm (especially those you or your executive would dread having to answer) and prepare, get approved and practice the answers in quote and sound-bite formats. Consider and choose appropriate language.
- Admit when you are not the right person to interview (due to lack of knowledge, legal parameters, etc.).
- Offer to direct them to an appropriate Subject Matter Expert (SME).
- Inquire about the format and duration.

WHAT NOT TO DO BEFORE AN INTERVIEW—TIPS

- Tell the news organization which reporter you prefer.
- Ask for specific questions in advance.

- Insist they do not ask about certain subjects.
- Demand your remarks not be edited.
- Insist an adversary not be interviewed.
- Assume it will be easy.
- Panic or get uptight and nervous!

DURING YOUR INTERVIEW—TIPS

- Be honest and accurate.
- Be open, transparent and forthcoming.
- Stay calm and focused—breathe deeply.
- Stick to your three key messages.
- State your conclusions first, then provide supporting data.
- Be forthcoming to the extent you decide beforehand.
- Offer to get the information you don't have.
- Explain the subject and content.
- Stress the facts and tell your story.
- Give a reason if you can't discuss a subject.
- Correct mistakes by stating you would like an opportunity to clarify.
- If you don't know an answer, say so and agree to get back with the reporter in a timely fashion.
- Do not use acronyms.
- Speak as if you are explaining the subject to my 80-year-old grandmother with a sixth-grade education.

THINGS NOT TO DO DURING AN INTERVIEW

- Lie or try to cloud the truth.
- Lose your cool.
- Improvise or dwell on negative allegations.
- Raise issues you don't want to see in the story.
- Fail to think it through ahead of time.
- Guess.
- Use jargon or assume the facts speak for themselves.
- Speculate or discuss hypothetical situations.
- Say, "no comment."
- Demand an answer not be used.

AFTER THE INTERVIEW—TIPS

- Remember, you are always on the record, and microphones could always be "hot."
- Do not ask how you did!

- Inquire about publication or airdate.
- Be helpful.
- Volunteer to get information.
- Make yourself available.
- Respect deadlines.
- Watch for and read the resulting report.
- Call the reporter to point out politely inaccuracies, if any.
- When appropriate, call the reporter and thank them for a "fair and balanced" report.

How to Work Effectively with Reporters

Reporters are no different from you or me. They have a job to do. It is not an easy job. They have a deadline to meet and editors to please. They do not set out to intimidate or get you, usually. Having dealt with programs such as *60 Minutes* and *20/20* in past lives, we understand how you could believe the media to be your "enemy." We suggest you try to not generalize and come to feel that all reporters are troublesome.

While it may seem that some reporters are not nice people, most are just doing their job. Working with reporters is not about liking one another; it is about respecting each other. A reporter has their role, and you have another. Each of you has specific responsibilities. You both want to get a story out to people that need to hear it.

The following is our advice based on four decades of experience on how to work with reporters. Use this to develop a set of clear guidelines and include them in your Communications Governance (CG) document. When reporters call:

- Ask who they represent.
- What is the nature of the story they are working?
- What is their deadline?
- Agree, not promise, to call back at a specific time to enable them to meet their deadline and then work with your team on how to best handle the situation.

Respond as quickly as you can. Always be honest and transparent, and ensure the information you are providing is correct. The sooner you respond to a reporter, the more likely they will believe you do not have anything to hide. When you ask for their deadline, they know you care about helping them. The reality is that their job is to get a story, and you want to help them to tell it correctly, fairly and balanced.

Do not ask the reporter to review or read their story in advance. Do not be led to believe that because the reporter is friendly and interested in you as a person that they are not there to do a job. Thank the reporter when appropriate for their interest and time.

If a reporter unfairly maligns you and your organization, you should call them and correct any errors. If the errors are egregious, ask to meet with them face-to-face to focus on getting the story right. If you do this with genuine respect and without an attitude, you are more than likely going to get a correction. Should the reporter be "incorrigible," go to their senior management and discuss the situation.

NaBITA Risk Rubric

NaBITA Risk Rubric

D-SCALE

Life Stress and Emotional Health

DECOMPENSATING

▲ Behavior is severely disruptive, directly impacts others, and is actively dangerous. This may include life-threatening, self-injurious behaviors such as:
  ▲ Suicidal ideations or attempts, an expressed lethal plan, and/or hospitalization
  ▲ Extreme self-injury, life-threatening disordered eating, repeated DUIs
  ▲ Repeated acute alcohol intoxication with medical or law enforcement involvement, chronic substance abuse
  ▲ Profoundly disturbed, detached view of reality and at risk of grievous injury or death and/or inability to care for themselves (self-care/protection/judgment)
  ▲ Actual affective, impulsive violence or serious threats of violence such as:
    ▲ Repeated, severe attacks while intoxicated; brandishing a weapon
    ▲ Making threats that are concrete, consistent, and plausible
    ▲ Impulsive stalking behaviors that present a physical danger

4

DETERIORATING

Destructive actions, screaming or aggressive/harassing communications, rapid/odd speech, extreme isolation, stark decrease in self-care
  Responding to voices, extremely odd dress, high risk substance abuse; troubling thoughts with paranoid/delusional themes; increasingly medically dangerous binging/purging
  Suicidal thoughts that are not lethal/imminent or non-life threatening self-injury
  Threats of affective, impulsive, poorly planned, and/or economically driven violence
  Vague but direct threats or specific but indirect threat; explosive language
  Stalking behaviors that do not **cause physical** harm, but are disruptive and concerning

3

DISTRESSED

⌘ Distressed individuals engage in behavior that concerns others, and have an impaired ability to manage their emotions and actions. Possible presence of stressors such as:
  ⌘ Managing chronic mental illness, mild substance abuse/misuse, disordered eating
  ⌘ Situational stressors that cause disruption in mood, social, or academic areas
  ⌘ **Difficulty coping/adapting to stressors/trauma; behavior may subside when** stressor is removed, or trauma is addressed/processed
⌘ If a threat is present, the threat is vague, indirect, implausible, and lacks detail or focus

2

DEVELOPING

⊕ Experiencing situational stressors but demonstrating appropriate coping skills
⊕ **Often first contact or referral to the BIT/CARE team, etc.**
⊕ Behavior is appropriate given the circumstances and context
⊕ No threat made or present

0/1

↑ TRAJECTORY?

OVERALL SUMMARY

E-SCALE
Hostility and Violence to Others

CRITICAL

iis stage, there is a serious risk of suicide, life-threatening self-injury, dangerous risk taking
, driving a motorcycle at top speed at night with the lights off) and/or inability to care for
self. They may display racing thoughts, high risk substance dependence, intense anger, and/
erceived unfair treatment or grievance that has a major impact on the students' academic,
al, and peer interactions. The individual has clear target for their threats and ultimatums,
ess to lethal means, and an attack plan to punish those they see as responsible for perceived
ngs. Without immediate intervention (such as law enforcement or psychiatric hospitalization),
likely violence will occur. There may be leakage about the attack plan (social media posts
say "I'm going to be the next school shooter" or telling a friend to avoid coming to campus
a particular day). There may be stalking behavior and escalating predatory actions prior to
ence such as intimidation, telegraphing, and "test-runs" such as causing a disruption to better
erstand reaction time of emergency response.

EMERGENCE OF VIOLENCE

▲ Behavior is moving towards a plan of targeted violence, sense of hopelessness,
and/or desperation in the attack plan; locked into an all or nothing mentality
▲ Increasing use of military and tactical language; acquisition of costume for attack
▲ Clear fixation and focus on an individual target or group; feels justified in actions
▲ Attack plan is credible, repeated, and specific; may be shared, may be hidden
▲ Increased research on target and attack plan, employing counter-surveillance
measures, access to lethal means; there is a sense of imminence to the plan
▲ Leakage of attack plan on social media or telling friends and others to avoid
locations

4

ELEVATED

avior at the elevated stage is increasingly disruptive (with multiple incidents) and involves
tiple offices such as student conduct, law enforcement, and counseling. The individual may
age in suicidal talk, self-injury, substance intoxication. Threats of violence and ultimatums
r be vague but direct or specific but indirect. A fixation and focus on a target often emerge
son, place, or system) and the individual continues to attack the target's self-esteem, public
ge, and/or access to safety and support. Others may feel threatened around this individual,
any threat lacks depth, follow-through, or a narrowing against an individual, office, or com-
ity. More serious social, mental health, academic, and adjustment concerns occur, and the
vidual is in need of more timely support and resources to avoid further escalation. Conditional
natums such as "do this or else" may be made to instructors, peers, faculty, and staff.

ELABORATION OF THREAT

Fixation and focus on a singular individual, group, or department; depersonalization of target, intimidating target to lessen their ability to advocate for safety
Seeking others to support and empower future threatening action; may find
extremists looking to exploit vulnerability; encouraging violence
Threats and ultimatums may be vague or direct and are motivated by a hardened
viewpoint; potential leakage around what should happen to fix grievances and
injustices
There is rarely physical violence here, but rather an escalation in the dangerousness and lethality in the threats; they are more specific, targeted, and repeated

3

MODERATE

or to this stage, conflict with others has been fairly limited. The hallmark of moderate is an
rease in conflict with others through aggressive speech, actions, and mannerisms. They
y become frustrated and engage in non-verbal behaviors or begin to post things on social
dia, put up posters around campus, or storm away from conversations. Stress, illness,
k of friends, and support are now becoming an increasing concern. The individual may be
rful, sad, hopeless, anxious, or frustrated. This may be caused by difficulty adjusting, dating
ess, failure in class assignments, and/or increasing social isolation. If there is a threat or
rsical violence such as carelessly pushing someone out of their way while storming off,
violence is typically limited and driven by adrenaline and impulsiveness, rather than any
aper plan to hurt others.

ESCALATING BEHAVIORS

⌘ Driven by hardened thoughts or a grievance concerning past wrongs or perceived
past wrongs; increasingly adopts a singular, limited perspective
⌘ When frustrated, storms off, disengaged, may create signs or troll on social media
⌘ Argues with others with intent to embarrass, shame, or shut down
⌘ Physical violence, if present, is impulsive, non-lethal, and brief; may seem similar to affective violence, but driven here by a hardened perspective rather than
mental health and/or environmental stress

2

MILD

e individual here may be struggling and not doing well. The impact of their difficulty is limited
und others, with the occasional report being made to the BIT/CARE team out of an abun-
nce of caution and concern rather than any direct behavior or threats. They may be having
uble fitting in, adjusting to college, making friends, or may rub people the wrong way. They
anate others with their thoughts or mannerisms, and there may be minor bullying and conflict.
th support and resources, it is likely the individual will be successful adapting and overcoming
stacles. Without support, it is possible they will continue to escalate on the rubric.

EMPOWERING THOUGHTS

☉ Passionate and hardened thoughts; typically related to religion, politics, academic
status, money/power, social justice, or relationships
☉ Rejection of alternative perspectives, critical thinking, empathy, or perspective-
taking
☉ Narrowing on consumption of news, social media, or friendships; seeking only
those who share the same perspective
☉ No threats of violence

0/1

TRAJECTORY?

BASELINE

INTERVENTION OPTIONS TO ADDRESS RISK AS CLASSIFIED

CRITICAL (4)

- Initiate wellness check/evaluation for involuntary hold or police response for arrest
- Coordinate with necessary parties (student conduct, police, etc.) to create plan for safety, suspension, or other interim measures
- Obligatory parental/guardian/emergency contact notification unless contraindicated
- Evaluate need for emergency notification to community
- Issue mandated assessment once all involved are safe
- Evaluate the need for involuntary/voluntary withdrawal
- Coordinate with university police and/or local law enforcement
- Provide guidance, support, and safety plan to referral source/stakeholders

ELEVATED (3)

- Consider a welfare/safety check
- Provide guidance, support, and safety plan to referral source/stakeholders
- Deliver follow up and ongoing case management or support services
- Required assessment such as the SIVRA-35, ERIS, HCR-20, WAVR-21 or similar; assess social media posts
- Evaluate parental/guardian/emergency contact notification
- Coordinate referrals to appropriate resources and provide follow-up
- Likely referral to student conduct or disability support services
- Coordinate with university police/campus safety, student conduct, and other departments as necessary to mitigate ongoing risk

MODERATE (2)

- Provide guidance and education to referral source
- Reach out to student to encourage a meeting
- Develop and implement case management plan or support services
- Connect with offices, support resources, faculty, etc. who interact with student to enlist as support or to gather more information
- Possible referral to student conduct or disability support services
- Offer referrals to appropriate support resources
- Assess social media and other sources to gather more information
- Consider VRAW² for cases that have written elements
- Skill building in social interactions, emotional balance, and empathy; reinforcement of protective factors (social support, opportunities for positive involvement)

MILD (0/1)

- No formal intervention; document and monitor over time
- Provide guidance and education to referral source
- Reach out to student to offer a meeting or resources, if needed
- Connect with offices, support resources, faculty, etc. who interact with student to enlist as support or to gather more information

CRITICAL

ELEVATED

MODERATE

MILD

**INTERVENTION OPTIONS TO ADDRESS RISK
AS CLASSIFIED**

CRITICAL (4)

- Initiate wellness check/evaluation for involuntary hold or police response for arrest
- Coordinate with necessary parties (student conduct, police, etc.) to create plan for safety, suspension, or other interim measures
- Obligatory parental/guardian/emergency contact notification unless contraindicated
- Evaluate need for emergency notification to community
- Issue mandated assessment once all involved are safe
- Evaluate the need for involuntary/voluntary withdrawal
- Coordinate with university police and/or local law enforcement
- Provide guidance, support, and safety plan to referral source/stakeholders

ELEVATED (3)

- Consider a welfare/safety check
- Provide guidance, support, and safety plan to referral source/stakeholders
- Deliver follow up and ongoing case management or support services
- Required assessment such as the SIVRA-35, ERIS, HCR-20, WAVR-21 or similar; assess social media posts
- Evaluate parental/guardian/emergency contact notification
- Coordinate referrals to appropriate resources and provide follow-up
- Likely referral to student conduct or disability support services
- Coordinate with university police/campus safety, student conduct, and other departments as necessary to mitigate ongoing risk

MODERATE (2)

- Provide guidance and education to referral source
- Reach out to student to encourage a meeting
- Develop and implement case management plan or support services
- Connect with offices, support resources, faculty, etc. who interact with student to enlist as support or to gather more information
- Possible referral to student conduct or disability support services
- Offer referrals to appropriate support resources
- Assess social media and other sources to gather more information
- Consider VRAW[2] for cases that have written elements
- Skill building in social interactions, emotional balance, and empathy; reinforcement of protective factors (social support, opportunities for positive involvement)

MILD (0/1)

- No formal intervention; document and monitor over time
- Provide guidance and education to referral source
- Reach out to student to offer a meeting or resources, if needed
- Connect with offices, support resources, faculty, etc. who interact with student to enlist as support or to gather more information

Scoring Guide Examples for Looking Glass

		Element	1-point score	2-point score
		Escalation	Elements	
Author Qualities	1.	Suicidal Content	No one understands me; sometimes I think it would be better if I disappear. I think that too, more often than I like.	You all will look back on this time, after I take my revenge and kill myself, with regret. The time to care for me has passed.
	2.	Isolation and Hopelessness	Each time I look for a path to something better, the world shits on me. I don't know... will it ever get better for me?	I haven't talked to anyone in a week. Literally a week. It will never change. I am tired of being alone all the time. There is no escape.
	3.	Fame/ Meaning-Seeking	I look at those kids on TV, the ones who kill everyone. I think they have it right. They matter now.	You will have my name on your lips for the rest of your life. You won't be able to look at a school without knowing me and thinking of my face.
	4.	Injustice/ Grievance-Collecting	It feels like every time I try, I get pushed down. The world is unfair to me. There isn't a way to change my future.	It was Mr. Kochat. Him above all others. He thinks he is smarter than me. We will see how smart he is when his brains are all over the wall. Then it will be right. Then he will be punished for what he did to me.

continued...

		Element	1-point score	2-point score
Tone	5.	Hardened, Black/white thinking	I just wish, for once, that some of the girls looked at me. Treated me like something more than every other kid.	Those bitches. Those whores. They will never be with someone who treats them good. Someone like me.
	6.	Overall use of graphic and violent descriptions	I get so angry that I just want to smash everything in my house. Break it all and just scream and scream. No one listens. No one cares. Maybe they would care if I smashed some things.	I think of those sick people. What it would feel like to walk by one on the street? To slip my knife in and up, saying, "oh, sorry," as I pierce their heart. And then collapse as I walk by. The blood pooling, wide-eyed terror as they face death.
Content	7.	Target Detail	The professors at this school are the most libtard, stupid, Clinton-worshiping pieces of crap. Someone should drown them all in a bucket of kittens.	Dr. Van Brunt, that hippy, NPR-listening-to son-of-a-bitch should be taken out back and shot in the head. He thinks he's untouchable. Well, maybe I'll reach out and show him that's not the case. #timesup #MAGA
	8.	Weapon Detail	There are times when I wonder if a gun would be the thing that would help me solve lots of my problems at school.	This is war and I am ready. I'm gonna take out all of the f$%#ers with my new Sig MPX 9 mm. Doesn't pack a punch, but those 30 rounds clips will get me accuracy by volume.

continued...

		Element	1-point score	2-point score
	9.	Threat Plan Detail	I think next year will be different at this school. Maybe some clean up, like they saw in Australia and California. #firetime	I know where she lives. What car she drives. Where the car is (thanks spytech GPS tracker!). If she isn't going to be with me, well, I think she's gonna have a little accident with her tires on Route 34 this weekend.
	10	Previous Attack Detail	I know other people out there do school shootings to make sense of their life. Maybe there is something to that. Some time to find some larger meaning out there. And make some people pay for their sins.	Good old Elliot got it right. Hmm, and Grandpa Sodini. Make them bitches pay. But not with guns, I'm going all Shinji Aoba on these bitches. Burn, baby, burn.
		Mitigating	**Elements**	
Author Disposition	1.	Trolling	A student posts against anti-abortion information on the pro-life Facebook page. There are numerous arguments and name-calling ensues.	A student identifies someone they disagree with about politics and identifies their rival on social media and shares their address and phone number online.
	2.	Developmental Delay	A student writes a story for class based on the *Friday the 13th* movie, but he changes all the names of the people who are killed into his classmates.	A student is upset at a professor and writes an essay about how much they would like to punch him in the face. The essay is five pages long and extremely detailed.

continued...

272

		Element	1-point score	2-point score
	3.	Tangential, Rambling or Incoherent	A student leaves a journal at a local restaurant. The journal contains odd symbols and all of the teacher's names. The journal is found and turned into the BIT/CARE team.	A student posts on Instagram pictures of zoomed in eyes. There is odd writing and pictures of animals, weapons and snakes. A classmate reports the post when they noticed the pictures were all of her eyes.
	4.	International, Native Language	An international male student continues to send unwanted text messages, pictures and requests to have sex. The female tells him to stop and he says she just doesn't know what she wants.	A student gets into an argument in an online discussion board. The student threatens to come into class with a bazooka and finish everyone off.
	5.	Creative Author	A student posts a story on Facebook that is a loosely veiled retelling of a recent school shooting from the point of view of someone who was killed.	A student writes an essay in class on "The person I admire most" about his teacher. The story involves a twist on a modest proposal where he describes how he would kill and eat her, piece by piece.
Content	6.	Writing for Class	A student shares a writing assignment on a gaming discussion board, and it is flagged by an admin and forwarded to the FBI. It's an explanation of why school shooters do it. The assignment for class was, "write an opinion piece defending something you disagree with strongly."	A student writes about something they believe strongly about in class. The essay is a defense of white supremacism and an argument for minorities to be kept in isolation. He reads the story out loud to the class, and there is a very angry reaction.

continued...

	Element	1-point score	2-point score
7.	Therapeutic Journal	A student posts on their Vent app all the people at school he thinks should be "removed from earth." Another student recognizes some of the details and asks the student if these were his posts. He says yes, but it was something his therapist asked him to do.	While in therapy, a student is asked to express his thoughts and then rip them up. Instead, he wrote a lengthy story outlining all of the women that he would rape. The story includes very graphic details and names specific students.
8.	Rhetoric or Opinion Piece	A student writes a piece for the school newspaper that argues for a return to eugenics regarding trans students because their behavior is immoral.	A student records a TikTok video entitled, "50 ways to kill a liberal." Other students report the anonymous school tip line.
9.	Retaliatory Expression	On a video game message board, a student is arguing with another about a recent Esports match. He says, "If I chop off your thumbs with this machete I have in my room, you won't be starting next week, will you?" The friend replies, "For real? Did you just write this?" He shares it with the BIT/CARE.	A female student, angry that her girlfriend broke up with her, writes a story about a teddy bear she received as a gift and how it was killed. She sends he ex the story and a video of a teddy bear being stabbed with a knife. The video includes stuffing and ketchup everywhere.

continued...

	Element	1-point score	2-point score
10.	Affective/ Reactive	A student is embarrassed by a teacher in a public argument and then begins to draw pictures in his notebook of various ways a stick figure could be killed. Another student sees this and reports it to the BIT/CARE team.	A student is asked to leave class because of their language. He storms out of class and stops and the blackboard, picks up some chalk and writes "Die all of you!" and then walks out, slamming the door.

Index

Page numbers in **bold** indicate items in tables. Page numbers in *italic* indicate items in figures.

Made in the USA
Middletown, DE
26 January 2023

23162256R00166